A CRITICAL EXPOSITION
OF THE
PHILOSOPHY OF LEIBNIZ

1896 *German Social Democracy*
1897 *An Essay on the Foundations of Geometry* (Constable)
1900 *The Philosophy of Leibniz*
1903 *The Principles of Mathematics*
1910 *Philosophical Essays*
1912 *Problems of Philosophy* (Oxford U.P.)
1910–13 *Principia Mathematica* 3 vols. (with A. N. Whitehead) (Cambridge U.P.)
1914 *Our Knowledge of the External World*
1916 *Justice in Wartime* (out of print)
1916 *Principles of Social Reconstruction*
1917 *Political Ideals*
1918 *Roads to Freedom*
1918 *Mysticism and Logic*
1919 *Introduction to Mathematical Philosophy*
1920 *The Practice and Theory of Bolshevism*
1921 *The Analysis of Mind*
1922 *The Problem of China*
1923 *Prospects of Industrial Civilization* (with Dora Russell)
1923 *The ABC of Atoms* (out of print)
1924 *Icarus or the Future of Science* (USA only)
1925 *The ABC of Relativity*
1925 *What I Believe*
1926 *On Education*
1927 *An Outline of Philosophy*
1927 *The Analysis of Matter*
1928 *Sceptical Essays*
1929 *Marriage and Morals*
1930 *The Conquest of Happiness*
1931 *The Scientific Outlook*
1932 *Education and the Social Order*
1934 *Freedom and Organization: 1814-1914*
1935 *In Praise of Idleness*
1935 *Religion and Science* (Oxford U.P.)
1936 *Which Way to Peace?* (out of print)
1937 *The Amberley Papers* (with Patricia Russell)
1938 *Power*
1940 *An Inquiry into Meaning and Truth*
1945 *History of Western Philosophy*
1948 *Human Knowledge: Its Scope and Limits*
1949 *Authority and the Individual*
1950 *Unpopular Essays*
1951 *New Hopes for a Changing World*
1952 *The Impact of Science on Society*
1953 *The Good Citizen's Alphabet* (Gabberbochus)
1953 *Satan in the Suburbs*
1954 *Nightmares of Eminent Persons*
1954 *Human Society in Ethics and Politics*
1956 *Logic and Knowledge* (ed. by R. C. Marsh)
1956 *Portraits from Memory*
1957 *Why I am Not a Christian* (ed. by Paul Edwards)
1957 *Understanding History and other essay* (USA only)
1958 *Vital Letters of Russell, Khrushchev and Dulles* (Macgibbon & Kee)
1958 *Bertrand Russell's Best* (ed. by Robert Egner)
1959 *Common Sense and Nuclear Warfare*
1959 *Wisdom of the West* (ed. by Paul Foulkes) (Macdonald)
1959 *My Philosophical Development*
1960 *Bertrand Russell Speaks his Mind* (USA only)
1961 *Fact and Fiction*
1961 *Has Man a Future?*
1961 *The Basic Writings of Bertrand Russell* (ed. by R. E. Egner and L. Dennon)
1963 *Unarmed Victory*
1967 *War Crimes in Vietnam*
1967 *The Archives of Bertrand Russell* (ed. by B. Feinberg, Continuum) (out of print)
1967 *Autobiography 1872-1914*
1968 *Autobiography 1914-1944*
1969 *Autobiography 1944-1967*
1969 *Dear Bertrand Russell...* (ed. by B. Feinberg and R. Kasrils)

A CRITICAL EXPOSITION
OF THE

PHILOSOPHY OF LEIBNIZ

With an Appendix of
Leading Passages

by

BERTRAND RUSSELL

LONDON
GEORGE ALLEN & UNWIN LTD
MUSEUM STREET

FIRST PUBLISHED IN 1900
NEW EDITION 1937
THIRD IMPRESSION (SECOND EDITION) 1949
FOURTH IMPRESSION (SECOND EDITION) 1951
FIFTH IMPRESSION 1958
SIXTH IMPRESSION 1964
SEVENTH IMPRESSION 1967
EIGHTH IMPRESSION 1971

PRINTED IN GREAT BRITAIN BY
JOHN DICKENS & CO LTD, NORTHAMPTON

PREFACE TO THE SECOND EDITION.

SHORTLY after the publication of the first edition of this book, its principal thesis—namely, that Leibniz's philosophy was almost entirely derived from his logic—received overwhelming confirmation from the work of Louis Couturat. His " La Logique de Leibniz " (1901), supported by his collection of MSS. overlooked by previous editors, entitled " Opuscules et Fragments inédits de Leibniz " (1903), showed that the " Discours de Métaphysique " and the letters to Arnauld, upon which I had to rely almost exclusively for my interpretation, were mere samples of innumerable writings expressing the same point of view, which had remained buried among the mass of documents at Hanover for over two centuries. No candid reader of the " Opuscules " can doubt that Leibniz's metaphysic was derived by him from the subject-predicate logic. This appears, for example, from the paper " Primae Veritates " (Opuscules, pp. 518-523), where all the main doctrines of the " Monadology " are deduced, with terse logical rigour, from the premiss :

" Semper igitur praedicatum seu consequens inest subjecto seu antecedenti, et in hoc ipso consistit natura veritatis in universum . . . . . Hoc autem est in omni veritate affirmativa universali aut singulari, necessaria aut contingente " (Ib. p. 518).*

Wherever my interpretation of Leibniz differed from that of previous commentators, Couturat's work afforded conclusive confirmation, and showed that the few previously published texts upon which I had relied had all the importance that I had attributed to them. But Couturat carried inorthodoxy further than I had done, and where his interpretation differed from mine, he was able to cite passages which seemed conclusive. The Principle of Sufficient Reason, he maintains, asserts simply that every true proposition is analytic, and is the exact converse of the Law of Contradiction, which asserts that every analytic proposition is true. The Identity of Indiscernibles, also, is expressly deduced by Leibniz from the analytic character of all true propositions ; for after asserting this he proceeds : " Sequitur etiam hinc *non dari posse duas res singulares solo numero differentes :* utique enim oportet rationem reddi posse cur sint diversae, quae ex aliqua in ipsis differentia petenda est "** (Ib. p. 519).

* " Always therefore the predicate or consequent inheres in the subject or antecedent, and in this fact consists the nature of truth in general . . . But this is true in every affirmative truth, universal or singular, necessary or contingent."

** " It even follows from this that *there cannot be two singular things which differ only numerically ;* for it must be possible to give a reason why they are diverse, which is to be sought in some difference between them."

Leibniz's logic was, therefore, at least in his most lucid moments, simpler than that with which I have credited him. In particular, the Law of Sufficient Reason is interpreted in §14 of the present work in a manner which is quite different from Couturat's, not compatible with the texts upon which he relies, and less consistent with Leibniz's logic. At the same time, there are abundant texts to support the view which I took. This is an instance of Leibniz's general duality : he had a good philosophy which (after Arnauld's criticisms) he kept to himself, and a bad philosophy which he published with a view to fame and money. In this he showed his usual acumen : his bad philosophy was admired for its bad qualities, and his good philosophy, which was known only to the editors of his MSS., was regarded by them as worthless, and left unpublished. For example, he composed, in 1686, a work on mathematical logic, and wrote on the margin " hic egregie progressus sum " ; but no editor before Couturat accepted his estimate of his own work. In another MS., he sent out Euler's diagrams for all the moods of the syllogism ; in yet another, he gave De Morgan's formula : A or B=not (not A and not B). These are merely samples of results or methods, known by the names of subsequent discoverers, which should have been known as Leibniz's, but for the bad taste of his editors and his own preference for cheap popularity. I think it probable that as he grew older he forgot the good philosophy which he had kept to himself, and remembered only the vulgarized version by which he won the admiration of Princes and (even more) of Princesses. If Couturat's work could have been published in his lifetime, he would, I feel sure, have hated it, not as being inaccurate, but as being indiscreetly accurate.

Buried among his fragments on logic, there is a curious definition of existence. " Definiri potest Existens, quod cum pluribus compatibile est quam quodlibet aliud incompatibile cum ipso "* (Opuscules, p. 360). Again, after saying " The existent is what has being or possibility, and something more," he proceeds : " Ajo igitur Existens esse Ens quod cum plurimis compatibile est, seu Ens maxime possibile, itaque omnia coexistentia aeque possibilia sunt "** (Ib. p. 376). Strange consequences follow if Leibniz intended this to be, in the strict sense, a *definition* of " existence." For, if it was so intended,

---

* " The existent may be defined as that which is compatible with more things than is anything incompatible with itself."

** " I say therefore that the existent is the being which is compatible with most things, or the most possible being, so that all coexistent things are equally possible."

there was no act of Creation : the relations of essences are among eternal truths, and it is a problem in pure logic to construct that world which contains the greatest number of coexisting essences. This world, it would follow, exists by definition, without the need of any Divine Decree ; moreover, it is a part of God, since essences exist in God's mind. Here, as elsewhere, Leibniz fell into Spinozism whenever he allowed himself to be logical ; in his published works, accordingly, he took care to be illogical.

Mathematics, and especially the infinitesimal calculus, greatly influenced Leibniz's philosophy. The truths which we call contingent are, according to him, those in which the subject is infinitely complex, and only an infinitely prolonged analysis can show that the predicate is contained in the subject. Every substance is infinitely complex, for it has relations to every other, and there are no purely extrinsic denominations, so that every relation involves a predicate of each of the related terms. It follows that " every singular substance involves the whole universe in its perfect notion " (Opuscules, p. 521). For us, accordingly, propositions about particular substances are only empirically discoverable ; but to God, who can grasp the infinite, they are as analytic as the proposition " equilateral triangles are triangles." We can, however, approximate indefinitely to the perfect knowledge of individual substances. Thus, speaking of St. Peter's denial of Christ, Leibniz says : " The matter can be demonstrated from the notion of Peter, but the notion of Peter is complete, and so involves infinites, and so the matter can never be brought to perfect demonstration, but this can be approached more and more nearly, so that the difference shall be less than any given difference." Couturat comments on " this quite mathematical locution, borrowed from the infinitesimal method " (La Logique de Leibniz, p. 213n). Leibniz is fond of the analogy of irrational numbers. A very similar question has arisen in the most modern philosophy of mathematics, that of the finitists. For example, does π at any point have three successive 7's in its decimal expression ? So far as people have gone in the calculation, it has not. It may be proved hereafter that there *are* three successive 7's at a later point, but it cannot be proved that there are not, since this would require the completion of an infinite calculation. Leibniz's God could complete the sum, and would therefore know the answer, but we can never know it if it is negative. Propositions about what exists, in Leibniz's philosophy, could be known *a priori* if we could complete an infinite analysis, but, since we cannot, *we* can only know them empirically, though God can deduce them from logic.

At the time when I wrote "The Philosophy of Leibniz," I knew little of mathematical logic, or of Georg Cantor's theory of infinite numbers. I should not now say, as is said in the following pages, that the propositions of pure mathematics are "synthetic." The important distinction is between propositions deducible from logic and propositions not so deducible; the former may advantageously be defined as "analytic," the latter as "synthetic." Leibniz held that, for God, all propositions are analytic; modern logicians, for the most part, regard pure mathematics as analytic, but consider all knowledge of matters of fact to be synthetic.

Again, I should not now say: "It is evident that not *every* monad can have an organic body, if this consists of other subordinate monads" (p. 150). This assumes that the number of monads must be finite, whereas Leibniz supposed the number to be infinite. "In every particle of the universe," he says, "a world of infinite creatures is contained" (Opuscules, p. 522). Thus it is possible for *every* monad to have a body composed of subordinate monads, just as every fraction is greater than an infinite number of other fractions.

It is easy to construct an arithmetical scheme representing Leibniz's view of the world. Let us suppose that to each monad is assigned some rational proper fraction m, and that the state of each monad at time t is represented by $m f(t)$, where $f(t)$ is the same for all the monads. There is then a correspondence, at any given time, between any two monads and also between any one monad and the universe; we may thus say that every monad mirrors the world and also mirrors every other monad. We might suppose the body of the monad whose number is m to be those monads whose numbers are powers of m. The number m may be taken as measuring the intelligence of the monad; since m is a proper fraction, its powers are less than m, and therefore a monad's body consists of inferior monads. Such a scheme is of course merely illustrative, but serves to show that Leibniz's universe is logically possible. His reasons for supposing it actual, however, since they depend upon the subject-predicate logic, are not such as a modern logician can accept. Moreover, as is argued in the following pages, the subject-predicate logic, taken strictly, as Leibniz took it, is incompatible with plurality of substances.

Except in regard to the points mentioned above, my views as to the philosophy of Leibniz are still those which I held in 1900. His importance as a philosopher has become more evident than it was at that date, owing to the growth of mathematical logic and the simultaneous discovery of his MSS.

on that and kindred subjects. His philosophy of the empirical world is now only a historical curiosity, but in the realm of logic and the principles of mathematics many of his dreams have been realized, and have been shown at last to be more than the fantastic imaginings that they seemed to all his successors until the present time.

September, 1937

PREFACE TO THE FIRST EDITION

THE history of philosophy is a study which proposes to
itself two somewhat different objects, of which the first is
mainly historical, while the second is mainly philosophical.
From this cause it is apt to result that, where we look for
history *of* philosophy, we find rather history *and* philosophy.
Questions concerning the influence of the times or of other
philosophers, concerning the growth of a philosopher's
system, and the causes which suggested his leading ideas—
all these are truly historical: they require for their answer
a considerable knowledge of the prevailing education, of the
public to whom it was necessary to appeal, and of the scientific
and political events of the period in question. But it may
be doubted how far the topics dealt with in works where these
elements predominate can be called properly philosophical.
There is a tendency—which the so-called historical spirit has
greatly increased—to pay so much attention to the *relations*
of philosophies that the philosophies themselves are neglected.
Successive philosophies may be compared, as we compare
successive forms of a pattern or design, with little or no
regard to their meaning: an influence may be established by
documentary evidence, or by identity of phrase, without any
comprehension of the systems whose causal relations are under
discussion. But there remains always a purely philosophical
attitude towards previous philosophers—an attitude in which,

without regard to dates or influences, we seek simply to discover what are the great types of possible philosophies, and
guide ourselves in the search by investigating the systems
advocated by the great philosophers of the past. There is
still, in this inquiry--what is, after all, perhaps the most important of the historical questions—the problem as to the
actual views of the philosopher who is to be investigated. But
these views are now examined in a different spirit. Where we
are inquiring into the opinions of a truly eminent philosopher,
it is probable that these opinions will form, in the main, a
closely connected system, and that, by learning to understand
them, we shall ourselves acquire knowledge of important philosophic truths. And since the philosophies of the past belong
to one or other of a few great types—types which in our own
day are perpetually recurring—we may learn, from examining
the greatest representative of any type, what are the grounds
for such a philosophy. We may even learn, by observing the
contradictions and inconsistencies from which no system hitherto
propounded is free, what are the fundamental objections to
the type in question, and how these objections are to be
avoided. But in such inquiries the philosopher is no longer
explained psychologically: he is examined as the advocate of
what he holds to be a body of philosophic truth. By what
process of development he came to this opinion, though in
itself an important and interesting question, is logically irrelevant to the inquiry how far the opinion itself is correct; and
among his opinions, when these have been ascertained, it
becomes desirable to prune away such as seem inconsistent
with his main doctrines, before those doctrines themselves are
subjected to a critical scrutiny. Philosophic truth and falsehood, in short, rather than historical fact, are what primarily
demand our attention in this inquiry.

It is this latter task, and not the more strictly historical
one, that I have endeavoured to perform towards Leibniz. The

historical task has been admirably performed by others, notably Professor Stein, in works to which I have nothing to add; but the more philosophical task appears to be still unperformed. Erdmann's excellent account of Leibniz in his larger history (1842), from which I have learnt more than from any other commentary, was written in ignorance of the letters to Arnauld, and of much other important material which has been published since the date of Erdmann's edition of Leibniz (1840). And since his day, the traditional view of our philosopher's system appears to have been so deeply rooted in the minds of commentators that the importance of new manuscripts has not, I think, been duly recognized. Dillmann, it is true, has written a book whose object is similar to that of the present work, and has emphasized—rightly as it seems to me—the danger of obtaining our opinions of Leibniz from the *Monadology*. But it may be doubted whether Dillmann has succeeded as well in understanding the meaning of Leibniz as in mastering the text of his writings.

A few personal remarks may serve to explain why I believe a book on Leibniz to be not wholly uncalled for. In the Lent Term of 1899 I delivered a course of lectures on the Philosophy of Leibniz at Trinity College, Cambridge. In preparing these lectures, I found myself, after reading most of the standard commentators and most of Leibniz's connected treatises, still completely in the dark as to the grounds which had led him to many of his opinions. Why he thought that monads cannot interact; how he became persuaded of the Identity of Indiscernibles; what he meant by the law of Sufficient Reason—these and many other questions seemed to demand an answer, but to find none. I felt—as many others have felt—that the *Monadology* was a kind of fantastic fairy tale, coherent perhaps, but wholly arbitrary. At this point I read the *Discours de Métaphysique* and the letters to Arnauld. Suddenly a flood of light was thrown on all the inmost recesses of Leibniz's philosophical edifice. I saw how its foundations were laid, and how its superstructure rose out of them. It appeared that this seemingly fantastic system could be deduced from a few simple premisses, which, but for the conclusions which Leibniz had drawn from them, many, if not most, philosophers would have been willing to admit. It seemed not unreasonable to hope that the passages which had seemed illuminating to me would seem so also to others. I have therefore, in what follows, begun with the doctrines contained in these passages, and endeavoured as far as possible to exhibit the theory of monads as a rigid deduction from a small number of premisses. The monad thus appears, not at the beginning of the exposition, but after a long preliminary chain of reasoning. And it must, I think, be allowed that, if this account be correct, Leibniz's value as a philosopher is very much greater than that which would result from the customary expositions.

I have added an Appendix of classified extracts, in which it has been my object to include at least one definite pronouncement, wherever one could be found, on every point in Leibniz's philosophy. On moot points, or points on which he is inconsistent, I have in general given several quotations. I have given the date of a passage whenever it is not later than 1686, or seems important for some other reason. Passages referred to in the text are generally quoted in the corresponding paragraph of the Appendix, except when they have been already referred to and quoted in an earlier paragraph; but passages quoted in the text are in general not repeated in the Appendix. For convenience of reference, I have made an index of the Appendix, so that any passage contained in it can be found at once by the reference. I have translated all passages quoted, and have nowhere assumed any knowledge of a foreign language. I have also endeavoured to assume no previous acquaintance with Leibniz beyond what can be obtained from

Mr. Latta's excellent translations. In quoting passages translated by him I have in general followed his translation; but the translations of Mr. Duncan and Mr. Langley I have usually found it necessary to correct. In quoting from the papers against Clarke, I have followed Clarke's translation wherever this is not seriously inaccurate.

I have to thank Mr. G. E. Moore, of Trinity College, Cambridge, for reading the proofs and for many valuable suggestions, as also for the serious labour of revising all translations from the Latin, both in the text and in the appendix. I have also to thank Professor James Ward for reading a portion of the work in manuscript and for several important criticisms.

September, 1900.

TABLE OF CONTENTS

CHAPTER I

LEIBNIZ'S PREMISSES.

CHAPTER II

NECESSARY PROPOSITIONS AND THE LAW OF CONTRADICTION.

CHAPTER III

CONTINGENT PROPOSITIONS AND THE LAW OF SUFFICIENT REASON.

CHAPTER IV

THE CONCEPTION OF SUBSTANCE.

CHAPTER V

THE IDENTITY OF INDISCERNIBLES AND THE LAW OF CONTINUITY. POSSIBILITY AND COMPOSSIBILITY.

CHAPTER VI

WHY DID LEIBNIZ BELIEVE IN AN EXTERNAL WORLD?

CHAPTER VII

THE PHILOSOPHY OF MATTER: (*a*) AS THE OUTCOME OF THE
PRINCIPLES OF DYNAMICS.

CHAPTER VIII

THE PHILOSOPHY OF MATTER (CONTINUED), (*b*) AS EXPLAINING
CONTINUITY AND EXTENSION.

CHAPTER IX

THE LABYRINTH OF THE CONTINUUM.

CHAPTER X

THE THEORY OF SPACE AND TIME AND ITS RELATION TO MONADISM.

CHAPTER XI

THE NATURE OF MONADS IN GENERAL.

CHAPTER XII

SOUL AND BODY.

CHAPTER XIII

CONFUSED AND UNCONSCIOUS PERCEPTION.

CHAPTER XIV

LEIBNIZ'S THEORY OF KNOWLEDGE.

CHAPTER XV

PROOFS OF THE EXISTENCE OF GOD.

CHAPTER XVI

LEIBNIZ'S ETHICS.

ABBREVIATIONS

G.   *Die philosophischen Schriften von G. W. Leibniz,* herausgegeben von C. J. Gerhardt. Berlin, 1875—90.

G. M. *Leibnizens mathematische Schriften,* herausgegeben von C. J. Gerhardt. Halle, 1850—63.

F. de C. *Réfutation inédite de Spinoza par Leibniz,* précédée d'un mémoire par A. Foucher de Careil. Paris, 1854.

D.   *The Philosophical Works of Leibnitz,* with notes by George Martin Duncan. New Haven, 1890.

L.   *Leibniz: The Monadology and other philosophical writings,* translated, with introduction and notes, by Robert Latta. Oxford, 1898.

N. E. *New Essays concerning human understanding by Gottfried Wilhelm Leibnitz, together with an Appendix consisting of some of his shorter pieces,* translated by Alfred Gideon Langley. New York and London, 1896.

CHAPTER I

1. THE philosophy of Leibniz, though never presented to the world as a systematic whole, was nevertheless, as a careful examination shows, an unusually complete and coherent system. As the method of studying his views must be largely dependent upon his method of presenting them, it seems essential to say something, however brief, as to his character and circumstances, and as to the ways of estimating how far any given work represents his true opinions.

The reasons why Leibniz did not embody his system in one great work are not to be found in the nature of that system. On the contrary, it would have lent itself far better than Spinoza's philosophy to geometrical deduction from definitions and axioms. It is in the character and circumstances of the man, not of his theories, that the explanation of his way of writing is to be found. For everything that he wrote he seems to have required some immediate stimulus, some near and pressing incentive. To please a prince, to refute a rival philosopher, or to escape the censures of a theologian, he would take any pains. It is to such motives that we owe the *Théodicée*, the *Principles of Nature and of Grace*[1], the *New Essays*, and the *Letters to Arnauld*. But for the sole purposes of exposition he seems to have cared little. Few of his works are free from reference to some particular person, and almost all are more concerned to persuade readers than to provide the most valid

---

[1] Accepting Gerhardt's opinion that this work, and not the *Monadology*, was written for Prince Eugene (G. VI. 483).

arguments. This desire for persuasiveness must always be borne in mind in reading Leibniz's works, as it led him to give prominence to popular and pictorial arguments at the expense of the more solid reasons which he buried in obscurer writings. And for this reason we often find the best statement of his view on some point in short papers discovered among his manuscripts, and published for the first time by modern students, such as Erdmann or Gerhardt. In these papers we find, as a rule, far less rhetoric and far more logic than in his public manifestoes, which give a very inadequate conception of his philosophic depth and acumen.

Another cause which contributed to the dissipation of his immense energies was the necessity for giving satisfaction to his princely employers. At an early age, he refused a professorship at the University of Altdorf[1], and deliberately preferred a courtly to an academic career. Although this choice, by leading to his travels in France and England, and making him acquainted with the great men and the great ideas of his age, had certainly a most useful result, it yet led, in the end, to an undue deference for princes and a lamentable waste of time in the endeavour to please them. He seems to have held himself amply compensated for laborious researches into the genealogy of the illustrious House of Hanover by the opportunities which such researches afforded for the society of the great. But the labours and the compensations alike absorbed time, and robbed him of the leisure which might have been devoted to the composition of a *magnum opus*. Thus ambition, versatility, and the desire to influence particular men and women, all combined to prevent Leibniz from doing himself justice in a connected exposition of his system.

2. By this neglect, the functions of the commentator are rendered at once more arduous and more important than in the case of most philosophers. What is first of all required in a commentator is to attempt a reconstruction of the system which Leibniz should have written—to discover what is the beginning, and what the end, of his chains of reasoning, to exhibit the interconnections of his various opinions, and to fill in from his other writings the bare outlines of such works as

---

[1] Guhrauer, *Leibnitz: Eine Biographie*, Vol. i. p. 44.

the Monadology or the *Discours de Métaphysique*. This unavoidable but somewhat ambitious attempt forms one part—perhaps the chief part—of my purpose in the present work. To fulfil it satisfactorily would be scarcely possible, and its necessity is my only excuse for the attempt. As I wish to exhibit a coherent whole, I have confined myself, as far as possible, to Leibniz's mature views—to the views, that is, which he held, with but slight modifications, from January 1686 till his death in 1716. His earlier views, and the influence of other philosophers, have been considered only in so far as they seemed essential to the comprehension of his final system.

But, in addition to the purely historical purpose, the present work is designed also, if possible, to throw light on the truth or falsity of Leibniz's opinions. Having set forth the opinions which were actually held, we can hardly avoid considering how far they are mutually consistent, and hence—since philosophic error chiefly appears in the shape of inconsistency—how far the views held were true. Indeed, where there is inconsistency, a mere exposition must point it out, since, in general, passages may be found in the author supporting each of two opposing views. Thus unless the inconsistency is pointed out, any view of the philosopher's meaning may be refuted out of his own mouth. Exposition and criticism, therefore, are almost inseparable, and each, I believe, suffers greatly from the attempt at separation.

3. The philosophy of Leibniz, I shall contend, contains inconsistencies of two kinds. One of these kinds is easily removed, while the other is essential to any philosophy resembling that of the Monadology. The first kind arises solely through the fear of admitting consequences shocking to the prevailing opinions of Leibniz's time—such are the maintenance of sin and of the ontological argument for God's existence. Where such inconsistencies are found, we, who do not depend upon the smiles of princes, may simply draw the consequences which Leibniz shunned. And when we have done this, we shall find that Leibniz's philosophy follows almost entirely from a small number of premisses. The proof that his system does follow, correctly and necessarily,

from these premisses, is the evidence of Leibniz's philosophical
excellence, and the permanent contribution which he made
to philosophy. But it is in the course of this deduction that
we become aware of the second and greater class of inconsistencies. The premisses themselves, though at first sight compatible, will be found, in the course of argument, to lead to
contradictory results. We are therefore forced to hold that
one or more of the premisses are false. I shall attempt to
prove this from Leibniz's own words, and to give grounds for
deciding, in part at least, which of his premisses are erroneous.
In this way we may hope, by examining a system so careful
and so thorough as his, to establish independent philosophical
conclusions which, but for his skill in drawing deductions,
might have been very difficult to discover.

4. The principal premisses of Leibniz's philosophy appear
to me to be five. Of these some were by him definitely laid
down, while others were so fundamental that he was scarcely
conscious of them. I shall now enumerate these premisses,
and shall endeavour to show, in subsequent chapters, how the
rest of Leibniz follows from them. The premisses in question
are as follows:

I.   Every proposition has a subject and a predicate.

II.   A subject may have predicates which are qualities
      existing at various times. (Such a subject is called
      a *substance*.)

III. True propositions not asserting existence at particular
      times are necessary and analytic, but such as assert
      existence at particular times are contingent and
      synthetic. The latter depend upon final causes.

IV.   The Ego is a substance.

V.   Perception yields knowledge of an external world, *i.e.*
      of existents other than myself and my states.

The fundamental objection to Leibniz's philosophy will be
found to be the inconsistency of the first premiss with the
fourth and fifth; and in this inconsistency we shall find a
general objection to Monadism.

5. The course of the present work will be as follows:
Chapters II.—V. will discuss the consequences of the first four
of the above premisses, and will show that they lead to the

whole, or nearly the whole, of the necessary propositions of the system. Chapters VI.—XI. will be concerned with the proof and description of Leibniz's Monadism, in so far as it is independent of final causes and the idea of the good. The remaining chapters will take account of these, and will discuss Soul and Body, the doctrine of God, and Ethics. In these last chapters we shall find that Leibniz no longer shows great originality, but tends, with slight alterations of phraseology, to adopt (without acknowledgment) the views of the decried Spinoza. We shall find also many more minor inconsistencies than in the earlier part of the system, these being due chiefly to the desire to avoid the impieties of the Jewish Atheist, and the still·greater impieties to which Leibniz's own logic should have led him. Hence, although the subjects dealt with in the last five chapters occupy a large part of Leibniz's writings, they are less interesting, and will be treated more briefly, than the earlier and more original portions of his reasoning. For this there is the additional reason that the subjects are less fundamental and less difficult than the subjects of the earlier chapters.

6. The influences which helped to form Leibniz's philosophy are not directly relevant to the purpose of the present work, and have, besides, been far better treated by commentators[1] than the actual exposition of his final system. Nevertheless, a few words on this subject may not be amiss. Four successive schools of philosophy seem to have contributed to his education; in all he found something good, and from each, without being at any time a mere disciple, he derived a part of his views. To this extent, he was an eclectic; but he differed from the usual type of eclectic by his power of transmuting what he borrowed, and of forming, in the end, a singularly harmonious whole. The four successive influences were: Scholasticism, Materialism, Cartesianism, and Spinozism. To these we ought to add a careful study, at a critical period, of some of Plato's Dialogues.

---

[1] See especially Guhrauer, *Leibnitz : Eine Biographie*, Breslau, 1846 ; Stein, *Leibniz und Spinoza*, Berlin, 1890; Selver, *Entwicklungsgang der Leibnizschen Monadenlehre*, Leipzig, 1885; Tönnies, *Leibniz und Hobbes*, *Phil. Monatshefte*, Vol. xxiii. ; Trendelenburg, *Historische Beiträge*, Vol. ii., Berlin, 1855.

Leibniz was educated in the scholastic tradition, then still unbroken at most of the German universities. He obtained a competent knowledge of the schoolmen, and of the scholastic Aristotle[1], while still a boy; and in his graduation thesis, *De Principio Individui*, written in 1663, he still employs the diction and methods of scholasticism. But he had already, two years before this time (if his later reminiscences are to be trusted), emancipated himself from what he calls the "trivial schools[2]," and thrown himself into the mathematical materialism of the day. Gassendi and Hobbes began to attract him, and continued (it would seem) greatly to influence his speculations until his all-important journey to Paris. In Paris (with two brief visits to England) he lived from 1672 to 1676, and here he became acquainted, more intimately than he could in Germany, with Cartesianism both in mathematics and philosophy—with Malebranche, with Arnauld the Jansenist theologian, with Huygens, with Robert Boyle, and with Oldenburg, the Secretary of the Royal Society. With these men he carried on correspondence, and through Oldenburg some letters (the source of 150 years of controversy[3]) passed between him and Newton. It was during his stay in Paris that he invented the Infinitesimal Calculus, and acquired that breadth of learning, and that acquaintance with the whole republic of letters, which afterwards characterized him. But it was only on his way back from Paris that he learnt to know the greatest man of the older generation. He spent about a month of the year 1676 at the Hague, apparently in constant intercourse with Spinoza; he discussed with him the laws of motion and the proof of the existence of God, and he obtained a sight of part (at any rate) of the *Ethics* in manuscript[4]. When the *Ethics* soon afterwards was posthumously published, Leibniz made notes of it, and undoubtedly bestowed very careful thought

---

[1] Leibniz appears, in spite of the great influence which Aristotle exerted upon him, to have never studied him carefully in the original. See Stein, *op. cit.* p. 163 ff.

[2] Guhrauer, *Leibnitz*, Vol. 1. pp. 25, 26; G. III. 606.

[3] These letters were said, by Newton's friends, to have given Leibniz the opportunity for plagiarizing the Calculus—a charge now known to be absolutely groundless.

[4] See Stein, *Leibniz und Spinoza*, Chapter IV.

upon its demonstrations. Of his thoughts during the years which followed, down to 1684 or even 1686 (since the *Thoughts on Knowledge, Truth and Ideas* deal only with one special subject), only slight traces remain, and it seems probable that, like Kant in the years from 1770 to 1781, he was in too much doubt to be able to write much. He certainly read Plato[1], and he certainly desired to refute Spinoza. At any rate, by the beginning of 1686 he had framed his notion of an individual substance, and had sufficiently perfected his philosophy to send Arnauld what is perhaps the best account he ever wrote of it—I mean the *Discours de Métaphysique* (G. IV. 427—463). With this and the letters to Arnauld his mature philosophy begins; and not only the temporal, but the logical beginning also is, in my opinion, to be sought here. The argument which forms the logical beginning, and gives the definition of substance, will be found in the four following chapters.

[1] Cf. Stein, *op. cit.* p. 119.

CHAPTER II

NECESSARY PROPOSITIONS AND THE LAW OF CONTRADICTION.

7. THAT all sound philosophy should begin with an analysis of propositions, is a truth too evident, perhaps, to demand a proof. That Leibniz's philosophy began with such an analysis, is less evident, but seems to be no less true. The system, which he afterwards uniformly maintained, was completed, in all essentials, by the beginning of the year 1686. In his writings during this year, when the grounds of his new opinions were still freshly present to his mind, there occurs an argument of great importance, derived, as he himself says (G. II. 73), from the general nature of propositions, and capable, in his opinion, if the plurality of substances be admitted, of alone establishing the remainder of his system. This argument is to be found in the letters to Arnauld, in the *Discours de Métaphysique*, written for Arnauld in January, 1686 (G. IV. 427—463)[1], and in a short undated paper, entitled *Specimen Inventorum de Admirandis naturae generalis arcanis* (G. VII. 309—318). Although the same reasoning does not, so far as I am aware, occur explicitly in any other passages, it is often suggested[2], and is alone capable of explaining why Leibniz held that substances do not interact. That Leibniz did not repeat, in his published works, this purely logical argument, is explained, in view of his invariable habit of choosing the reasons most likely to convince his readers, by a passage in one of his letters to Arnauld (G. II. 73, 74). "I expected," he writes, "that the argument drawn

---

[1] See G. II. 11 ff; also IV. 409, 410.
[2] *e.g.* L. 326; G. IV. 496.

from the general nature of propositions would make some impression on your mind; but I confess also that few people are capable of appreciating such abstract truths, and that perhaps no one but you would have so easily perceived its force." We know, however, that Leibniz often expressed an intention of publishing his correspondence with Arnauld (G. II. 10), and must, consequently, have regarded this correspondence as adequately expressing his philosophical opinions. There is thus no reason to suppose that, after the date of these letters, his views on fundamental points underwent any serious alteration.

The argument in question, whose examination will occupy the present and the three following chapters, yields the whole, or nearly the whole, of the necessary part of Leibniz's philosophy—of the propositions, that is to say, which are true of all possible worlds. In order to obtain further the propositions describing the actual world, we need the premiss that perception gives knowledge of an external world, whence follow space and matter and the plurality of substances. This premiss is derived, apparently, from no better basis than common sense, and with its introduction, in Chapter VI., we shall pass to a new division of Leibniz's philosophy. But since the *meaning* of substance is logically prior to the discussion of the plurality or the perceptions of substances, it is plain that the present argument, from which the meaning of substance is derived, must first be expounded and examined. I shall first state the argument quite briefly, and then proceed to set forth its various parts in detail.

8. Every proposition is ultimately reducible to one which attributes a predicate to a subject. In any such proposition, unless existence be the predicate in question, the predicate is somehow contained in the subject. The subject is defined by its predicates, and would be a different subject if these were different. Thus every true judgment of subject and predicate is analytic—*i.e.* the predicate forms part of the notion of the subject—unless actual existence is asserted. Existence, alone among predicates, is not contained in the notions of subjects which exist. Thus existential propositions, except in the case of God's existence, are synthetic, *i.e.* there would be no contra-

diction if the subjects which actually do exist did not exist. Necessary propositions are such as are analytic, and synthetic propositions are always contingent.

When many predicates can be attributed to one and the same subject, while this subject cannot be made the predicate of any other subject, then the subject in question is called an individual substance. Such subjects involve, *sub ratione possibilitatis*, a reference to existence and time; they are possible existents, and they have predicates expressing their states at different times. Such predicates are called contingent or concrete predicates, and they have the peculiarity that no one of them follows analytically from any others, as *rational* follows from *human*. Thus when a subject is defined by means of a certain number of such predicates, there is no contradiction in supposing it to be without the remainder. Nevertheless, in the subject which has these predicates, they are all contained, so that a perfect knowledge of the subject would enable us to deduce all its predicates. Moreover there is a connection, though not a necessary one, between the various concrete predicates; sequences have reasons, though these incline without necessitating. The need of such reasons is the principle of sufficient reason. Subjects whose notion involves a reference to time are required by the idea of persistence. Thus in order to say that I am the same person as I was, we require, not merely internal experience, but some *à priori* reason. This reason can only be that I am the same subject, that my present and past attributes all belong to one and the same substance. Hence attributes which exist in different parts of time must be conceived, in such a case, as attributes of the same subject, and must therefore be contained, somehow, in the notion of the subject. Hence the notion of me, which is timeless, involves eternally all my states and their connections. Thus to say, all my states are involved in the notion of me, is merely to say, the predicate is in the subject. Every predicate, necessary or contingent, past, present or future, is comprised in the notion of the subject. From this proposition it follows, says Leibniz, that every soul is a world apart; for every soul, as a subject, has eternally, as predicates, all the states which time will bring it; and thus these states follow from its notion alone, without any need of action from without. The principle, according to which the states of a substance change, is called its activity; and since a substance is essentially the subject of predicates which have a reference to time, activity is essential to every substance. The notion of an individual substance. differs from a mere collection of general notions by being complete, as Leibniz puts it, *i.e.* by being capable of wholly distinguishing its subject, and involving circumstances of time and place. The nature of an individual substance, he says, is to have so complete a notion as to suffice for comprehending and deducing all its predicates. Hence he concludes that no two substances can be perfectly alike. From this stage, by the help of the empirical premiss mentioned above, the doctrine of monads follows easily.

9. Such is, in outline, the logical argument by which Leibniz obtains his definition of an individual substance. In the above brief account, I have made no endeavour to conceal the gaps and assumptions involved. We must now enquire whether the gaps can be filled and the assumptions justified. For this purpose the following seem to be the most important questions.

(1) Are all propositions reducible to the subject-predicate form ?

(2) Are there any analytic propositions, and if so, are these fundamental and alone necessary ?

(3) What is the true principle of Leibniz's distinction between necessary and contingent propositions ?

(4) What is the meaning of the principle of sufficient reason, and in what sense do contingent propositions depend upon it ?

(5) What is the relation of this principle to the Law of Contradiction ?

(6) Does the activity of substance unduly presuppose time ?

(7) Is there any validity in Leibniz's deduction of the Identity of Indiscernibles ?

It is only by a critical discussion of these points that Leibniz's meaning can be grasped; for unless we have clear ideas about philosophy, we cannot hope to have clear ideas about Leibniz's philosophy. When all these questions have been discussed, we may proceed to enquire why Leibniz believed in a plurality of substances, and why he held that each mirrored the universe. But until we are clear as to his logic, we cannot hope to understand its applications.

10. The question whether all propositions are reducible to the subject-predicate form is one of fundamental importance to all philosophy, and especially to a philosophy which uses the notion of substance. For this notion, as we shall see, is derivative from the logical notion of subject and predicate. The view that a subject and a predicate are to be found in every proposition is a very ancient and respectable doctrine; it has, moreover, by no means lost its hold on philosophy, since Mr Bradley's logic consists almost wholly of the contention that every proposition ascribes a predicate to Reality, as the only ultimate subject[1]. The question, therefore, whether this form is universal, demands close attention, not only in connection with Leibniz, but also in connection with the most modern philosophy. I cannot here, however, do more than indicate the grounds for rejecting the traditional view.

The plainest instances of propositions not so reducible are the propositions which employ mathematical ideas. All assertions of numbers, as *e.g.* "There are three men," essentially assert plurality of subjects, though they may also give a predicate to each of the subjects. Such propositions cannot be regarded as a mere sum of subject-predicate propositions, since the number only results from the singleness of the proposition, and would be absent if three propositions, asserting each the presence of one man, were juxtaposed. Again, we must admit, in some cases, relations between subjects—*e.g.* relations of position, of greater and less, of whole and part. To prove that these are irreducible would require a long argument, but may be illustrated by the following passage from Leibniz himself (D. pp. 266—7; G. VII. 401):

"The ratio or proportion between two lines L and M may be conceived three several ways; as a ratio of the greater L to the lesser M; as a ratio of the lesser M to the greater L; and lastly, as something abstracted from both, that is, as the ratio

---

[1] Cf. *Logic*, Book I. Chap. II., especially pp. 49, 50, 66.

between L and M, without considering which is the antecedent, or which the consequent; which the subject, and which the object.... In the first way of considering them, L the greater is the subject, in the second M the lesser is the subject of that accident which philosophers call *relation* or *ratio*. But which of them will be the subject, in the third way of considering them? It cannot be said that both of them, L and M together, are the subject of such an accident; for if so, we should have an accident in two subjects, with one leg in one, and the other in the other; which is contrary to the notion of accidents. Therefore we must say that this relation, in this third way of considering it, is indeed *out of* the subjects; but being neither a substance, nor an accident, it must be a mere ideal thing, the consideration of which is nevertheless useful."

This passage is of capital importance for a comprehension of Leibniz's philosophy. After he has seemed, for a moment, to realize that *relation* is something distinct from and independent of subject and accident, he thrusts aside the awkward discovery, by condemning the third of the above meanings as "a mere ideal thing." If he were pushed as to this "ideal thing," I am afraid he would declare it to be an accident of the mind which contemplates the ratio. It appears plainly from his discussion that he is unable to admit, as ultimately valid, any form of judgment other than the subject-predicate form, although, in the case he is discussing, the necessity of relational judgments is peculiarly evident.

It must not be supposed that Leibniz neglected relational propositions. On the contrary, he dealt with all the main types of such propositions, and endeavoured to reduce them to the subject-predicate form. This endeavour, as we shall see, was one of the main sources of most of his doctrines. Mathematician as he was, he could hardly neglect space, time and number. As regards propositions asserting numbers, he held aggregates to be mere phenomena: they are what he calls "semi-mental entities." Their unity, which is essential to the assertion of any number, is, he says, added by perception alone, by the very fact of their being perceived at one time (G. II. 517). All that is true, then, in such judgments, is the individual assertions of subject and predicate, and the psychological assertion of simultaneous perception as a predicate of the percipient. Again, we are told that numbers have the nature of relations, and hence are in some manner beings (G. II. 304). But relations, though founded in things, derive their reality from the supreme reason (N. E. p. 235 ; G. v. 210) ; God sees not only individual monads and their various states, but their relations also, and in this consists the reality of relations (G. II. 438). And as regards space and time, Leibniz always endeavoured to reduce them to attributes of the substances in them. Position, he says, like priority or posteriority, is nothing but a mode of a thing (G. II. 347). The whole doctrine is collected in the *New Essays* (N. E. p. 148 ; G. v. 132). " Units are separate, and the understanding gathers them together, however dispersed they may be. Yet, although relations are from the understanding, they are not groundless or unreal. For the primitive understanding is the origin of things; and indeed the reality of all things, simple substances excepted, consists only in the foundation of the perceptions of phenomena in simple substances." Thus relations and aggregates have only a mental truth ; the true proposition is one ascribing a predicate to God and to all others who perceive the relation[1].

Thus Leibniz is forced, in order to maintain the subject-predicate doctrine, to the Kantian theory that relations, though veritable, are the work of the mind. As applied to various special relations—as *e.g.* those of space, time, and number—I shall criticize special forms of this doctrine in their proper places. The view, implied in this theory, and constituting a large part of Kant's Copernican revolution, that propositions may acquire truth by being believed[2], will be criticized in connection with the deduction of God's existence from the eternal truths. But as applied to relations, the view has, in Leibniz's case, a special absurdity, namely, that the relational propositions, which God is supposed to know, must be strictly meaningless. The only ground for denying the independent

---

[1] Cf. Lotze, *Metaphysic*, beginning of § 109.

[2] I am aware that this is not an orthodox statement of the Kantian theory. The kind of grounds which lead me to think it correct, will be found indicated in Chaps. XIV. and XV., especially § 113.

reality of relations is, that propositions must have a subject and a predicate. If this be so, a proposition without a subject and a predicate must be no proposition, and must be destitute of meaning. But it is just such a proposition which, in the case of numbers, or of relations between monads, God is supposed to see and believe. God, therefore, believes in the truth of what is meaningless. If the proposition which he believes, on the other hand, be truly a proposition, then there are propositions which do not have a subject and a predicate. Thus the attempt to reduce relations to predicates of the percipient suffers from one or other of two defects. Either the percipient is deceived into seeing truth in a meaningless form of words, or there is no reason to suppose the truth dependent upon his perception of it.

A thorough discussion of the present question would, at this point, proceed to show that judgments of subject and predicate are themselves relational, and include, moreover, as usually understood, two fundamentally different types of relation. These two types are illustrated by the two propositions: "This is red," and "red is a colour." In showing that these two propositions express relations, it would be shown that *relation* is more fundamental than the two special types of relation involved. But such a discussion is beset with difficulties, and would lead us too far from the philosophy of Leibniz.

In the belief that propositions must, in the last analysis, have a subject and a predicate, Leibniz does not differ either from his predecessors or from his successors. Any philosophy which uses either substance or the Absolute will be found, on inspection, to depend upon this belief. Kant's belief in an unknowable thing-in-itself was largely due to the same theory. It cannot be denied, therefore, that the doctrine is important. Philosophers have differed, not so much in respect of belief in its truth, as in respect of their consistency in carrying it out. In this latter respect, Leibniz deserves credit. But his assumption of a plurality of substances made the denial of relations peculiarly difficult, and involved him in all the paradoxes of the pre-established harmony[1].

---

[1] Cf. Bradley, *Appearance and Reality*, 1st ed. pp. 29—30.

11. I pass now to a question which is no less fundamental, and more difficult, than that which we have just discussed. This is the question—as it has been called since Kant—of analytic and synthetic judgments and their relation to necessity. Leibniz's position on this question determined, not only his departure from his predecessors, but also, by its obvious untenability, Kant's great departure from him. On this point it will be necessary to begin with an account of Leibniz's views.

Two questions must be carefully distinguished in this connection. The first concerns the meaning and range of analytic judgments, the second concerns their claim to exclusive necessity. On the second question, Leibniz agreed wholly with his predecessors; on the first, by the discovery that all causal laws are synthetic, he made an important change, which prepared the way for Kant's discovery that all the propositions of Mathematics are synthetic.

In discussing the first of these questions, I shall use the terms analytic and synthetic, though they are not used by Leibniz in this sense. He uses the terms necessary and contingent; but this use prejudges, in his own favour, the second question, which forms one of the principal issues between him and Kant. It is therefore unavoidable to depart from Leibniz's usage, since we need two pairs of terms, where he required only one pair.

As regards the range of analytic judgments, Leibniz held that all the propositions of Logic, Arithmetic and Geometry are of this nature, while all existential propositions, except the existence of God, are synthetic. The discovery which determined his views on this point was, that the laws of motion, and indeed all causal laws (though not, as I shall show in the next chapter, the law of Causality itself), are synthetic, and therefore, in his system, also contingent (cf. G. III. 645).

As regards the meaning of analytic judgments, it will assist us to have in our minds some of the instances which Leibniz suggests. We shall find that these instances suffer from one or other of two defects. Either the instances can be easily seen to be not truly analytic—this is the case, for example, in

Arithmetic and Geometry—or they are tautologous, and so not properly propositions at all. Thus Leibniz says, on one occasion (N. E. p. 404 ; G. v. 343), that primitive truths of reason are identical, because they appear only to repeat the same thing, without giving any information. One wonders, in this case, of what use they can be, and the wonder is only increased by the instances which he proceeds to give. Among these are " A is A," " I shall be what I shall be," " The equilateral rectangle is a rectangle," or, negatively, " A B cannot be non-A." Most of these instances assert nothing ; the remainder can hardly be considered the foundations of any important truth. Moreover those which are true presuppose, as I shall now show, more fundamental propositions which are synthetic. To prove this, we must examine the meaning of analytic judgments, and of the definitions which they presuppose.

The notion that all *à priori* truths are analytic is essentially connected with the doctrine of subject and predicate. An analytic judgment is one in which the predicate is contained in the subject. The subject is supposed defined by a number of predicates, one or more of which are singled out for predication in an analytic judgment. Thus Leibniz, as we have just seen, gives as an instance the proposition : "The equilateral rectangle is a rectangle " (N. E. p. 405 ; G. v. 343). In the extreme case, the subject is merely reasserted of itself, as in the propositions : " A is A," " I shall be what I shall be" (*ib.*). Now two points seem important in this doctrine. In the first place, the proposition must be of what I distinguished above as the second type of subject-predicate proposition, *i.e.* of the type " red is a colour," " man is rational," not of the type " this is red," or " Socrates is human." That is to say, the proposition is concerned with the relation of genus and species, not of species and individual. This is the reason why every proposition about actual individuals is, in Leibniz's opinion, contingent. I do not wish at present to discuss whether the distinction of these two types is ultimately tenable—this question will be better discussed when we come to the Identity of Indiscernibles. For the present, I only wish to point out, what Leibniz frequently asserts, that analytic propositions are necessarily concerned with essences and species, not with assertions as to individuals[1]. The second point concerning analytic propositions is, that the subject, except in such pure tautologies as "A is A," must always be complex. The subject is a collection of attributes, and the predicate is a part of this collection. If, however, the reference to individuals be deemed essential to the distinction of subject from predicate, we shall have to say that the subject is any individual having a certain collection of predicates. In this way, we might attempt to reduce the second type to the first. But now the proposition becomes hypothetical: "If a thing is red, it is coloured." This Leibniz admits. The eternal truths, he says, are all hypothetical, and do not assert the existence of their subjects (N. E. p. 515; G. v. 428). But this makes it evident that our reduction to the first type has failed. The above hypothetical proposition evidently presupposes the proposition "red is a colour"; and thus Leibniz goes on to say that the truth of hypothetical propositions lies in the connection of ideas (N. E. p. 516; G. v. 429). Thus in analytic judgments, when they are not expressed in the derivative hypothetical form, the subject is a complex idea, *i.e.* a collection of attributes, while the predicate is some part of this collection.

The collection, however,—and this is the weak point of the doctrine of analytic judgments—must not be any haphazard collection, but a collection of compatible or jointly predicable predicates (predicability being here of the first type). Now this compatibility, since it is presupposed by the analytic judgment, cannot itself be analytic. This brings us to the doctrine of definition, in which we shall find that Leibniz, like all who have held analytic propositions to be fundamental, was guilty of much confusion.

Definition, as is evident, is only possible in respect of complex ideas. It consists, broadly speaking, in the analysis of complex ideas into their simple constituents. Since one idea can only be defined by another, we should incur a vicious circle if we did not admit some indefinable ideas. This obvious truth

---

[1] Foucher de Careil, *Réfutation inédite de Spinoza par Leibniz*, Paris, 1854, p. 24 (D. 175); G. v. 268 (N. E. 309); G. ii. 49. In this latter passage, it is specially instructive to observe Leibniz's corrections, as indicated in Gerhardt's notes.

is fully recognized by Leibniz, and the search for the simple ideas, which form the presuppositions of all definition, constitutes the chief part of his studies for the Universal Characteristic. Thus Leibniz says (*Monadology*, §§ 33, 35) : " When a truth is necessary, its reason can be found by analysis, resolving it into more simple ideas and truths, until we come to those which are primary....In short, there are *simple ideas*, of which no definition can be given; there are also axioms and postulates, in a word, *primary principles*, which cannot be proved, and indeed have no need of proof; and these are *identical propositions*, whose opposite involves an express contradiction" (L. 236—7 ; D. 223 ; G. vi. 612). The same view is expressed whenever Leibniz treats of this question. What I wish to show is, that Leibniz's theory of definition, as consisting of analysis into indefinable simple ideas, is inconsistent with the doctrine that the " primary principles" are identical or analytic ; and that the former is correct, while the latter is erroneous.

Leibniz often urges that the objects of definitions must be shown to be *possible*. It is thus that he distinguishes what he calls *real* definitions from such as are only *nominal* (*e.g.* D. p. 30 ; G. iv. 424). And thus he says that Arithmetic is analytic, because the number 3, for example, is *defined* as $2 + 1$, but he confesses that 3, so defined, must be seen to be possible (N. E. p. 410 ; G. v. 347). In one passage (G. i. p. 385), he even confesses that ideas in general involve a judgment, namely the judgment that they are possible. This confession, one might suppose, would be inconsistent with the doctrine of analytic judgments; it is rendered consistent, however, by Leibniz's definition of possibility. A possible idea, for him, is one which is not self-contradictory. But if this were all that is meant, any collection of simple ideas would be compatible, and therefore every complex idea would be possible. In an early proof of the existence of God (G. vii. 261) submitted by Leibniz to Spinoza at the Hague, this argument is actually used to show that God is possible[1]. He here defines God as the subject

---

[1] We shall find, when we come to deal with the proofs of God's existence, that this paper, in spite of its early date (1676), contains no views which Leibniz did not hold in his maturity.

which has all positive predicates. He takes two simple predicates, A and B, and shows, what is sufficiently evident, that they cannot be mutually contradictory. Hence he concludes that God, so defined, is possible. But since all ideas, when correctly analyzed, must, for Leibniz, be ultimately predicates, or collections of predicates, it follows that all ideas will be possible. And indeed, as Leibniz himself urges in this proof, any relation between simple ideas is necessarily synthetic. For the analytic relation, as we saw, can only hold between ideas of which one at least is complex. Hence if there were no synthetic relations of compatibility and incompatibility, all complex ideas would be equally possible. Thus there is always involved, in definition, the synthetic proposition that the simple constituents are compatible. If this be not the case, the constituents are incompatible—e.g. good and bad, or two different magnitudes of the same kind—and this is also a synthetic relation, and the source of negative propositions[1].

This conclusion may be enforced by examining some idea which is self-contradictory, such as a round square. In order that an idea may be self-contradictory, it is evidently necessary that it should involve two judgments which are mutually contradictory, i.e. the truth and falsehood of some judgment. For the Law of Contradiction applies, not to ideas, but to judgments: it asserts that every proposition is true or false (N. E. p. 405; G. v. 343). Hence a mere idea, as such, cannot be self-contradictory. Only a complex idea which involves at least two propositions can be self-contradictory. Thus the idea "round square" involves the proposition "round and square are compatible," and this involves the compatibility of having no angles, and of having four angles. But the contradiction is only possible because round and square are both complex, and round and square involve synthetic propositions asserting the compatibility of their constituents, while round

---

[1] Leibniz seems to have sometimes realized the difficulty involved in the compatibility of all single predicates. Thus he says: "It is yet unknown to men what is the reason of the incompossibility of different things, or how it is that different essences can be opposed to each other, seeing that all purely positive terms seem to be compatible" inter se (G. VII. 195; quoted by Caird, Critical Philosophy of Kant, I. pp. 93—4). (The date is before 1686.)

involves the incompatibility of its constituents with the possession of angles. But for this synthetic relation of incompatibility, no negative proposition would occur, and therefore there could be no proposition involved which would be directly contradictory to the definition of a square. This is almost admitted by Leibniz, when he urges that truths are not arbitrary, as Hobbes supposed, because " notions are not always reconcilable among themselves" (D. 30; G. IV. 425). Since the possibility of God, as defined by Leibniz, depends upon the fact that all *simple* ideas *are* " reconcilable among themselves," and since all notions are composed of simple ideas, it is difficult to see how the two views are to be combined. Thus Leibniz's criterion of possible and impossible ideas can never apply to simple ideas, and moreover always presupposes those simple ideas and their relations—relations which can only be expressed in synthetic propositions. Two simple ideas can never be mutually contradictory in Leibniz's sense, since mere analysis will not reveal any further predicate possessed by the one and denied by the other. Thus a self-contradictory idea, if it be not a mere negative, such as a non-existent existent, must always involve a synthetic relation of incompatibility between two simple notions. The impossible idea, in Leibniz's sense, presupposes the idea which is impossible on account of some synthetic proposition; and conversely, the possible complex idea is possible on account of a synthetic proposition asserting the compatibility of its simple constituents. Thus to return to Arithmetic, even if $2 + 1$ be indeed the *meaning* of 3, still the proposition that $2 + 1$ is possible is necessarily synthetic. A possible idea cannot, in the last analysis, be *merely* an idea which is not contradictory; for the contradiction itself must always be deduced from synthetic propositions. And hence the propositions of Arithmetic, as Kant discovered, are one and all synthetic.

In the case of Geometry, which Leibniz also regards as analytic, the opposite view is even more evidently correct. The triple number of dimensions, he says, follows analytically from the fact that only three mutually perpendicular lines can be drawn through one point (G. VI. 323). No instance, he says, could be more proper for illustrating a blind necessity independent of God's will. It is amazing that he did not perceive, in this instance, that the proposition from which the three dimensions are supposed to be deduced is in fact precisely the same as the three dimensions, and that, so far from being proved, it is wholly incapable of deduction from any other proposition, and about as synthetic as any proposition in the whole range of knowledge. This is so obvious as to need no further argument; and it is an interesting fact that Kant, in his first published work[1], points out the circularity of Leibniz's deduction in the above passage of the *Théodicée*, and proceeds, being still a Leibnizian, to infer that the number of dimensions is synthetic and contingent, and might be different in other possible worlds (ed. Hartenstein, 1867, I. p. 21 ff.).

We may argue generally, from the mere statement of the Law of Contradiction, that no proposition can follow from it alone, except the proposition that there is truth, or that some proposition is true. For the law states simply that any proposition must be true or false, but cannot be both. It gives no indication as to the alternative to be chosen, and cannot of itself decide that any proposition is true. It cannot even, of itself, yield the conclusion that such and such a proposition is true or false, for this involves the premiss "such and such is a proposition," which does not follow from the law of contradiction. Thus the doctrine of analytic propositions seems wholly mistaken.

It may be worth pointing out that even those propositions which, at the beginning of the enquiry, we took as the type of analytic propositions, such as "the equilateral rectangle is a rectangle," are not wholly analytic. We have already seen that they are logically subsequent to synthetic propositions asserting that the constituents of the subject are compatible. They cannot, therefore, in any case, give the premisses of any science, as Leibniz supposed (cf. N. E. p. 99; G. v. 92). But further, in so far as they are significant, they are judgments of whole and part; the constituents, in the subject, have a certain kind of unity—the kind always involved in numeration, or in assertions of a whole—which is taken away by analysis. Thus even here, in so far as the subject is *one*, the judgment does not

---

[1] *Gedanken von der wahren Schützung der lebendigen Kräfte*, 1747.

follow from the Law of Contradiction alone. And in the closely allied judgments, such as "red is a colour," "2 is a number," "number is a concept," the subject is not even complex, and the proposition is therefore in no sense analytic. But this last assertion is one which I cannot here undertake to prove.

12. As regards the second point which was to be discussed, namely the connection of the necessary and the analytic, it is evident, from what has been said already, that if there are to be any necessary propositions at all there must be necessary synthetic propositions. It remains to enquire what we mean by necessity, and what distinction, if any, can be made between the necessary and the contingent.

Necessity itself is never discussed by Leibniz. He distinguishes kinds of necessity—metaphysical, hypothetical, and moral—but he nowhere explains metaphysical necessity, which is here in question, otherwise than as the property of analytic propositions. Nevertheless, necessity must mean something other than connection with the Law of Contradiction; the statement that analytic propositions are necessary is significant, and the opposite statement—that synthetic propositions are contingent—is certainly so regarded by Leibniz. It would seem that necessity is ultimate and indefinable. We may say, if we choose, that a necessary proposition is one whose contradictory is impossible; but the impossible can only be defined by means of the necessary, so that this account would give no information as to necessity. In holding necessary propositions to be analytic, Leibniz agreed with all his predecessors, and with those of his successors who preceded Kant. But by the discovery that the laws of motion are synthetic, and by his strict determinism, he rendered the denial of necessary synthetic propositions highly paradoxical in its consequences, and prepared the way for Kant's opposite assertion. (For Leibniz, by the way, the necessary is not, as for Kant, the same as the *à priori*; we shall find that contingent propositions also have *à priori* proofs. The *à priori* is, as in Kant, what is independent of particular experience, but the necessary is not coextensive with this.) Leibniz and Kant both held that there is a fundamental distinction between propositions that are necessary, and those that are contingent, or, in Kant's language, empirical. Thus the propositions of mathematics are necessary, while those asserting particular existence are contingent. It may be questioned whether this distinction is tenable, whether, in fact, there is any sense in saying, of a true proposition, that it might have been false. As long as the distinction of analytic and synthetic propositions subsisted, there was some plausibility in maintaining a corresponding distinction in respect of necessity. But Kant, by pointing out that mathematical judgments are both necessary and synthetic, prepared the way for the view that this is true of *all* judgments. The distinction of the empirical and the *à priori* seems to depend upon confounding sources of knowledge with grounds of truth. There is no doubt a great difference between *knowledge* gained by perception, and *knowledge* gained by reasoning; but that does not show a corresponding difference as to what is known. The further discussion of this point, however, must be postponed till we come to Leibniz's theory of perception. And it must be confessed that, if *all* propositions are necessary, the notion of necessity is shorn of most of its importance.

Whatever view we adopt, however, as regards the necessity of existential propositions, it must be admitted that arithmetical propositions are both necessary and synthetic, and this is enough to destroy the supposed connection of the necessary and the analytic.

In the next Chapter we shall have a less destructive task. We shall have to show the true principle and the true importance of Leibniz's division of propositions into two kinds, and the meaning of the Law of Sufficient Reason, which he invoked as the source of his contingent propositions.

CHAPTER III

13. WE have now seen that Leibniz's division of propositions into two classes, in the form in which he gave it, is untenable. Necessary propositions are not to be defined as those that follow from the Law of Contradiction; and as regards propositions which are not necessary, it may be questioned whether any such are to be found. Nevertheless, there is a most important principle by which propositions may be divided into two classes. This principle, we shall find, leads to the same division of propositions as that to which Leibniz was led, and may, by examination of his words, be shown to be the true principle upon which his division proceeded. His division does, therefore, correspond to what is perhaps the most important classification of which propositions are capable. I shall first explain this classification, and then examine the Law of Sufficient Reason, which Leibniz held to be the supreme principle of contingent propositions.

Contingent propositions, in Leibniz's system, are, speaking generally, such as assert actual existence. The exception which this statement requires, in the case of the necessary existence of God, may be provided for by saying that contingent propositions are such as involve a reference to parts of time. This seems to be Leibniz's meaning when he says (G. III. 588): "The notion of eternity in God is quite different from that of time, for it consists in necessity, and that of time in contingency." Thus necessary propositions are such as have no reference to actual time, or such as—except in the case of God—do not assert the existence of their subjects. " As for the eternal truths," Leibniz says, " we must observe that at bottom they are all conditional, and say in fact : Such a thing posited, such another thing is" (N. E. p. 515; G. v. 428). And again: " Philosophers, who distinguish so often between what belongs to *essence* and what to *existence,* refer to existence all that is *accidental* or *contingent*" (N. E. p. 498 ; G. v. p. 414). He points out also that the truth of a necessary proposition does not depend upon the existence of its subject (N. E. p. 516 ; G. v. 429). The designation as *eternal* truths, which he always adopts, must be meant to indicate that no special time is referred to in the proposition; for the proposition itself, of whatever nature, must of course be eternally true or eternally false.

But propositions about contingency itself, and all that can be said generally about the nature of possible contingents, are not contingent; on the contrary, if the contingent be what actually exists, any proposition about what *might* exist must be necessary. Thus Leibniz says (G. II. 39): " The notion of a species involves only eternal or necessary truths, but the notion of an individual involves, *sub ratione possibilitatis,* what is of fact, or related to the existence of things and to time." He proceeds to explain that the notion of the sphere which Archimedes caused to be placed on his tomb involves, besides its form, the matter of which it was made, as well as the place and time. This passage is very important, for it involves the distinction, afterwards urged by Kant against the ontological argument, between the notion of an existent and the assertion of actual existence. The notion of an individual, as Leibniz puts it, involves reference to existence and time *sub ratione possibilitatis, i.e.* the notion is exactly what it would be if the individual existed, but the existence is merely possible, and is not, in the mere notion, judged to be actual. " Possibles are possible," he says, " before all actual decrees of God, but not without sometimes supposing the same decrees taken as possible. For the possibilities of individuals or of contingent truths contain in their notion the possibility of their causes, to wit, the free decrees of God; in which they are different from the possibilities of species or eternal truths, which depend only upon the understanding of God, without involving his will" (G. II. 51). That is to say, possible existents involve possible causes, and the connection between a possible cause and a possible effect is similar to that between an actual cause and an actual effect. But so long as we do not assert actual existence, we are still in the region of eternal truths, and although, as we shall see, the law of sufficient reason does apply to possibles, still it is not, in such applications, coordinate with the principle of contradiction, but only a consequence of that principle. It is in taking the further step, in judging the actual existence of the individual whose notion is in question, that the law of sufficient reason becomes indispensable, and gives results to which the law of contradiction is, by itself, inadequate. The individual once posited, all its properties follow: "every predicate, necessary or contingent, past, present, or future, is comprised in the notion of the subject" (G. II. 46). But it does not follow that this notion represents a subject which exists: it is merely the idea of a subject having the general qualities distinguishing existents. Existence is thus unique among predicates. All other predicates are contained in the notion of the subject, and may be asserted of it in a purely analytic judgment. The assertion of existence, alone among predicates, is synthetic, and therefore, in Leibniz's view, contingent. Thus existence has, for him, just as peculiar a position as it has in Kant's criticism of the ontological proof, and it must be regarded as a sheer inconsequence, in Leibniz, that he failed to apply his doctrine also to God. But for the fact that Leibniz definitely asserts the contrary (N. E. 401; G. v. 339)[1], one would be tempted to state his position as tantamount to a denial that existence is a predicate at all.

But further, not only the existence of such and such a subject is contingent, but also the connection of any two predicates expressing the states of that subject at different times. Thus Leibniz says, in discussing the supposition that he is

[1] "When we say that a thing exists, or has real existence, this existence itself is the predicate, *i.e.* it has a notion joined to the idea in question, and there is connection between these two notions."

going, at some future time, to make a journey, "the connection of events, though certain, is not necessary, and it is open to me to make or not to make this journey, for though it is included in my notion that I shall make it, it is also included in it that I shall make it freely. And there is nothing in me, of all that can be conceived generally, or by essence, or by a specific or incomplete notion, whence it can be concluded that I shall do so necessarily, whereas from my being a man it can be concluded that I am capable of thinking; and consequently, if I do not make this journey, that will not combat any eternal or necessary truth. Nevertheless, since it is certain that I shall do so, there must be some connection between me, who am the subject, and the execution of the journey, which is the predicate; for, in a true proposition, the notion of the predicate is always in the subject. Consequently, if I did not do so, there would be a falsity, which would destroy my individual or complete notion" (G. II. 52). Thus those predicates which are concretes, *i.e.* those expressing states of a substance at particular parts of time, are in a different position from such abstract predicates as *human* and *rational*. Concrete predicates, though they are connected with each other, are not necessarily connected; the connections, as well as the predicates, are contingent. All the predicates are necessarily connected with the subject, but no concrete predicates are necessarily connected with each other. And hence Leibniz often speaks of them as contingent predicates. If the series of predicates were different, the subject would be different; hence the necessary connection of predicates and subject amounts to little more than the law of identity[1]. A subject is defined by its predicates, and therefore, if the predicates were different, the subject could not be the same. Thus it follows, from a subject's being the subject it is, that it will have all the predicates that it will have; but from one or more of its predicates, this does not follow necessarily. The existence of each separate predicate at each separate instant is a contingent truth, for each is presupposed in the assertion that just such a subject exists. There is a difficulty, on this view, in distinguishing

[1] "It would not have been our Adam, but another, if he had had other events" (G. II. 42).

a subject from the sum of its predicates—a difficulty to which I shall return when I come to the doctrine of substance. For the present, I am content to point out that, in asserting the existence of an individual substance, *i.e.* of a subject whose notion is complete, there are involved just as many separate contingent propositions as there are moments through which the substance persists. For the state of the substance at each moment exists, and its existence is a contingent proposition. It is thus existential propositions that are contingent, and propositions not asserting existence that are necessary. Leibniz's division of propositions into two kinds does, therefore, correspond to a very important division—perhaps the most important—of which propositions are susceptible.

Some explanation seems, however, to be called for by the connections of contingent predicates. These connections can hardly be said to *exist*, and yet they are always contingent, not only in free substances, but also in such as have no freedom. In substances which are not free, the connections of successive states are given by the laws of motion, and these laws are most emphatically contingent. Leibniz even goes so far as to say that it is in Dynamics that we learn the distinction of necessary and contingent propositions (G. III. 645). Besides these, there is the general law, equally contingent, but equally without exception, "that man will always do, though freely, what seems the best" (G. IV. 438). The fact seems to be, that these general but not necessary laws are regarded by Leibniz as essentially referring to *every* part of actual time. That is to say, they do not hold of the sequences in other *possible* time-orders, but only of *actual* sequences. Moreover they are deduced from elements in the actual preceding state, which elements lead to the sequence, and are logically prior to it— this is, as we shall see, essential to the doctrine of activity. Thus these laws, though they have an *à priori* proof by means of final causes, are yet of the *nature* of empirical generalisations. They have held, they hold now, and they will hold hereafter. They apply to every moment of actual time, but they cannot be stated without such reference. This is a conception which I shall have to criticize when we come to deal with Leibniz's philosophy of Dynamics. For the present, I only wish to point out that, in his system, the laws of motion and the law of volition are existential, and do have an essential reference to the parts of actual time. They are peculiar only in referring to *all* parts of time. They may be contrasted, in this respect, with the properties of time itself, which are metaphysically necessary, and the same in all possible worlds; whereas the *existence* of time is contingent, since it depends upon God's free resolve to create a world.

Leibniz's dichotomy of propositions amounts, therefore, to the following assertions. All true propositions not involving actual existence, but referring only to essences or possibles, are necessary; but propositions asserting existence—except in the case of God—are never necessary, and do not follow necessarily from any other existential proposition, nor yet from the fact that the subject has all the qualities distinguishing existents[1]. If, then, existential propositions are to have any interrelations, and are to be in any way systematized, there must be some principle by which their merely particular and contingent character is mitigated.

14. This brings me to the principle of sufficient reason. This principle is usually supposed to be, by itself, adequate to the deduction of what actually exists. To this supposition, it must be confessed, Leibniz's words often lend colour. But we shall find that there are really two principles included under the same name, the one general, and applying to all possible worlds, the other special, and applying only to the actual world. Both differ from the law of contradiction, by the fact that they apply specially—the former, however, not exclusively—to existents, possible or actual. The former, as we shall see, is a form of the law of causality, asserting all possible causes to be desires or appetites; the latter, on the other hand, is the assertion that all *actual* causation is determined by desire for the good. The former we shall find to be metaphysically necessary, while the latter is contingent, and applies only to contingents. The former is a principle of possible contingents, the latter a principle of actual contingents only. The importance of this distinction will appear as soon as we

---

[1] On the connection of contingency with infinite complexity (which many commentators regard as defining contingency) see Chap. V. § 26.

begin to examine Leibniz's accounts of what he means by sufficient reason[1].

The law of sufficient reason is variously stated by Leibniz at various times. I shall begin with his later statements, which are better known, and more in accordance with the traditional view of its import; I shall then refer to the earlier statements, especially those of 1686, and examine whether these can be reconciled with the later forms of the principle.

The statement in the *Monadology* is as follows (§§ 31, 32, 33, 36): "Our reasonings are founded upon two great principles, that of contradiction, ...and that of sufficient reason, in virtue of which we judge that no fact can be found true or existent, no statement veritable, unless there is a sufficient reason why it should be so and not otherwise, although these reasons usually cannot be known to us. There are also two kinds of truths, those of reasoning, and those of fact. Truths of reasoning are necessary, and their opposite is impossible; truths of fact are contingent, and their opposite is possible. When a truth is necessary, the reason of it can be found by analysis.... But there must also be a sufficient reason for contingent truths or truths of fact, *i.e.* for the sequence of things which are dispersed throughout the universe of created beings, in which the resolution into particular reasons might go on into endless detail" (D. 222—3; L. 235—7; G. vi. 612). This leaves us entirely uninformed as to what is meant by a sufficient reason. The same vagueness appears in the *Principles of Nature and of Grace* (§ 7): "Thus far we have spoken only as mere physicists: now we must rise to metaphysics, by making use of the great principle, little employed in general, which affirms that nothing happens without a sufficient reason; *i.e.* that nothing happens without its being possible for one who should know things sufficiently to give a reason sufficient to determine why things are so and not otherwise. This principle being laid down, the first question we are entitled to put will be, why is there something rather than nothing? For *nothing* is simpler and easier than *something*. Further, supposing that things

---

[1] I do not maintain that Leibniz himself was perfectly clear as to these two principles of sufficient reason, but that he did, as a matter of fact, designate two distinct principles (perhaps not distinguished by him) by this same name.

must exist, we must be able to give a reason why they must exist thus and not otherwise" (D. 212—3; L. 414—5; G. vi. 602). This statement, though it brings out very clearly the connection of contingency and existence, gives us no further information as to the meaning of sufficient reason. In the paper " On the Ultimate Origination of Things" (1697) Leibniz is a little more definite. He says: " In eternal things, even though there be no cause, there must be a reason, which, for permanent things, is necessity itself, or essence; but for the series of changing things, if it be supposed that they succeed one another from all eternity, this reason is, as we shall presently see, the prevailing of inclinations, which consist not in necessitating reasons, *i.e.* reasons of an absolute and metaphysical necessity, the opposite of which involves a contradiction, but in inclining reasons" (L. 338; D. 100; G. vii. 302). What is meant by these inclining reasons cannot be properly explained until we come to deal with the activity of substance. In dealing with actual existents, the inclining reason is the perception of the good, either by the substance itself, if it be free, or by God, if the substance be not free. But the law as above stated, even in the form which applies only to the series of changing things, is true, as we shall soon see, not only of the actual world, but of all possible worlds. It is, therefore, itself metaphysically necessary, and unable to distinguish the actual from the possible. Even in the form which applies only to the series of changing things, the law is still a law of all *possible* contingents; and any true proposition about *possible* contingents must itself be not contingent, but necessary.

Before developing this topic, let us examine Leibniz's earlier statements of the law. In the year 1686, when he was more inclined than in later years to go to the bottom of his principles, he gives a statement at first sight very different from those which he usually gives, and refers to his usual formula as a " vulgar axiom" which follows as a corollary. He says : " There must always be some foundation of the connection of terms in a proposition, which must be found in their notions. This is my great principle, with which I believe all philosophers must agree, and of which one of the corollaries is this vulgar axiom, that nothing happens without a reason...though often this reason inclines without necessitating" (G. II. 56). And again he says that in Metaphysics he presupposes hardly anything but two great principles, namely (1) the law of contradiction, and (2) "that nothing is without a reason, or that every truth has its *à priori* proof, drawn from the notion of the terms, although it is not always in our power to make this analysis" (G. II. 62).

There is another passage, in an undated paper, which however, on internal evidence, would seem to belong to the same period, in which Leibniz is even more definite on the *à priori* proof of contingent propositions. "Generally, every true proposition," he says, "(which is not identical or true *per se*) can be proved *à priori* by the help of axioms, or propositions true *per se*, and by the help of definitions or ideas. For as often as a predicate is truly affirmed of a subject, some real connection is always judged to hold between the predicate and the subject, and thus in any proposition: A is B (or, B is truly predicated of A), B is always in A itself, or its notion is in some way contained in the notion of A itself; and this either with absolute necessity, in propositions of eternal truth, or with a kind of certainty, depending upon a supposed decree of a free substance, in contingent things; and this decree is never wholly arbitrary and destitute of foundation, but always some reason for it (which however inclines, and does not necessitate), can be given, which could itself be deduced from analysis of the notions (if this were always within human power), and certainly does not escape the omniscient substance, which sees everything *à priori* by means of ideas themselves and its own decrees. It is certain, therefore, that all truths, even the most contingent, have an *à priori* proof, or some reason why they are rather than are not. And this is itself what people commonly say, that nothing happens without a cause, or that nothing is without a reason." (G. VII. 300, 301)[1].

---

[1] The principle of sufficient reason, in so far as it is independent of final causes, occurs in Spinoza (*Ethics*, I. 11, 2nd dem.): "For the existence or non-existence of anything, it must be possible to assign a cause or reason." Leibniz was aware of this agreement, as appears from the following comment on Schuller's account of Spinoza: "This is rightly observed, and agrees with what I am wont to say, that nothing exists unless a sufficient reason of its existence can be given, which is easily shown not to lie in the series of causes." [G. I. 138.]

These statements, as they stand, seem different from Leibniz's later statements of the law of sufficient reason. But it would seem that he intends, in contingent matter, to include, in "the notion of the terms," the pursuit of the apparently best. This appears quite plainly in a passage also written in 1686, where he says that the actions of Caesar, though contained in his notion, depend upon God's free choice to create men, and to make them such that they would always choose, though freely, what seemed best to them. It is only thus, he says, that such predicates can be shown *à priori* to belong to Caesar (G. IV. 438).

Thus the law of sufficient reason, as applied to actual existents, reduces itself definitely to the assertion of final causes, in the sense that actual desires are always directed towards what appears the best. In all actual changes, the consequent can only be deduced from the antecedent by using the notion of the good. Where the change depends only upon God, it really is for the best; where it depends upon a free creature, it is such as seems best to the creature, but is often, owing to confused perception, not really the best possible change. Such a connection can only be regarded as contingent by admitting, as Leibniz does, that a law may be general, *i.e.* may apply to every part of time, without being necessary, *i.e.* without being capable of a statement in which no actual part of time is referred to. To pursue this topic is impossible until we come to the doctrine of substance. At present I will only point out that this principle confers upon the good a relation to existence such as no other concept possesses. In order to infer actual existence, whether from another existent, or from mere notions, the notion of the good must always be employed. It is in this sense that contingent propositions have *à priori* proofs[1]. "As possibility is the principle of essence," Leibniz says, "so perfection, or a degree of essence (by which the greatest number of things are compossible), is the principle

---

[1] The *à priori*, in Leibniz, is opposed to the empirical, not to the contingent. A proof employing the notion of the good may show, without appealing to experience, that something exists, but does not thereby render this proposition necessary. Thus the *à priori* is not, as in Kant, synonymous with the necessary.

of existence " (D. 103; L. 342—3; G. VII. 304)[1]. This connection of existence with the good, the principle that all actual causation is determined by desire for what appears best, is a most important proposition, which we shall have to consider again at a later stage. It gives the essence of the law of sufficient reason as applied to actual existents. At the same time we shall see that the law has also a wider meaning, in which it applies to possible existents as well. The confusion of these two has rendered the connection of the law with the principle of contradiction very difficult to understand. The distinction will, I think, enable us to clear up the connection of Leibniz's two principles.

15. When we enquire into the relation of the law of sufficient reason to the law of contradiction, we find that Leibniz makes very few remarks on the subject, and that those few give a meaning to the law of sufficient reason, in which it applies equally to all possible worlds. We then require a further principle, applicable only to the actual world, from which actual existence may be inferred. This is to be found in final causes. But let us see what Leibniz says.

"I certainly maintain," he writes to Des Bosses, "that a power of determining oneself without any cause, or without any source of determination, implies contradiction, as does a relation without foundation; but from this the metaphysical necessity of all effects does not follow. For it suffices that the cause or reason be not one that metaphysically necessitates, though it is metaphysically necessary that there should be some such cause" (G. II. 420). In this passage he is evidently thinking of the volitions of free creatures; in a letter to the Princess of Wales, accompanying the fourth paper against Clarke, he makes the same statement concerning God. "God himself," he says, "could not choose without having a reason of his choice" (G. VII. 379). But we know that God, being free, might have chosen otherwise, and therefore, since he must have a reason for his choice, there must have been possible reasons for possible

---

[1] Perfection here has its metaphysical sense, as the "amount of positive reality" (*Monadology*, § 41, D. 224), but Leibniz certainly thought metaphysical perfection good. In the sentence preceding the one quoted in the text, he speaks of "imperfection or moral absurdity" as synonymous, and means by imperfection the opposite of metaphysical perfection. See Chap. XVI.

choices, as well as actual reasons for actual choices. The same consequence follows as regards free creatures. And this consequence, as appears from a passage quoted above (G. II. 51 ; § 13), was actually drawn by Leibniz. In order that a notion may be the notion of a possible existent, there must be another notion which, if it existed, would be a sufficient reason for such an imagined existent. "There were," Leibniz continues, "an infinity of possible ways of creating the world, according to the different designs which God might form, and each possible world depends upon certain principal designs or ends of God proper to itself" (G. II. 51).

But if the principle applies to possible as well as actual existents, how is it to help in determining what does actually exist ? It gives merely, on this view, a general quality of what *might* exist, not a source of actual existents[1]. This Leibniz would admit. And we may now clearly state the distinction between actual and possible sufficient reasons. The part of the principle which is metaphysically necessary, which applies equally to possible and to actual existents, is the part which asserts all events to be due to design. From the passage at the end of the preceding paragraph, it appears that, whichever of the possible worlds God had created, he would always necessarily have had some design in doing so, though his design might not have been the best possible. And similarly volition, in free creatures, *must* have a motive, *i.e.* must be determined by some prevision of the effect. The relation of cause and effect can never be a purely external one ; the cause must be always, in part, a desire for the effect. This form of causality is the essence of activity, which Leibniz, as we shall see, declares to be metaphysically necessary to substance. And in this form, the law of sufficient reason is necessary and analytic, not a principle coordinate with that of contradiction, but a mere consequence of it.

The principle which applies only to actuals, which is really coordinate with the law of contradiction, and gives the source

---

[1] Cf. G. II. 225 : De Volder objects to Leibniz that to conceive the existence of a substance we require a cause, but not to conceive its essence. "I retort," Leibniz replies, " to conceive its essence we require the conception of a possible cause, to conceive its existence we require the conception of an actual cause."

of the world which does exist, is the principle that designs are always determined by the idea of the good or the best. God might have desired any of the possible worlds, and his desire would have been a sufficient reason for its creation. But it is a contingent fact that he desired the best, that the actual sufficient reason of creation was the desire for the maximum of good, and not for anything that the other possible worlds would have realised. So Leibniz says: "It is reasonable and assured that God will always do the best, though what is less perfect does not imply contradiction" (G. IV. 438)[1]. The same holds of free creatures, with the limitation that they are often mistaken about the good. It would be possible to desire what does not appear best, but it is a contingent fact that actual desires, which are actual sufficient reasons, are always directed to what the free spirit holds to be the best possible[2]. It might be supposed that, if God is necessarily good, his acts also must *necessarily* be determined by the motive of the best. But this Leibniz evades by the common notion that freedom is essential to goodness, that God is good only because the evil which he rejects is possible—a notion which this is not the place to discuss.

We may now sum up the results of our discussion of contingency and sufficient reason. Leibniz, holding fast to the doctrine that a necessary proposition must be analytic, discovered that existential propositions are synthetic, and also, like Hume and Kant, that all causal connections among existents differing in temporal position are synthetic. He inferred, accordingly, that the actual world does not exist necessarily, and that, within this world, causes do not produce their effects

[1] Cf. G. VII. 309, text and note. Also the following passages in the fifth paper against Clarke [G. VII.] : No. 9 : "But to say, that God can only choose what is best; and to infer from thence, that what he does not choose, is impossible; this, I say, is confounding of terms : 'tis blending power and will, metaphysical necessity and moral necessity, essences and existences. For what is necessary, is so by its essence, since the opposite implies a contradiction; but a contingent which exists, owes its existence to the principle of what is best, which is a sufficient reason of things." No. 73 : "God can do everything that is possible, but he will do only what is best." Cf. also No. 76.

[2] This appears also from a passage [G. II. 40] where Leibniz explains that the present state of the world follows from the first state only in virtue of certain laws freely decreed by God. These laws, therefore, among which is the pursuit of the best, must be contingent.

necessarily. The reason, as he perpetually repeats, inclines without necessitating. This was his solution of the problem raised by the fact, which he perceived as clearly as Hume and Kant, that causal connections are synthetic. Hume inferred that causal connections do not really connect, Kant inferred that the synthetic may be necessary, Leibniz inferred that a connection may be invariable without being necessary. As he never dreamt of denying that the necessary must be analytic, this was his only possible escape from a total denial of causal connections.

Thus the proposition that anything except God exists is contingent, and so is the proposition that one existent is the cause of another. At the same time, causality itself is necessary, and holds in all possible worlds. In all possible worlds, moreover, causality can only be rendered intelligible by regarding the cause as being in part a prevision or desire of the effect. This follows, as we shall see in the next chapter, from the general doctrine that "every extrinsic denomination has an intrinsic one for its foundation" (G. II. 240), *i.e.* that no relation is purely external. So far as this is asserted by the law of sufficient reason, that law is metaphysically necessary. The effect *must* be the end in the psychological sense, *i.e.* the object of desire. But in the actual world, owing to God's goodness, the effect also is, or seems to be, the end in the ethical sense. The psychological end is, as a matter of fact, what the agent believes to be the ethical end, *i.e.* what he believes to be the best possible effect. (In substances which are not free, the sufficient reason does not lie in them, but in God.) This is what distinguishes the actual from any other possible world. God might have created one of the possible worlds, but he could not have been ignorant of its not being the best. For its degree of excellence is an eternal truth, and an object of his understanding. But we are told (G. II. 51) that whatever world God had created, he would have had a design in so doing, and that some design is metaphysically necessary to his acts. It only remains, therefore, to interpret design psychologically, not ethically, when design is said to be necessary.

God's good actions then are contingent, and true only within the actual world. They are the source, from which all explanation of contingents by means of sufficient reason proceeds. They themselves, however, have their sufficient reason in God's goodness, which one must suppose metaphysically necessary[1]. Leibniz failed to show why, since this is so, God's good actions are not also necessary. But if they were necessary, the whole series of their consequences would have been also necessary, and his philosophy would have fallen into Spinozism. The only remedy would have been, to declare God's existence, like all other existence, contingent—a remedy irresistibly suggested by his logic, but regarded by him, for obvious reasons, as worse than the disease of Spinozism which his doctrine of contingency was designed to cure.

[1] Leibniz nowhere, so far as I know, definitely asserts God's goodness to be necessary, but this conclusion seems to follow from his philosophy. For God's goodness is an eternal truth, not referring solely, as do his acts, to the actual world. We can hardly suppose that, in other possible worlds, God would not have been good, or that it is a merely contingent fact that God is good. But if we were to make this supposition, we should merely remove the difficulty one stage further, since we should then require a sufficient reason for God's goodness. If this reason were necessary, God's goodness would also be necessary; if contingent, it would itself require a sufficient reason, concerning which the same difficulty would recur.

CHAPTER IV

THE CONCEPTION OF SUBSTANCE.

16. THE question to be discussed in this chapter is: What did Leibniz mean by the word substance, and how far can this meaning be fruitfully employed in philosophy? This question must be carefully distinguished from the question which is answered by the doctrine of Monads, namely, what existential judgments can we make, in which the notion of substance is employed? Our present question is simply, what *is* the notion of substance? Not, what judgments about the world can be made by the help of this notion?

The conception of substance dominated the Cartesian philosophy, and was no less important in the philosophy of Leibniz. But the meaning which Leibniz attached to the word was different from that which his predecessors had attached to it, and this change of meaning was one of the main sources of novelty in his philosophy. Leibniz himself emphasized the importance of this conception in his system. As against Locke, he urged that the idea of substance is not so obscure as that philosopher thought it (N. E. 148; G. v. 133). The consideration of it, he says, is one of the most important and fruitful points in philosophy: from his notion of substance follow the most fundamental truths, even those concerning God and souls and bodies (D. 69; G. IV. 469). To explain this notion is, therefore, an indispensable preliminary to a discussion of his views on matter or of his theory of Monads.

The Cartesians had defined substance as that which needs, for its existence, only God's concurrence. By this they meant, practically, that its existence was not dependent upon relations to any other existents; for God's concurrence was an awkward

condition, which had led Des Cartes to affirm that God alone
was properly and strictly a substance. Thus although, practically, they admitted two substances, mind and matter, yet,
whenever they took God seriously, they were compelled to deny
the substantiality of everything except God. This inconsistency
was remedied by Spinoza, to whom substance was *causa sui*,
the self-caused, or that which is in itself and is conceived
through itself. Substance to him, was therefore God alone—a
remedy which Leibniz regarded as condemning the original
definition (G. VI. 582). To Spinoza, extension and thought did
not constitute separate substances, but attributes of the one
substance. In Spinoza as in Des Cartes, the notion of substance, though not by them clearly analyzed into its elements,
was not an ultimate simple notion, but a notion dependent, in
some undefined manner, upon the purely logical notion of
subject and predicate. The attributes of a substance are the
predicates of a subject; and it is supposed that predicates
cannot exist without their subject, though the subject can
exist without them. Hence the subject becomes that whose
existence does not depend upon any other existent.

There is an interesting discussion of this definition, in
connection with Malebranche, in the Dialogue between Philarète and Ariste (G. VI. pp. 579—594). In this dialogue, the
representative of Malebranche begins by defining substance as
whatever can be conceived alone, or as existing independently
of other things (G. VI. 581). Leibniz points out, in objection,
that this definition, at bottom, applies only to God. "Shall we
then say," he proceeds, "with an innovator who is but too well-
known, that God is the only substance, and creatures are mere
modifications of him?" If the independence is to extend only
to created things, then, Leibniz thinks, force and life, abstractly
at least, can be so conceived. Independence in conception, he
says, belongs not only to substance, but also to what is essential
to substance. Malebranche's supporter then confines his definition to concretes: substance is a concrete independent of every
other created concrete. To this Leibniz retorts (1) that the
concrete can *perhaps* only be defined by means of substance, so
that the definition may involve a vicious circle[1]; (2) that

---

[1] This objection however is subsequently withdrawn (*Ib.* 583).

extension is not a concrete, but the abstract of the extended, which is the subject of extension (*Ib.* 582). But he avoids, in this place, any definition of his own, contenting himself, in a characteristically conciliatory manner, with pointing out that the above rectified definition will apply to Monads alone (*Ib.* 585—6).

17. Leibniz perceived, however, that the relation to subject and predicate was more fundamental than the doubtful inference to independent existence (cf. G. II. 221). He, therefore, definitely brought his notion of substance into dependence upon this logical relation. He urges against Locke that there is good reason to assume substance, since we conceive several predicates in one and the same subject, and this is all that is meant by the words *support* or *substratum*, which Locke is using as synonymous with substance (N. E. p. 225; G. v. 201—2).

But when we examine further, we find that this, though an essential part of the meaning of substance, is by no means *all* that this word means. Besides the logical notion of subject, there has been, as a rule, another element in the meaning people have attached to the word substance. This is the element of persistence through change. Persistence is involved, indeed, in the very notion of change as opposed to mere becoming. Change implies something which changes; it implies, that is, a subject which has preserved its identity while altering its qualities. This notion of a subject of change is, therefore, not independent of subject and predicate, but subsequent to it; it is the notion of subject and predicate applied to what is in time. It is this special form of the logical subject, combined with the doctrine that there are terms which can only be subjects and not predicates, which constitutes the notion of substance as Leibniz employs it. If we are to hold, he says, that I am the same person as I was, we must not be content with mere internal experience, but must have an *à priori* reason. This can only be that my present and past attributes are predicates of the same subject (G. II. 43). The necessity of substance in the sense of a subject of change has been pointed out by Kant in the first analogy of experience. But to Kant, this subject is as phenomenal as its predicates. The distinctive feature of substance, when used as the basis of a dogmatic metaphysic, is the belief that certain terms are only and essentially subjects. When several predicates can be attributed to a subject, *and this in turn cannot be attributed to any other subject*, then, Leibniz says, we call the subject an individual substance (G. IV. 432). This point is important; for it is plain that any term *may* be made a subject. I may say " two is a number," " red is a colour," and so on. But such terms can be attributed to others, and therefore are not substances. The ultimate subject is always a substance (G. II. 457—8). Thus the term *I* appears incapable of attribution to any other term; I have many predicates, but am not in turn a predicate of anything else. I, therefore, if the word *I* does denote anything distinct from the mere sum of my states, and if I persist through time, fulfil Leibniz's definition of a substance. Space, as Leibniz often admits, would, if it were real, which he denies, be a substance; for it persists through time, and is not a predicate[1].

Substance, then, is that which can only be subject, not predicate, which has many predicates, and persists through change. It is, in short, the subject of change. The different attributes which a substance has at different times are all predicates of the substance, and though any attribute exists only at a certain time, yet the fact of its being an attribute at that time is eternally a predicate of the substance in question. For the substance is the same subject at all times, and therefore has always the same predicates, since the notion of the predicate, according to Leibniz, is always contained in the notion of the subject. All my states and their connections have always been in the notion of that subject which is *I*. Thus to say that all my states are involved in the notion of me, is merely to say that the predicate is in the subject (G. II. 43). From this proposition, Leibniz continues, it follows that every soul is a world apart, independent of everything else except God (G. II. 46, 47). For since all my predicates have always belonged to me, and since among these predicates are contained all my states at the various moments of time, it follows that my development in time is a mere consequence of my notion, and cannot depend upon any other substance. Such a subject as I

---

[1] In his youth, Leibniz was inclined to admit space as a substance. See G. I. 10 (1668), and Selver, *op. cit.* p. 28.

am may not exist; but if such a subject does exist, all my states follow from the fact that I am such as I am, and this suffices to account for my changes, without supposing that I am acted upon from without[1].

18. We can now understand what Leibniz means by *activity*. The activity of substances, he says, is metaphysically necessary (G. II. 169). It is in this activity that the very substance of things consists. Without a force of some duration, no created substance would remain numerically the same, but all things would be only modifications of one divine substance (D. 117; G. IV. 508)[2]. Substance, again, is a being capable of action (D. 209; L. 406; G. VI. 598). But he does not often explain clearly what he means by activity. Activity is, as a rule, a cover for confused thinking; it is one of those notions which, by appealing to psychological imagination, appear to make things clear, when in reality they merely give an analogy to something familiar. Leibniz's use of activity, however, does not seem open to this charge. He definitely rejects the appeal to imagination. The indwelling force of substances, he says, may be conceived distinctly, but not explained by images, for force must be grasped by the understanding, not the imagination (D. 116; G. IV. 507). What then is this activity, which can be clearly conceived, but not imagined?

Without an internal force of action, Leibniz explains, a thing could not be a substance, for the nature of substance consists in this regulated tendency, from which phenomena are born in order (G. III. 58). Again he says (L. 300, *n.*; G. IV.

---

[1] Arnauld's judgment upon this theory, immediately after reading the *Discours de Métaphysique*, deserves quotation as a warning to philosophers who feel tempted to condemn their juniors. "I have at present," he writes, "such a cold, that all I can do is tell your Highness, in two words, that I find in these thoughts so many things which alarm me, and which almost all men, if I am not mistaken, will find so shocking, that I do not see of what use a writing can be, which apparently all the world will reject. I shall only give as an instance what he says in Art. 13: 'That the individual notion of each person involves once for all everything that will ever happen to him'" (G. II. 15). The selection of this remark as specially shocking may perhaps help to account for Leibniz's omission of it from his published works.

[2] Cf. Spinoza, *Ethics*, III. 6, 7. For him also, individuality consists in activity. Cf. Pollock's *Spinoza*, 1st ed. pp. 217, 221; 2nd ed. pp. 201, 205.

472): "By force or power (*puissance*), I do not mean the capacity (*pouvoir*) or mere faculty, which is nothing but a near possibility of acting, and which, being as it were dead, never produces an action without being stimulated from without, but I mean something between the capacity (*pouvoir*) and action, something which includes an effort, an act, an entelechy, for force passes of itself into action, in so far as nothing hinders it. Wherefore I regard force as constitutive of substance, since it is the principle of action, which is the characteristic of substance." We can thus see what Leibniz means by activity, and we can see also that this notion is a necessary and legitimate consequence of his notion of substance. A substance, we have seen, is a subject which has predicates consisting of various attributes at various parts of time. We have seen also that all these predicates are involved in the notion of the subject, and that the ground of its varying attributes is, therefore, within the substance, and not to be sought in the influence of the outside world. Hence there must be, in every state of a substance, some element or quality in virtue of which that state is not permanent, but tends to pass into the next state. This element is what Leibniz means by activity[1]. Activity is to be distinguished from what we mean by causation. Causation is a relation between two phenomena in virtue of which one is succeeded by the other. Activity is a quality of one phenomenon in virtue of which it tends to cause another. Activity is an *attribute* corresponding to the *relation* of causality; it is an attribute which must belong to the subject of changing states, in so far as those states are developed out of the nature of the subject itself. Activity is not a mere relation; it is an actual quality of a substance, forming an element in each state of the substance, in virtue of which that state is not permanent, but tends to give place to another. Since a substance, as we have seen, is essentially the permanent subject of changing attributes, it follows that activity, in the above sense, is essential to substance, and thus metaphysically necessary. It follows also that, as Leibniz says, without activity a substance could not preserve its numerical identity; for without activity a substance would cease to have new attributes at new moments of

[1] Cf. D. 115; G. IV. 506—7.

time, and would thus cease to exist. Activity thus follows
from the general doctrine, which Leibniz shares with many
other philosophers (*e.g.* Lotze), that every relation must be
analyzable into adjectives of the related terms. Two states
have a relation of succession and causality; therefore there
must be corresponding adjectives of the states. The adjective
of the preceding state is activity. Passivity, however, is not
the adjective of the succeeding state, but is something quite
different[1].

19. We may now return to the law of sufficient reason,
and interpret it in connection with activity. Although, as we
saw, all the states of a substance are contained in its notion,
and could, by perfect knowledge, be deduced from its notion,
yet this, as Leibniz means it, amounts to little more than the
law of identity[2]. Whatever my future actions may be, it must
be true now that they will be such as they will be. Whoever
acted otherwise would not be the same person. But that I
shall act in any specific manner cannot be inferred from any
general proposition about me. My specific actions are connected with the notion of me, but are not related *necessarily* to
any of my general qualities or to each other. There is nothing
in me, Leibniz says, of all that can be conceived generally, or
by essence, or by a specific or incomplete notion, from which
my future actions follow necessarily. Nevertheless, if I am
going to take a journey, it is certain that I shall take it, and
therefore, if I did not take it, there would be falsity, which
would destroy the individual or complete notion of me (G. II.
52). That is to say, whoever did otherwise would not be the
same person. This really amounts to no more than (1) the
assertion of permanent substances, (2) the obvious fact that
every proposition about the future is already determined either
as true or as false, though we may be unable to decide the
alternative. Thus we have no means, in all this, of determining,
from a given state of substance, what its future states will be;
and for this purpose, according to Leibniz, we require the principle of sufficient reason.

The principle fulfils, therefore, the same function as that

[1] Cf. Chap. XII, § 84.
[2] Cf. G. II. 42, beginning of paragraph.

for which causality is now used; it gives a connection between events at different times. But unlike causality, it endeavours to show *why*, and not merely *that*, certain sequences occur. In an early letter, written before Leibniz had discovered his notion of substance (1676 ?), he urges that a single thing cannot be the cause of its changes, since everything remains in the state it is in, if there is nothing to change it; for no reason can be given in favour of one change rather than another (G. I. 372). By the contrast between this and his later opinions, we see clearly the connection between activity and sufficient reason. The sufficient reason for one change rather than another is to be found in the nature of activity. In substances which are not free, this activity is regulated by general laws, which themselves have a sufficient reason in God's perception of fitness; in free substances, the sufficient reason lies in the more or less confused perception of the good on the part of the substance itself. But in no case is the connection between two states in itself necessary; it always arises from the perception, either in God or in the creature (if this be free), that the change is good (G. II. 38). This topic, however, cannot be fully discussed until we have examined the doctrine of Monads.

20. From what has been said of activity, it is plain that those predicates of a given substance which are existents in time form one causal series. Leibniz sometimes goes so far in this direction as to approach very near to Lotze's doctrine that things are laws[1]. All singular things, he says, are subject to succession, nor is there anything permanent but the law itself, involving continual succession. Successions, he continues, like such series as numbers, have the property that, given the first term and the law of progression, the remaining terms arise in order. The only difference is, that in successions the order is temporal, but in numbers the order is that of logical priority (G. II. 263). Further, the persistence of the same law is the ground for asserting that a new temporal existent belongs to the same substance as a past existent. The identity of a substance at different times is recognized, he says, " by the persistence of the same law of the series, or of continuous simple transition, which leads us to the opinion that one and the

---

[1] See Lotze's *Metaphysic*, Book I. Chap. III., especially § 32.

same subject or monad is changing. That there should be a persistent law, involving the future states of that which we conceive as the same, is just what I assert to constitute it the same substance" (G. II. 264). These passages explain very definitely what Leibniz means by his phrase, that each monad contains in its nature the law of the continuation of the series of its operations (D. 38; G. II. 136). They enable us, also, to see what would remain of the doctrine of monads if the appeal to substance were dropped. All the predicates of a given substance form one causal series : this series might, therefore, be taken as defining what we are to mean by one substance, and the reference to subject and predicate might be dropped. The plurality of substances would then consist in the doctrine, that a given existent at a given moment is caused, not by the whole preceding state of the universe, but by some one definite existent in the preceding moment. This assumption is involved in the ordinary search for causes of particulars. It is supposed, for instance, that two simultaneous existents A and B have been caused, respectively, by two different preceding existents a and β, not that each was caused by the whole preceding state of the universe. This assumption, if justified, would be sufficient to establish something very like Leibniz's philosophy. For A and B will in turn cause, respectively, different existents A′ and B′, and so on. The denial of the interaction of substances thus reduces itself, when the series is substituted for the single subject, to the assertion that there are many causal series, and not one only. I shall return to this assertion when I come to Leibniz's grounds for a plurality of substances[1]. At present I wish to point out how easily Leibniz could have got rid, at this stage, of the appeal to subject and predicate, and have substituted the unity of the law or series for that of the logical subject—a doctrine from which, as from his own, the persistence and independence of substances necessarily follows.

21. At this point it may be well to enquire how, in Leibniz's view, a substance differs from the sum of its predicates. If the monad had been reduced to a mere causal series, it would have been identified with the sum of its predicates. It would then have had a purely formal unity; there would not

[1] See end of Chap. VII.

have been an actual subject, the same at all points of time, but only a series of perpetually new terms. There would still have been simple substances, in the sense of independent causal series, but there would have been no reason for regarding the soul as one of these simple substances, or for denying causal interaction between my states and other existents. On the contrary, it is because the Ego appeared to Leibniz to be evidently one subject, that its various states were held to constitute one independent causal series. We must not say, therefore, as is often loosely done, that Leibniz *identified* substance and activity; activity is the *essence* of substances, but substances themselves are not essences, but the subjects of essences and other predicates[1]. Thus a substance is not, for Leibniz, identical with the sum of its states[2]; on the contrary, those states cannot exist without a substance in which to inhere. The ground for assuming substances—and this is a very important point—is purely and solely logical. What Science deals with are *states* of substances, and it is these only that can be given in experience. They are assumed to be states of *substances*, because they are held to be of the logical nature of predicates, and thus to demand subjects of which they may be predicated. The whole doctrine depends, throughout, upon this purely logical tenet. And this brings us back to the distinction, which we made in Chapter II., between two kinds of subject-predicate proposition. The kind which is appropriate to contingent truths, to predications concerning actual substances, is the kind which says "This is a man," not "man is rational." Here *this* must be supposed defined, not primarily by predicates, but simply as that substance which it is. The

---

[1] Cf. D. 118; G. iv. 509: "As for me, as far as I believe myself to have grasped the notion of action, I hold that that most received philosophical dogma, that *actions belong to subjects (esse suppositorum)*, follows from it, and is proved by it; and I think that this principle is so true that it is also reciprocal, so that not only whatever acts is a single substance, but also that every single substance acts without intermission." It appears plainly, from this passage, that the substance is conceived as a permanent subject, so that the assertion of activity is significant, and not a mere tautology.

[2] Cf. G. ii. 263: "Substances are not wholes which contain parts *formaliter*, but complete things which contain partial ones *eminenter*." Cf. also G. vi. 350.

substance is not an idea, or a predicate, or a collection of predicates; it is the substratum in which predicates inhere (cf. N. E. pp. 225—6; G. v. 201—3; esp. § 2). It would seem, however, that the word *this* must mean something, and that only a meaning is capable of distinguishing which substance we are speaking of. What is usually meant is some reference to time or place, so that "this is human" would reduce itself to "humanity exists here." The reference to time and place is to some extent countenanced by Leibniz (see *e.g.* G. II. 49), but he regarded time and place as themselves ultimately reducible to predicates. Thus the substance remains, apart from its predicates, wholly destitute of meaning[1]. As to the way in which a term wholly destitute of meaning can be logically employed, or can be valuable in Metaphysics, I confess that I share Locke's wonder[2]. When we come to the Identity of Indiscernibles, we shall find that Leibniz himself, by holding a substance to be defined by its predicates, fell into the error of confounding it with the sum of those predicates. That this was from his stand-point an error, is sufficiently evident, since there would be no ground for opposing subjects to predicates, if subjects were nothing but collections of predicates. Moreover, if this were the case, predications concerning actual substances would be just as analytic as those concerning essences or species, while the judgment that a substance exists would not be one judgment, but as many judgments as the subject has temporal predicates. Confusion on this point seems, in fact, to be largely responsible for the whole theory of analytic judgments.

22. The relation of time to Leibniz's notion of substance is difficult clearly to understand. Is the reality of time assumed as a premiss, and denied as a conclusion? A substance, we have seen, is essentially a subject persisting in time. But by the doctrine that all the states of a substance are eternally its predicates, Leibniz endeavours to eliminate the dependence

---

[1] Mr Bradley, in attempting to reduce all judgment to predication about Reality, is led to the same view concerning his ultimate subject. Reality, for him, is not an idea, and is therefore, one must suppose, meaningless. See his *Logic*, pp. 43, 49, 50, 66.

[2] *Essay*, Book II. Chap. XXIII. §§ 1, 2; N. E. pp. 225—6.

upon time. There is, however, no possible way, so far as I can discover, in which such an elimination can be ultimately effected. For we must distinguish between the state of the substance at a given moment, and the fact that such is its state at the given moment. The latter only is eternal, and therefore the latter only is what Leibniz must take as the predicate of the substance. The present state exists now, and does not exist the next moment; it cannot itself, therefore, be eternally a predicate of its substance. The eternal predicate is *that* the substance has such and such a state at such and such a moment. The pretended predicate, therefore, resolves itself into a proposition, which proposition itself is not one of subject and predicate. This point is well illustrated by a passage in which Leibniz endeavours to explain how an eternal predicate may refer to one part of time. What follows from the nature of a thing, he says, may follow perpetually or for a time. When a body moves in a straight line under no forces, it follows that at a given moment it will be at a given point, but not that it will stay there for ever (G. II. 258). What follows, in this case, for a time, is itself a proposition, and one logically prior to the attempted subsequent predication. This instance should make it plain that such propositions cannot be validly reduced to predications.

The doctrine of activity, however, seems designed to free such propositions from all reference to actual parts of time, and thus to render the propositions concerning states of a substance at different times merely complex predicates. It is necessary for Leibniz to maintain that *to exist now* and *to exist then* do not differ intrinsically, but only differ in virtue of some relation between what exists now and what existed then; and further, that this relation is due to the quality of what exists in these different times. This is attempted by the notion of activity. In order to avoid the relation to moments of time, these moments must be reduced to elements or parts of the corresponding states. Now activity is supposed to make a difference of quality between preceding and succeeding states, by means of which we could interpret their order of succession as a result of their own natures. The preceding state is the desire, the succeeding state the desired—such is, roughly speaking, the difference of states, to which it is sought to reduce the temporal difference. But this attempt, I think, cannot be successful. In the first place, few people would be willing to admit, what follows from the doctrine, that it is a pure tautology to say that activity or desire is directed to the future. In the second place, the present doctrine cannot explain what is meant by the simultaneity of states of different substances. If simultaneity be admitted, it follows that the present or any other time is not merely in my mind, but is something single and unique in respect of which simultaneous states agree. There is, in short, *one* time, not as many times as there are substances. Hence the time-order cannot be merely something in *my* mind, or a set of relations holding between *my* states. In the third place, it may be questioned what we gain by substituting the order due to activity for that due to time. We have a series of states A, B, C, D,..., such that A's activity refers to B, B's refers to C, and so on. We then say that the order thus obtained is what the time-order really means. The difficulty is, to understand the relation of the activity of A to the B which it refers to. It seems essential that the object of activity or desire should be non-existent, but should be regarded as capable of becoming existent. In this way, reference to future time seems to be a part of the meaning of activity, and the attempt to infer time from activity thus involves a vicious circle. Then again, the definition of *one* state of a substance seems impossible without time. A state is not simple; on the contrary, it is infinitely complex. It contains traces of all past states, and is big with all future states. It is further a reflection of all simultaneous states of other substances. Thus no way remains of defining one state, except as the state at one time. And finally, all states consist of perceptions, and desires for perceptions, either of the world or of the eternal truths. Now the perceptions involved in mirroring the universe—from which all knowledge of actual existence is derived—presuppose simultaneity in their definition. This point will be proved when we come to deal with perception, and the general doctrine of time will be dealt with again in connection with space. I shall then endeavour to show, that there must be one and the same order among the states of all substances, and that this

order, consequently, cannot depend upon the states of any one
substance.

Thus time is necessarily presupposed in Leibniz's treatment
of substance. That it is denied in the conclusion, is not a
triumph, but a contradiction. A precisely similar result will
appear as regards space, when we come to the grounds for the
plurality of substances. We shall find that Leibniz made
a constant endeavour to eliminate, by subsequent fruitless
criticism, these indispensable, but, for him, inadmissible
premisses.

CHAPTER V

THE IDENTITY OF INDISCERNIBLES AND THE LAW OF CONTINUITY.

POSSIBILITY AND COMPOSSIBILITY.

23. I COME now to the last of Leibniz's general logical principles. The Identity of Indiscernibles and the Law of Continuity are closely connected, though not deducible one from the other. They are both included in the statement that all created substances form a series, in which every possible position intermediate between the first and last terms is filled once and only once. That every possible position is filled once is the Law of Continuity; that it is filled only once is added by the Identity of Indiscernibles. I shall discuss the latter principle first. We shall have to enquire (1) what it means, (2) how Leibniz established it, (3) how far his arguments in support of it were valid.

(1) There is no difficulty as to the meaning of the Identity of Indiscernibles. It is not, like the principle of sufficient reason, stated in different ways at different times. It asserts "that there are not in nature two indiscernible real absolute beings" (D. 259; G. VII. 393), or again that "no two substances are completely similar, or differ *solo numero*" (G. IV. 433). It applies to substances only; existent attributes, as Leibniz explains in discussing place (D. 266; G. VII. 400, 401), may be indiscernible. Leibniz's doctrine is not that urged by Mr Bradley, that all diversity must be diversity of content. If this were the principle, it would be far more fundamental, and

would have to be considered before the definition of substance. The principle, so far from maintaining diversity of content alone, presupposes material or numerical diversity as well as diversity of content proper. To both these it is logically subsequent. Diversity of content proper is the difference between one content and another. Material or numerical diversity is the difference between one subject, or one substance, and another. Leibniz's doctrine is, that two things which are materially diverse, *i.e.* two different substances, always differ also as to their predicates. This doctrine evidently presupposes both kinds of diversity, and asserts a relation between them. Diversity of content is sometimes also used in this latter sense, as meaning that difference, between two subjects, which consists in their having different predicates. But as this sense is complex, and composed of the two other kinds of diversity, it is better to restrict the term *diversity of content* to the former sense, *i.e.* the difference between contents. The doctrine is, therefore, that any two substances differ as to their predicates. It thus presupposes a knowledge of substance, and could not be discussed until substance had been defined.

24. (2) This principle is not, like the Law of Sufficient Reason, a premiss of Leibniz's philosophy. It is deduced and proved in many passages. But the proofs are various, not only in their methods but even in their results. For once at least the principle appears as merely contingent, like the laws of motion, at other times as metaphysically necessary. In such cases of inconsistency, it is well to decide, if possible, which alternative suits the rest of the system best, and which, if the inconsistency had been pointed out, the philosopher would have chosen. I hold that Leibniz should have regarded his principle as necessary. For the proof of this, we will examine his various grounds.

In the fifth letter to Clarke, Leibniz says : " This supposition of two indiscernibles......seems indeed to be possible in abstract terms; but it is not consistent with the order of things, nor with the divine wisdom, by which nothing is admitted without reason " (D. 259; G. VII. 394). He continues : " When I deny that there are two drops of water perfectly alike, or any two other bodies perfectly indiscernible from each other ; I don't say, 'tis absolutely impossible to suppose (*poser*) them; but that 'tis a thing contrary to the divine wisdom, and which consequently does not exist. I own that if two things perfectly indiscernible from each other did exist, they would be two; but that supposition is false, and contrary to the grand principle of reason" (D. 260; G. VII. 394—5). In the preceding paper (D. 247; G. VII. 371—2) he deduces the Identity of Indiscernibles from the Law of Sufficient Reason, saying that God could have no reason for placing one of two indiscernibles *here*, the other *there*, rather than for adopting the opposite arrangement. This argument, however, though it is, of all his arguments for the principle, the least *à priori* and the least cogent, yet gives metaphysical necessity, for we saw, in Chapter III., that the need for *some* sufficient reason is metaphysically necessary (G. II. 420). Thus negative conclusions from this principle—*i.e.* such a proposition is false, because it could have no sufficient reason—are necessary, though positive conclusions, where a specific sufficient reason is assigned, may be contingent. Accordingly, he concludes the above proof with the remark that to suppose two things indiscernible is to suppose the same thing under different names (D. 247; G. VII. 372). The passage asserting indiscernibles to be possible—which, so far as I know, is the only one—was probably due, therefore, to the fact that he was deducing their non-existence from the principle of Sufficient Reason, and that this principle generally gives contingent results. And it is difficult to be sure how great a reservation is implied by the words "in abstract terms."

The above argument for his principle is far from cogent as it stands, and does not adequately represent his meaning. It seems to presuppose *here* and *there* as sources of numerical diversity, and then to infer that there must be some further and apparently unconnected difference besides that of position. What he really means, however, is that *here* and *there* must themselves be reduced to predicates, in accordance with his general logic. This is attempted by his theory of space, which will be examined later. What I want to insist on, however, is, that the differentiation must not be supposed effected by difference of place, *per se*, but by difference as to the predicates to which, on Leibniz's theory, place must be reduced. Where difference of place *appears*, there must *be* difference of predicates, the latter being the truth of which the former is a confused expression. Thus to assert that two substances cannot be in the same place at the same time, is to assert a proposition logically subsequent to the Identity of Indiscernibles. The proof which starts from difference of place is, therefore, merely *ad hominem*, and does not represent the gist of the principle. Clarke is willing to admit that two things must differ in place; hence, since place is a predicate, they must have different predicates. Thus Leibniz says (N. E. 238; G. v. 213) that besides the difference of time and place there must be an internal principle of distinction, and adds that places and times are distinguished by means of things, not *vice versâ*. Again he says (G. II. 250) that things which differ in place must express their place, and thus differ not only in place or in an extrinsic denomination. He no doubt relied, as a rule, on his readers admitting that two things could not co-exist in one spatio-temporal point, and would thus deduce an intrinsic difference from this admission. But with his theory of space and time, he could not logically rely upon this argument, as he used the Identity of Indiscernibles to disprove the reality of space and time. He had also another and more abstract ground, derived from the nature of substance, and closely connected with the logical doctrines which we have already examined. If he had not had such a ground, he would have been involved in many hopeless difficulties. For he declares (D. 273; G. VII. 407) that God will never choose among indiscernibles, which is, indeed, a direct result of sufficient reason. Consequently we must infer that, among all actual substances, there is none to which another precisely similar substance can be even conceived. For if it were possible to conceive another, God would have conceived it, and therefore could not have created either. The proof that, where the notions concerned are notions of substances, indiscernibles are inconceivable, is to be found in Leibniz, and must now be examined.

The nature of an individual substance or complete being, Leibniz says, is to have so complete a notion that it suffices for comprehending and deducing all the predicates of the subject of the notion[1]. "From this," he continues, "follow several considerable paradoxes, as, among others, that it is not true that two substances resemble each other completely, and differ only numerically" (G. IV. 433). In this argument, several intermediate steps seem to have been omitted, I suppose because Leibniz thought them obvious. I cannot find these steps anywhere explicitly stated, but I imagine his argument might be put as follows. All that can be validly said about a substance consists in assigning its predicates. Every extrinsic denomination—*i.e.* every relation—has an intrinsic foundation, *i.e.* a corresponding predicate (G. II. 240). The substance is, therefore, wholly defined when all its predicates are enumerated, so that no way remains in which the substance could fail to be unique. For suppose A and B were two indiscernible substances. Then A would differ from B exactly as B would differ from A. They would, as Leibniz once remarks regarding atoms, be different though without a difference (N. E. p. 309; G. V. 268). Or we may put the argument thus: A differs from B, in the sense that they are different substances; but to be thus different is to have a relation to B. This relation must have a corresponding predicate of A. But since B does not differ from itself, B cannot have the same predicate. Hence A and B will differ as to predicates, contrary to the hypothesis. Indeed, if we admit that nothing can be said about a substance except to assign its predicates, it seems evident that to be a different substance is to have different predicates. For if not, there would be something other than predicates involved in determining a substance, since, when these were all assigned, the substance would still be undetermined.

25. (3) This argument is valid, I think, to the extent of proving that, if subject and predicate be the canonical form of propositions, there cannot be two indiscernible substances. The difficulty is, to prevent its proving that there cannot be two substances at all. For the numerical diversity of the substances

---

[1] See Appendix, § 17. So Wolff says (*Logic*, Chap. I. § 27): "All that we conceive, or all that is found, in an *individual*, is determined in every respect; and it is by this very fact, that a thing is determined, both as to what constitutes its essence, and as to what is accidental to it, that it acquires the quality of *individual*."

is logically prior to their diversity as to predicates : there can be no question of their differing in respect of predicates, unless they first differ numerically. But the bare judgment of numerical diversity itself is open to all the objections which Leibniz can urge against indiscernibles[1]. Until predicates have been assigned, the two substances remain indiscernible ; but they cannot have predicates by which they cease to be indiscernible, unless they are first distinguished as numerically different. Thus on the principles of Leibniz's logic, the Identity of Indiscernibles does not go far enough. He should, like Spinoza, have admitted only one substance. On any other logic, there can be no ground against the existence of the same collection of qualities in different places, since the adverse proof rests wholly on the denial of relations. But as a different logic destroys substance, it destroys also anything resembling Leibniz's statement of his principle.

But further, the argument seems to show an objection—the same which was suggested in the last Chapter—against the whole doctrine of substance. If a substance is *only* defined by its predicates—and this is essential to the Identity of Indiscernibles—then it would seem to be identical with the sum of those predicates. In that case, to say that such and such a substance exists, is merely a compendious way of saying that all its predicates exist. Predicates do not *inhere* in the substance in any other sense than that in which letters inhere in the alphabet. The logically prior judgments are those asserting the existence of the various predicates, and the substance is no longer something distinct from them, which they determine, but is merely all those predicates taken together. But this, as we have already seen, is not what Leibniz intends to say. The substance is a single simple indivisible thing, persisting through time ; it is not the same as the series of its states, but is the subject of them. But in this case, a substance is not properly speaking *defined* by its predicates. There is a difference between asserting a given predicate of one substance, and asserting it of another. The substance can only be *defined* as "this." Or rather—and this is where the doctrine of substance breaks down—the substance cannot be *defined* at all. To define is

---

[1] Cf. the proof of Prop. V. Book I. of Spinoza's *Ethics*.

to point out the meaning, but a substance is, by its very nature, destitute of meaning, since it is only the predicates which give a meaning to it. Even to say "this," is to indicate some part of space or time, or some distinctive quality; to explain in any way which substance we mean, is to give our substance some predicate. But unless we already know which substance we are speaking of, our judgment has no definiteness, since it is a different judgment to assert the same predicate of another substance. Thus we necessarily incur a vicious circle. The substance must be numerically determinate before predication, but only predicates give numerical determination. Either a substance is wholly meaningless, and in that case cannot be distinguished from any other: or a substance is merely all or some of the qualities which are supposed to be its predicates. These difficulties are the invariable result of admitting, as elements of propositions, any terms which are destitute of meaning, *i.e.* any terms which are not what may be called ideas or concepts. As against *many* substances, we may urge, with Mr Bradley, that all diversity must be diversity of meanings; as against *one* substance, we may urge that the same is true of identity. And this holds equally against the supposed self-identity of Mr Bradley's Reality.

26. Connected with the Identity of Indiscernibles is the assertion that every substance has an infinite number of predicates. That this must be the case, is evident from the mere fact that every substance must have a predicate corresponding to every moment of time. But Leibniz goes further than this. The state of a substance at each moment is analyzable into an infinite number of predicates. This *might* itself be deduced from the fact that the present state has relations to all past and future states, which relations, according to Leibniz, must affect the present state—indeed it is in this that their truth consists. But another factor is the representation of the whole universe, which necessarily involves infinite complexity in each state of each substance. This infinite complexity is a mark of the contingent. There is a difference, Leibniz says, between the analysis of the necessary and that of the contingent. The analysis from the subsequent by nature to the prior by nature comes to an end in necessary matter with the primitive notions, as the analysis of numbers ends with unity. But in contingents or existents, this analysis goes to infinity, without ever reaching primitive elements (G. III. 582). Again he points out that it is impossible for us to have knowledge of individuals, and to determine exactly the individuality of anything. For individuality includes infinity, and only one who understands infinity can know the principle of individuation of this or that thing (N. E. 309; G. V. 268). Necessary and contingent truths differ as rational numbers and surds. The resolution of the latter proceeds to infinity (G. VII. 309).

Again he says (G. VII. 200): "The difference between necessary and contingent truths is indeed the same as that between commensurable and incommensurable numbers. For the reduction of commensurable numbers to a common measure is analogous to the demonstration of necessary truths, or their reduction to such as are identical. But as, in the case of surd ratios, the reduction involves an infinite process, and yet approaches a common measure, so that a definite but unending series is obtained, so also contingent truths require an infinite analysis, which God alone can accomplish."

I am afraid Leibniz regarded this, to some extent, as a confirmation of his doctrine of contingency. He seems to have thought it natural that the contingent should be that which *we* cannot perfectly understand; he says, for example, that God alone sees *how* I and existence are joined, and knows *à priori* the cause of Alexander's death[1]. The world of contingents is characterized, not only by the fact that it exists, but also by the fact that everything in it involves infinity by its infinite complexity, and is thus inaccessible to exact human knowledge.

Such passages have led many commentators to think that the difference between the necessary and the contingent has an essential reference to our human limitations, and does not subsist for God. This view, I think, rests upon a confusion, and does quite undue damage to Leibniz's system. The confusion is between the general character of all contingents, actual as well as possible—for possible worlds involve the same infinite complexity, which indeed is a necessary result of time—and the meaning of contingency itself. It is metaphysically necessary

[1] G. IV. 433; V. 392 (N. E. 469).

that the contingent should be thus complex ; but what makes contingency is not complexity, but existence. Or, to put the matter otherwise, the confusion is between eternal truths *about* the contingent—*i.e.* the necessary propositions about the *natures* of substances—and the contingent truth that such substances exist. This distinction *must* be made—though Leibniz may have been guilty of some confusion in the matter—for many very weighty reasons. In the first place, truths about *possible* worlds cannot be contingent, and all truths about the actual world are, when robbed of the assertion of actual existence, truths about one among possible worlds. In the second place, God was free, in creation, because of the other possible worlds : his choice was contingent. And his freedom, as well as that of creatures, can only result if contingency is metaphysically true, and no mere delusion. In the third place, the Law of Sufficient Reason, in the sense in which it asserts final causes, is coordinate with the Law of Contradiction, and applies to God's acts just as much as to the actual world ; whereas, on the opposite view, Leibniz's belief that he used two principles has to be declared erroneous. The doctrines of final causes, of possible worlds, of the synthetic nature of causal connections, and of freedom—everything, in fact, that is characteristic of Leibniz— depends upon the ultimately irreducible nature of the opposition between existential and necessary propositions. Thus we must maintain that Leibniz does not only mean, by *contingent*, that which *we* cannot fully explain. But he cannot be absolved, I fear, from dwelling with pleasure on this supposed confirmation of the twofold nature of propositions.

Here again, I think, as throughout, Leibniz is not clear as to the difference between the relation of individual to species, and that of species to genus. He sometimes urges that there is no difference between these two relations—a view to which I see no objection, except that it is inconsistent with his notion of individual substance. This view underlies, as we saw, the Identity of Indiscernibles, and is suggested in the New Essays, where, however, it leads to results which he ought to have found very inconvenient. " In mathematical strictness," he says, "the least difference making two things in any respect dissimilar, makes them different in species....... In this sense, two physical individuals will never be perfectly similar, and what is more, the same individual will pass from species to species, for it is never wholly similar to itself even for more than a moment[1]" (N. E. 335—6; G. v. 287—8). His view seems to be that, in eternal truths, we start with essences and predicates, and determine their relations; while in contingent truths, we start with the existence of something undetermined, such as the Ego, and enquire into its predicates. The question is, in this case, what is the nature of this existent? And since every substance has an infinite number of predicates, the question is one which we can never fully answer. But it is evident—though Leibniz would seem not to have perceived it—that in starting with the Ego, or any other existent, we must already have determined some unique property of our substance, or else we should not know which we were speaking of, and the question would be wholly indeterminate. Spatio-temporal position is, I think, always covertly assumed in such questions, and it is this assumption alone which gives them a definite meaning and a definite answer.

27. The infinite complexity of substances will help us in dealing with our next topic, the *Law of Continuity*. This law usually holds a prominent place in expositions of Leibniz, but I cannot discover that, except as applied to Mathematics, it has any great importance. There are three distinct kinds of continuity, all of which Leibniz asserts. None of them, he thinks, has metaphysical necessity, but all are regarded as required by the "order of things." These three kinds are (1) spatio-temporal continuity, (2) what may be called continuity of cases, (3) the continuity of actual existents or of forms. Let us consider these in turn.

(1) Spatio-temporal continuity is itself twofold. There is the continuity of space and time themselves, which Leibniz admits to be metaphysically necessary; and there is the continuity of what exists *in* space and time. The former is not in question here. The latter includes motion and all other kinds of change. As regards change, it is generally admitted that

---

[1] It seems probable that Leibniz does not mean, by a "physical individual," a single substance, for if he did, the passage would contradict his whole philosophy. This is the more probable from his illustrations, which are drawn from circles and ellipses and other mathematical figures.

it must be gradual, that a change of position involves the intermediate occupation of a continuous series of intermediate positions, or a change of colour involves the passage through all intermediate colours. I do not know any reason for such a principle, unless it be that we only regard qualities in different parts of time as belonging to the same thing when they are connected by some such continuous series. Jumps from place to place and from state to state, according to Leibniz, are exactly on a level (G. II. 169); any *à priori* reason against the former will apply equally against the latter. Both, he thinks, are metaphysically possible, but are condemned by the same reason as a vacuum, rest, or a hiatus (G. II. 182), *i.e.* by what he vaguely calls the " order of things "—a sort of metaphysical perfection which seems to consist in all that gives pleasure to the metaphysician[1].

(2) Continuity of cases is the sole form of the law of continuity given in Leibniz's letter to Bayle, on a general principle useful in the explanation of the laws of nature (D. 33—36; G. III. 51—55). This principle states, that when the difference of two cases diminishes without limit, the difference in their results also diminishes without limit, or, more generally, when the data form an ordered series, their respective results also form an ordered series, and infinitesimal differences in the one lead to infinitesimal differences in the other (D. 33; G. III. 52). This is properly a mathematical principle, and was used as such by Leibniz, with great effect, against Cartesian mathematics, especially against the Cartesian theory of impact (*e.g.* G. III. 47). In Mathematics, though it has exceptions in cases of what is called instability, it is still in constant use. But in philosophy it seems of no very great moment.

(3) The third kind of continuity is peculiar to Leibniz, and seems destitute either of self-evident validity or of grounds from which it may be proved. That nature makes no leaps, which is the general statement of all forms of continuity, is held by Leibniz to apply also in the passage from one substance to another. If two substances differ by a finite difference, there must be, according to Leibniz, a continuous series of inter-

[1] Cf. G. III. 558: " There is order in proportion as there is much to remark in a multiplicity."

mediate substances, each of which differs infinitesimally from the next[1]. As he often expresses it, there is as little a hiatus, or vacuum of forms, as there is a vacuum in space (*e.g.* G. II. 168). He sometimes pretends (*e.g.* L. 377; N. E. p. 51; G. v. 49—50) to deduce the Identity of Indiscernibles from this principle, but such a deduction must be taken only as showing how the world can be explained consistently with the Identity of Indiscernibles. For continuity asserts that every place in the series is filled, whereas the Identity of Indiscernibles asserts that no place is filled twice over. The latter, we shall find, is logically prior to the former. Moreover the latter, as we saw, is metaphysically necessary, whereas the former is only demanded by order, *i.e.* is contingent. What Leibniz means to do, in such passages, is to point out that, since there are things which only differ infinitesimally, and infinitesimal differences are insensible, the discovery of things which appear to be indiscernible does not make against the denial that they are really indiscernible. And this is why Leibniz remarks parenthetically (L. 380; N. E. 52; G. v. 51) that he has *à priori* reasons for his view.

28. Why Leibniz held that substances form a continuous series, it is difficult to say. He never, so far as I know, offers a shadow of a reason, except that such a world seems to him pleasanter than one with gaps. I cannot help thinking, however, that spatial continuity was connected with this form of continuity. We shall see hereafter that every monad mirrors the world from a certain point of view, and that this point of view is often regarded as a spatial point. Accordingly neighbouring spatial points should give infinitesimally different points of view, and therefore, since the mirroring of the universe gives the whole of a monad's perceptions, neighbouring points in space should be occupied by infinitesimally different monads[2]. There are many objections to this interpretation, which will appear when we come to the relation of the monads to space.

[1] Cf. N. E. 712: "All the different classes of beings, whose union forms the universe, are in the ideas of God, who knows distinctly their essential gradations, only as so many ordinates of the same curve, the union of which does not allow the placing of others between them, because that would indicate disorder and imperfection." [Guhrauer, *Leibnitz: Eine Biographie*, Anmerkungen zum zweiten Buche, p. 32.]

[2] Cf. G. IV. 439.

But it will then appear also, I think, that these objections apply against the whole theory of monads, and cannot, therefore, prove that the confusions, involved in the above interpretation of the continuity of forms, did not actually exist in Leibniz's mind.

29. The continuity of forms does not assert that all possible forms are actual. On the contrary, it is vitally important to Leibniz's system to maintain that the possible is wider than the actual. Things are *possible* when they are not self-contradictory; two or more things are *compossible* when they belong to one and the same possible world, *i.e.* when they may coexist. All possible worlds have general laws, analogous to the laws of motion; what these laws are, is contingent, but that there are such laws is necessary (G. II. 51; cf. also G. II. 41). Hence two or more things which cannot be brought under one and the same set of general laws are not *compossible*. And so it is with species. Though actual species form a continuous series, there are other possible species outside the actual series, and these, though possible, are not compossible, with those that exist. Not all possible species, Leibniz says, are compossible, so that some species cannot exist. There are of necessity species which never have existed and never will exist, not being compatible with the series which God has chosen. There is no gap in the order of nature, but no one order contains all possible species (N. E. 334; G. v. 286).

The question of possibility and compossibility is important in Leibniz's philosophy, as his solution of the problem of evil turns on it. It may be well, therefore, to examine the meaning of compossibility in somewhat greater detail.

There are, according to Leibniz, an infinite number of possible worlds, *i.e.* of worlds internally free from self-contradiction. These worlds all agree in certain respects—*i.e.* as regards the eternal truths—while they differ in others. The notion of an existent is *possible* when it does not involve a contradiction. Any such notion forms part of the notion of *some* possible world. When several notions of possible existents form part of the notion of one and the same possible world, they are compossible, for in this case they may all exist (cf. G. III. 573). When they are not compossible, then, though each separately is possible, yet their coexistence is not possible.

The meaning of compossibility is thus sufficiently plain. But a difficulty remains as regards its application. For we saw that no two contingent predicates of a substance, according to Leibniz, are necessarily connected. Each is necessarily connected with the notion of the substance, in the sense that, given that substance, each predicate follows. But each separate contingent predicate might also have belonged to a different substance, and thus no two such predicates are necessarily connected with each other. Thus it would seem that any collection of possible existents must be compossible, since their coexistence cannot be self-contradictory (cf. *supra*, pp. 19, 20).

This difficulty is evaded by Leibniz by means of the necessity for *some* sufficient reason of the whole series. Although this or that sufficient reason is contingent, there must be some sufficient reason, and the lack of one condemns many series of existents as metaphysically impossible. "There were," he says, " an infinity of possible ways of creating the world, according to the different designs which God might form, and each possible world depends upon certain principal designs or ends of God proper to itself, *i.e.* certain free primitive decrees (conceived *sub ratione possibilitatis*), or laws of the general order of this possible universe, to which they belong, and whose notion they determine, as well as the notions of all the individual substances which must belong to this same Universe" (G. II. 51). This passage proves quite definitely that all possible worlds have general laws, which determine the connection of contingents just as, in the actual world, it is determined by the laws of motion and the law that free spirits pursue what seems best to them[1]. And without the need for *some* general laws, any two possibles would be compossible, since they cannot contradict one another. Possibles cease to be compossible only when there is no general law whatever to which both conform. What is called the "reign of law" is, in Leibniz's philosophy, metaphysically necessary, although the actual laws are contingent. If this is not realized, compossibility must remain unintelligible.

30. At this point it may be well, for the sake of clearness,

---

[1] This is a point on which, according to Lotze, Leibniz never pronounced. (*Metaphysics*, Book I. Chap. V. § 67.)

to enumerate the principal respects in which all possible worlds agree, and the respects in which other possible worlds might differ from the actual world. For this purpose, since Leibniz himself is not very explicit, we have to consider which propositions are necessary and which contingent. I shall content myself, at present, with stating opinions; the evidence will be given where the various questions concerned are dealt with in detail.

In the first place, God was free not to create any of the possible worlds. Hence even what exists in all of them does not exist necessarily. This applies especially to space, time, and motion. These are necessary as regards their properties, *i.e.* as regards the propositions of Geometry and Kinematics, but not as regards their existence. God could not have created a world in which space and time would be other than in the present world, and time, at least, would form part of *any* possible world, while space and motion would form part of any world in which there were many substances. All possible worlds, again, consist of monads, *i.e.* of individual substances endowed with activity; and in all possible worlds there are general causal laws. But the plurality of substances is not necessary; it would have been possible for God to create only one monad, and this one might have been any one of the actual created monads. All that is involved in perception and the pre-established harmony, including the existence of other substances, is contingent. It would seem, even, that any casual selection among the actual monads would give a possible world[1]. But worlds may differ from the actual world, not only in number and quantity, but in quality. Other worlds might have other laws of motion, and might, if I am not mistaken, contain free substances which would not always choose the apparently best. Every causal law, in fact (though not Causality itself), might have been different.

These seem to be the main points concerning the other possible worlds. By keeping them in mind, we obtain a kind of hierarchy among Leibniz's principles, as they are successively

---

[1] This appears not only from the mutual independence of the monads, but also from a discussion with Des Bosses concerning the successive days of the creation in Genesis: *e.g.* G. II. 368, 370.

specialized by the approach to the actual world. The inconsistencies in his logical doctrine of possibility will be best postponed until we come to the proofs of the existence of God.

31. In relation to possibility and compossibility, Leibniz distinguishes several kinds of necessity. There is first metaphysical or geometrical necessity, which alone is strictly called necessity. This is the sort we have hitherto discussed, where the opposite is self-contradictory. There is next hypothetical necessity, where a consequence follows with metaphysical necessity from a contingent premiss. Thus the motions of matter have hypothetical necessity, since they are necessary consequences of the laws of motion, while these are themselves contingent. There is lastly moral necessity, which is the necessity by which God and the angels and the perfect sage choose the good The actions of free spirits hold a peculiar place in relation to necessity. Not only do their states, in so far as they are the results of previous states, have only hypothetical necessity, but the consequence itself has only hypothetical necessity, as involving a psychological law which the spirits are not compelled to obey, though they always do obey it[1]. The difficulties in this conception will be discussed when we come to the problem of Freedom and Determination. For the present, it is time to leave the logical discussions upon which we have been engaged, and proceed to the Philosophy of Matter, from which, by the help of the logic with which we are now acquainted, Leibniz deduced the doctrine with which expositions usually begin, I mean the doctrine of monads.

---

[1] Cf. D. 170, 171; G. iii. 400, 401.

CHAPTER VI

WHY DID LEIBNIZ BELIEVE IN AN EXTERNAL WORLD?

32. I PASS now to an entirely new order of ideas. From questions of Logic—the nature of propositions, the definition of substance, how substances must differ *if* there be many—from these questions I come to questions as to the actual world : how can the notion of substance be applied in the world of existents ? Is there one substance or many ? What properties have actual substances beyond those involved in the definition of substance ? And how does this notion serve to explain the difficulties which the actual world presents to the metaphysician ?

In this problem, Leibniz, for reasons which apparently were only historical and psychological, began with matter as his datum. He would seem, when he first abandoned scholasticism, to have turned to Gassendi and Hobbes, to atomism and materialism (G. III. 620; IV. 209; VII. 377; IV. 478 and L. 300 and D. 72; G. I. 52—4). That he did not remain a materialist was due to difficulties which he found in the ordinary conception of matter. He therefore invented what may be called a spiritualistic or idealistic theory of matter: but what his theory started with was still matter. Accordingly, the problem with which he began was not: Does matter exist ? But, what is the nature of matter ? In this respect, Leibniz, whose ontology begins with Dynamics, which it gradually transforms into psychology, was less philosophical than Bishop Berkeley. The question: Does matter exist ? is thus one which Leibniz never thoroughly faced. Nevertheless, there are some remarks of his, on this question, which may help us to understand his position.

Two short works are, in this respect, peculiarly important. The first of these is a letter to Foucher, written in or about the year 1676, nine or ten years before Leibniz completed his philosophy (G. I. 369—374). The second is a paper without date, entitled "On the method of distinguishing real from imaginary phenomena" (G. VII. 319—322; N. E. 717—720). Though scattered remarks in his later writings seem in agreement with these two papers, I can find nothing dated, after his philosophy was complete, in which the existence of matter is seriously discussed, and it seems at least possible that Leibniz was only led to question its existence by the difficulties of the continuum, which, in his opinion, the doctrine of monads completely and satisfactorily solved. This view is supported by Leibniz's own account of the origin of his views in the *Système Nouveau*[1]: "At first, when I had freed myself from the yoke of Aristotle, I took to the void and the atoms, for that is the view which best satisfies the imagination. But having got over this, I perceived, after much meditation, that it is impossible to find *the principles of a real unity* in matter alone, or in that which is only passive, since it is nothing but a collection or aggregation of parts *ad infinitum*. Now a multiplicity can derive its reality only *from genuine units*, which come from elsewhere and are quite other than mathematical points, which are only extremities of the extended and modifications, of which it is certain that *the continuum* cannot be composed. Accordingly, in order to find these *real units*, I was constrained to have recourse to a *real and animated point*," etc. It would seem that a good many years elapsed between Leibniz's discovery that mere matter involved the insoluble difficulties of the continuum, and his invention of monads as real units by which the continuum was rendered discrete[2]. This theory, at any rate, accounts both for his views, and for his manner of exposition, much better than any other theory with which I am acquainted. But it is time to examine Leibniz's actual words.

[1] L. 300; D. 72; G. IV. 478; cf. also *Archiv. für Gesch. der Phil.* I. 577 [L. 351—2].
[2] See Chapter IX.

33. Leibniz does not clearly distinguish two totally different questions, namely, (1) why admit a world other than ourselves? (2) granted such a world, how shall we distinguish true perceptions from hallucinations? The latter, as the title indicates, is the main question discussed in the undated paper above quoted. This is not a fundamental question, and Leibniz answers it in the usual way—mutual consistency, and success in prediction, he says, are the best tests. He proceeds, however, to a radically unphilosophical remark on the first question. "Although the whole of this life were said to be nothing but a dream, and the visible world nothing but a phantasm, I should call this dream or phantasm real enough, if, using reason well, we were never deceived by it" (N. E. 718—9; G. VII. 320). In this passage, the unduly practical nature of Leibniz's interest in philosophy very plainly appears. He confesses, both here, and in many other passages, that there is no "exact demonstration" that the objects of sense are outside us, and that the existence of the external world has only moral certainty[1]. To obtain even this, he requires first the existence of God, which has absolute certainty. He says, for example: "That there should exist only one substance" (*created* substance, he seems to mean) "is among those things which are not conformable to the divine wisdom, and thus do not happen, although they might happen" (G. II. 307). And in one early passage (G. I. 372—3, *ca.* 1676), he actually suggests Berkeley's philosophy. All we know for certain, he says, is that our appearances are connected *inter se*, and that they must have a constant cause external to us; but there is no way of proving this cause to be other than God. Yet, though he seems never to have found arguments against this admission, he so far forgot his early unresolved doubts, that, when Berkeley's philosophy appeared, Leibniz had no good word for it. "The man in Ireland," he writes, "who impugns the reality of bodies, seems neither to give suitable reasons, nor to explain himself sufficiently. I suspect him to be one of that class of men who wish to be known by their paradoxes" (G. II. 492).

If any arguments for the existence of matter were to be found in Leibniz, they would evidently depend upon the ex-

[1] N. E. 318, 422, 719; G. v. 275, 355—6; VII. 320—321; I. 373; II. 378, 502.

istence of God, by which solipsism is destroyed. The Cartesian argument, however, which rests on the assertion that, if there were no matter, God would be a deceiver, is definitely rejected by Leibniz. "The argument by which Des Cartes seeks to demonstrate the existence of material things is weak. It would have been better therefore not to try" (D. 58; G. IV. 366). God might, he says, have excellent reasons for deceiving us, and, in any case, the deception could be undone by our own reason (D. 58; G. IV. 367; I. 373; V. 275; N. E. p. 318).

There is, it is true, a kind of pantheistic argument, according to which our view of the world is part of God's view, and therefore has the same truth as belongs to God's perceptions. "God...regards all the aspects of the world," Leibniz says, "in all possible ways...; the result of each view, as if seen from a certain place, is a substance expressing the universe from this point of view, if God sees fit to make his thought effective and produce this substance. And since God's view is always veritable, our perceptions are so too; but it is our judgments, which are from us, that deceive us" (G. IV. 439). This whole passage, however, is so extreme an example of Leibniz's pantheistic tendencies, as to be scarcely consistent with his usual monadism. He can hardly, therefore, have relied upon such an argument to any great extent.

The only other positive argument is one no better than that which is commonly urged for life on other planets. "We judge with the greatest probability," he says, "that we do not exist alone, not only by the principle of the Divine Wisdom, but also by that common principle which I always inculcate, that nothing happens without a reason, nor does a reason appear, why we alone should be preferred to so many other possibles" (G. II. 502)[1].

The ground upon which Leibniz seems to have mainly relied, in this question, is the same as that which led him to deny a vacuum, namely, that the more existence there is, the better (cf. D. 102, 103; L. 340, 341; G. VII. 303, 304). This is the principle of metaphysical perfection, which I shall discuss in connection with his Ethics. It led Leibniz to think that there must be as many monads as possible, and that there

[1] Cf. G. II. 516.

must, therefore, be an infinity of substances other than himself[1]. But historically and psychologically, I think, Leibniz started with matter and space in a purely common-sense spirit. The reason that a problem arises for him is, that by criticism of these notions he transformed them into something quite different, namely, unextended substances and their perceptions. But having arrived at the subjectivity of space, he did not, like Kant, confine knowledge to experience, and render all *à priori* knowledge really self-knowledge. He did not perceive that the denial of the reality of space compels us to admit that we know only phenomena, *i.e.* appearances to our minds. That Kant was able to assume even an unknowable thing-in-itself was only due to his extension of cause (or ground) beyond experience, by regarding something not ourselves as the source of our perceptions. This, which was an inconsistency in Kant, would have been a sheer impossibility to Leibniz, since he held perceptions to be wholly due to ourselves, and not in any sense caused by the objects perceived. The ordinary grounds for assuming an external world were thus destroyed by Leibniz, and I cannot discover that anything very solid was put in their place.

The existence of other substances, besides God and ourselves, is therefore only probable: it has only a moral certainty. This remark applies, consequently, to all existential propositions derived from the theory of matter, *i.e.* to the whole doctrine of monads, in so far as this asserts the actual existence of many monads. It is a pity that Leibniz did not devote more attention to this fundamental question, that he did not make himself the critic rather than the commentator of common sense. Had he done so, he might have invented some more satisfactory theory of space than one which, while based upon a common-sense assumption of its reality, arrives, on that very basis, at a complete denial of that reality. I have brought out this presupposition now, as the following Chapters will, with Leibniz, start from a common-sense belief in the reality of matter.

---

[1] Cf. L. 323; D. 86; G. IV. 495: "I am asked whence it comes that God does not think it enough to produce all the thoughts and modifications of the soul, without these useless bodies, which the soul, it is said, can neither move nor know. The answer is easy. It is, that it was God's will that there should be more substances rather than fewer, and He thought it right that these modifications should correspond to something outside."

CHAPTER VII

THE PHILOSOPHY OF MATTER.

(a) *As the outcome of the principles of Dynamics.*

34. THE word matter is, in philosophy, the name of a problem. Assuming that, in perception, we are assured of the existence of something other than ourselves—an assumption which, as we saw in the last chapter, Leibniz made on very inadequate grounds—the question inevitably arises: Of what nature is this something external to ourselves? In so far as it appears to be in space, we name it matter (cf. G. IV. 106). Our problem is, then, what is matter? how are we to conceive that which, in perception, appears as spatial and as other than ourselves? It was the attempt to answer this question, on the basis of the logic which we have already examined, that led Leibniz to the doctrine of monads. In this and the three succeeding chapters, I shall endeavour to follow the same course as Leibniz followed. I shall intersperse criticisms where they seem called for, but the chief criticism of Leibniz's procedure is, that he never examined its starting-point, the assumption, namely, that there is something other than ourselves to be perceived. The general trustworthiness of perception is a premiss of Leibniz's philosophy, but a faulty premiss, even if it be true, since arguments may be adduced for or against it.

35. Before I enter on any detail as to Leibniz's theory of Dynamics, I must warn readers that he uses the words *matter* and *body* in at least five different senses. These are not confused in his own thinking, and are often distinguished in his writings. At the same time, the words are often employed without any indication, except what the context provides, as to the sense to be attached to them, and this adds greatly to the difficulty of understanding Leibniz's theory of matter. Of these five senses, two are prior to the theory of monads, and three are subsequent. There is, in the first place, the distinction of primary and secondary matter; and this distinction is one thing in Dynamics, and another in the theory of monads. Thus we have four meanings of matter. In addition to these, there is the organic body of a monad, which consists of other monads subordinated to it. It is the object of Leibniz's theory to transform primary and secondary matter as they occur in Dynamics, into primary and secondary matter as they occur in the theory of monads. At the same time, since the first pair are data, while the second pair are results, it is important to distinguish them, and Leibniz's correctness may be tested by examining how far his criticism of dynamical matter does justify the transformation.

The five meanings, then, to be definite, are as follows.

(1) There is *primary matter* as that which, according to Leibniz, is presupposed by extension. Extension, as we shall see in the next chapter, is regarded by him as mere repetition. That which is repeated, taken *per se*, is *materia prima*. This is purely passive.

(2) There is *secondary matter* as it occurs in Dynamics, that is, matter endowed with *force*. The further explanation of these two meanings will occupy the remainder of this chapter.

(3) There is primary matter as an element in the nature of every created monad. In this sense, it is equivalent to passivity, or confusedness of perception.

(4) There is secondary matter as an aggregate of monads, or *mass* : this is a mere aggregate with only an accidental unity.

(5) There is the organic body of a monad, *i e.* the collection of monads which it dominates, and to which it gives a more than accidental unity (G. II. 252; N.E. p. 722 and G. VII. 501).

The transformation of the first pair of meanings into the second pair constitutes the proof of the doctrine of monads, and will occupy the next three chapters. The second and fourth senses are often called *mass* or *body*, the fifth with the dominant monad is often called *corporeal substance*; without the dominant monad, it is called the organic body, or simply the body, of the dominant monad. But there is little regularity in Leibniz's use of all these words, and the meaning must generally be gathered from the context.

36. Leibniz's theory of Dynamics was framed in conscious opposition to Des Cartes. Des Cartes held that the essence of matter is extension, that the quantity of motion in the universe is constant, and that *force* is proportional to quantity of motion. Leibniz, on the contrary, proved that the essence of matter is not extension, that the total quantity of motion is not constant, but that, what Des Cartes did not know, the quantity of motion in any given direction *is* constant. He also believed himself to have proved that Dynamics required, as an ultimate notion, the conception of *force*, which he identified with the activity essential to substance. Des Cartes and the Cartesians measured force by quantity of motion, from which they seem scarcely to have distinguished it. Leibniz, on the contrary, believing force to be an ultimate entity, and holding as an axiom that its quantity must be constant, introduced a different measure of it, by which it became proportional to what is now called energy. On this question of the true measure of force, a famous controversy arose, which was distinguished by the fact that it divided Voltaire and the Marquise du Chatelet, and that it formed the subject of Kant's first published work[1]. This controversy seems to modern mathematicians to be mere logomachy. To Leibniz and his contemporaries it seemed something more, because force was supposed to be an ultimate entity, and one whose quantity, like that of mass, must be constant.

37. That the essence of matter is not extension, is a proposition on which Leibniz loves to dwell. He seems to have discovered this proposition at least as early as 1672[2], so

---

[1] *Gedanken über die wahre Schätzung der lebendigen Kräfte*, 1747. Ed. Hart. Vol. i.

[2] This results *e.g.* from his saying that he has geometrical proofs of the existence of a vacuum (G. i. 58). That Leibniz was aware of the fact that a vacuum is inconsistent with the view that the essence of matter is extension, appears also from G. i. 321. Again in a letter to Antoine Arnauld, written

that it was probably one of the sources of his innovations. The proof of the proposition is about as thorough as it could be. It is derived (1) from the nature of extension, (2) from the nature of the extended, or *materia prima*, (3) from the fact that even *materia prima*, though not mere extension, is an abstraction, requiring to be supplemented by *force* or *activity*. The argument from the nature of extension, with its consequences, I leave for the next chapter; the other two arguments must now be given. Let us begin with the definition of *materia prima* as it occurs in Dynamics.

38. *Materia prima* is defined by what Leibniz calls *resistance*. This, he says, does not consist in extension, but is the principle of extension (G. II. 306), that is, it is the quality in virtue of which bodies occupy places. Resistance, again, involves two distinct properties, impenetrability or antitypia, and resistance (in the narrower sense) or inertia (G. II. 171)[1]. These two properties of *materia prima* might be defined as (1) the property of bodies in virtue of which they are in places (G. VII. 328), (2) the property in virtue of which they resist any effort to make them change their places. Passive force, Leibniz says, is a resistance, by which a body resists not only penetration, but also motion, so that another body cannot come into the place of the first unless the first gives way, and it does not give way without retarding the other. Thus there are two resistances or masses, impenetrability and inertia. These are uniform everywhere, and therefore proportional to extension (G. IV. 395; G. M. VI. 100 and N. E. p. 701). Inertia is spoken

probably at the end of 1671 or the beginning of 1672, Leibniz says (G. I. 72) that he has proved, among other things, "that the essence of body does not consist in extension, since empty space must be different from body, and yet is also extended"; further "that the essence of body consists rather in motion." Cf. G. IV. 106 (1669): "The definition of a body is that it exists in space." Also *Ib.* 171 (1670). See Selver, *Entwickelungsgang der Leibniz'schen Monadenlehre*, p. 49. Leibniz appears to have been led to this discovery by the search for a philosophical theory of the Eucharist. The Cartesian doctrine, that the essence of matter is extension, was found by him to be inconsistent with both transubstantiation and consubstantiation. See Guhrauer, *Leibnitz : Eine Biographie*, Vol. I. p. 77.

[1] The use of resistance in two senses, (1) as the whole essence of *materia prima*, (2) as inertia only, is very tiresome, and greatly confuses Leibniz's exposition.

of as a *passive force*, a somewhat difficult phrase, which we shall find to be equivalent to what, in the theory of monads, is called passivity simply. Thus Leibniz says (*ib.*): "Again τὸ δυναμικόν or power in body is twofold—passive and active. Passive force properly constitutes matter or mass, the active constitutes ἐντελέχεια or form. Passive force is that very resistance by which body resists not only penetration, but also motion." And passive force, as we shall find with active force also, "is twofold, either primitive or derivative. And indeed *the primitive force of enduring or resisting* constitutes that very thing which is called *materia prima*, rightly interpreted, in the schools, by which it happens that body is not penetrated by body, but forms an obstacle to it, and is endowed also with a certain laziness, so to speak, that is, repugnance to motion, and does not indeed suffer itself to be set in motion unless by the somewhat broken force of the active body. Whence afterwards the *derivative force of enduring* variously exhibits itself in *secondary matter*" (N. E. p. 672—3; G. M. VI. 236). Resistance, Leibniz says, is not merely not changing without cause, but having a force and inclination to retain the actual state and resist the cause of change. Thus in impact (which he has always in his mind in the mathematical discussion of *materia prima*), when one body is at rest, the impinging body loses some of its velocity in starting the other, and the other, when started, moves more slowly than the first did[1]. Resistance in this sense, he asserts, is not metaphysically necessary (G. II. 170).

As part of an actual theory of Dynamics, the above analysis is antiquated. But philosophically, it is easy to see what is meant by the two elements of *materia prima*. Not only is it impossible for one body to come into the place occupied by another, unless that other gives way, and moves into a new place, but also some of the first body's motion is absorbed by the second body, or some effort is required to cause the second body to abandon its place. The importance of the doctrine lies, as we shall afterwards see, in the connection with the *materia prima* of each monad. A difficulty, which I think is a bare inconsistency, is introduced by the statement that *materia*

[1] See L. 352—3; N. E. 678; G. M. VI. 240.

prima, as an element in each monad, *is* metaphysically necessary (G. II. 325). It is more consistent with Leibniz's philosophy, I think, to hold both necessary than to hold both
contingent; particularly as the necessity of the one is declared
much ·more emphatically than the contingency of the other.

Neither of the properties of *materia prima* can be deduced
from mere extension. That this is true of impenetrability,
follows from the simple consideration that place, though extended, is not impenetrable (G. III. 453). As regards inertia,
Leibniz points out that, if bodies were wholly indifferent to
rest and motion, a big body could be set in motion by a small
one without any loss of velocity, whereas what is really conserved is momentum, which involves mass. But for inertia, we
should have action without reaction, and no estimate of power
could be made, since anything might be accomplished by anything (L. 353; N. E. 678; G. M. VI. 241). Even if matter,
then, were purely passive, Des Cartes' theory, that the essence
of matter is extension, would be mistaken.

39. But this is still more evident when we pass to *materia
secunda*, *i.e.* to matter as active and endowed with force. The
doctrine of force is closely connected with every part of
Leibniz's philosophy—with the notion of contingent truths[1],
with the conception of substance as the source of all its
predicates[2], with the plurality of independent causal series
(D. 60, 61; G. IV. 369), with the psychical nature of all
substances[3], and with the whole theory of activity, liberty and

---

[1] "You are right in judging that (Dynamics) is to a great extent the foundation of my system; for it is there we learn the difference between truths whose
necessity is brute and geometrical, and truths which have their source in fitness
and final causes" (G. III. 645).

[2] "I am not astonished that you find insurmountable difficulties where you
seem to assume a thing so inconceivable as the passage of an accident from one
subject to another; but I see nothing which compels us to an assumption which
is scarcely less strange than that of the scholastics of accidents without a subject" (N. E. p. 233, G. v. 208); in answer to Locke's difficulties concerning
impact. Cf. also D. 124; G. IV. 515: in a series of impacts, "each ball, when
repelled from the next one impinging on it, is set in motion by its *own force*,
viz. its elasticity."

[3] "We see also, that thought, being the action of a thing on itself, cannot
happen in figures and motions, which can never show the principle of a truly
internal action" [G. III. 69]. Such a principle, however, *is* found in force.

determination. It is a central point in Leibniz's philosophy, and was by him recognized as such. Force is said to be prior to extension (N. E. 671; G. M. vi. 235), and to be the true ground for inferring the plurality of substances (G. ii. 372). In so far as force is the same as activity, we have already considered it. What we have now to examine, is the way in which Leibniz developed the idea of force from Dynamics.

Leibniz discovered the conservation of momentum, and believed himself to have discovered another law, the conservation of Vis Viva, both of which were unknown to Des Cartes (D. 88; L. 327; G. iv. 497). He was thus able theoretically—assuming perfectly elastic impact to be ultimately the only form of dynamical action—to determine completely the course of any motion, and to disprove, if the validity of his Dynamics was allowed, the possibility, admitted by Des Cartes, of a direct action of mind upon matter. Des Cartes had supposed that, though the *quantity* of motion is constant, its *direction* may be altered by a direct action of the mind upon the animal spirits. Had he known, Leibniz says, that the quantity of motion in every direction is constant, he would probably have discovered the pre-established harmony (D. 164; G. vi. 540); for he would have seen that an interaction between mind and matter is impossible. Why he should not have been led to the views of Geulincx or of Spinoza, which Leibniz does not mention, it is very difficult to see. That Leibniz was not led to occasionalism, or to Spinoza's theory that the mind is the idea of the body, was due to his conception of force, which led him to regard every piece of matter—or rather every collection of the real substances whose appearance is matter—as an independent source of all its own changes.

40. The necessity of force is variously deduced. Much of the argument—especially when it assumes the form of a polemic against the Cartesians—depends, as Wundt has pointed out[1], upon the axiom that the cause must be equal to the effect. The two measures of force only give the same result in the case of equilibrium, *i.e.* in Statics; and Leibniz attributes the

---

[1] *Die physikalischen Axiome und ihre Beziehung zum Causalprincip*, Erlangen, 1866, p. 60 ff. Many valuable observations on Leibniz's Dynamics are contained in this work.

persistence of the Cartesian measure to the fact that people
have devoted an undue share of attention to Statics as opposed
to Dynamics (N. E. 675; G. M. vi. 239). Since the quantity of
motion is not conserved (as Des Cartes had falsely assumed), the
true causes and effects cannot be motions. Motion in a given
direction might have been substituted, if purely mathematical
considerations had been alone employed. But for an ultimate
physical entity, Leibniz desired some one unique quantity,
which had a constant sum in any independent system ; and
this he believed himself to have found in Vis Viva, *i.e.* the
mass multiplied by the square of the velocity. Statics and
Dynamics are to be deduced from the law " that the total effect
must always be equivalent to its full cause." " As in Geometry
and numbers," he explains, "through the principle of the
equality of the whole to all its parts, Geometry is subjected to
an analytical Calculus, so in Mechanics, through the equality of
the effect to all its causes, or of the cause to all its effects, we
obtain certain equations, as it were, and a kind of mechanical
Algebra by the use of this axiom[1]." In a thorough discussion
of the principles of Dynamics, it would be necessary to examine
this supposed law, but here it is sufficient to point out its influence on Leibniz's views. For, as he himself appears to recognize
(*Archiv, loc. cit.*), it belongs more to the mathematics than to
the philosophy of the subject[2]. I therefore pass now to the
more strictly philosophical arguments.

While Leibniz was crossing from England to Holland, on
his way to visit Spinoza, he composed a highly interesting
dialogue on the difficulties arising from the continuity of
motion[3]. At the end of this dialogue he remarks : "Here I
have considered the nature of change and the continuum, in so
far as they belong to motion. It remains to consider, first the
subject of motion, that it may appear to which of two bodies,
which change their relative situation, the motion is to be

---

[1] L. 354; *Archiv fur Geschichte der Philosophie*, i. p. 576. The same maxim
was employed by Leibniz in arguing with Spinoza in 1676 against Des Cartes'
laws of motion : see L. p. 10, and Foucher de Careil, *Réfutation inédite de
Spinoza*, p. lxiv.

[2] Though in a letter to Bayle he speaks of it as a "wholly metaphysical
axiom " (G. iii. 46).

[3] See *Archiv f. Geschichte der Phil.* i. pp. 211—5,

ascribed; secondly, the cause of motion, or motor force"
(p. 215). The question of the continuum I leave for a later
chapter; the other two were solved together, in Leibniz's
opinion, by the notion of force which he afterwards gained.

That motion requires force, or a principle of change, in the
moving body, was deduced by Leibniz partly from abstract
metaphysical reasons, partly from the relativity of motion, and
partly from the so-called law of inertia, *i.e.* the law that every
body persists in any motion which it has acquired, except in so
far as it is hindered by outside causes. I shall begin with the
last of these arguments.

The law of inertia states, on the one hand, that a body will
not of itself begin a motion, but that, on the other hand, "body
retains of itself the impetus which it has once acquired, and
that it is constant in its levity, or has an endeavour to persevere in that very series of changes which it has entered upon"
(D. 120; G. IV. 511). A moving body is not merely successively in different places, but is at each moment in a *state* of
motion; it has velocity, and differs, in its state, from a body at
rest (D. 122; G. IV. 513). But this involves some effort to
change its place, whence the next state follows of itself from
the present. Otherwise, in the present, and therefore in every
moment, a moving body would differ in no way from one at
rest (*Ib.*). This argument is valid, I think, as against those
who, like Clerk Maxwell (*Matter and Motion*, Art. XLI.), endeavour to represent Newton's First Law as a self-evident
truth. Leibniz recognizes that, in a uniform rectilinear motion,
a body undergoes a series of changes, although its velocity is
unchanged. He infers that, since this series of changes is
possible without external influence, every body must contain in
itself a principle of change, *i.e.* force or activity, by means of
which a meaning is given to a *state* of change. But this
involves the continuity of change, concerning which we are
faced with those very difficulties to evade which, as regards
space, was a main purpose of the doctrine of monads. Accordingly, in other places, where Leibniz is thinking of the difficulties of the continuum, he holds all change to be discrete
once even asserting that motion is a continual transcreation[1].

[1] G. II. 279. Cf. the dialogue alluded to above, *Archiv*, Vol. I. p. 212 ff.

This is an instance of the vacillation into which, as we shall see in the next two chapters, Leibniz was led by his refusal to admit the antinomy of infinite division.

41. The most important dynamical argument in favour of force is connected with the relativity of motion. On this point, Leibniz's views present some suggestion of a vicious circle. He seems sometimes to argue that, because force is something real, it must have a subject, and be an attribute, not a mere relation ; whence it follows that, in a change of relative situation, the *cause* of change can be apportioned between the bodies, thus giving a sense to absolute motion (*e.g.* G. M. II. 184). But at other times, he argues that some real change, not merely relative, must underlie motion, and can only be obtained by means of force (*e.g.* D. 60, 61 ; G. IV. 369). This argument is interesting, both on account of its difference from the analogous arguments by which Newton proved the need of absolute space, and by the fact that Dynamics, at the present day, is still unable to reconcile the relativity of motion with the absoluteness of force[1]. In every motion, Leibniz says, the motion *per se* gives a mere change of relative situation, and it is impossible to say which body has moved, or whether both have moved. In order to be able to say this, we require to know in which is the cause of the change of relative situation. This cause we call force (*Ib.*). " When formerly," he says, " I regarded space as an immoveable real place, possessing extension alone, I had been able to define absolute motion as change of this real space. But gradually I began to doubt whether there is in nature such an entity as is called space ; whence it followed that a doubt might arise about absolute motion....... It seemed to follow that that which is real and absolute in motion consists not in what is purely mathematical, such as change of neighbourhood or situation, but in motive force itself ; and if there is none of this, then there is no absolute and real motion.......

---

[1] I cannot here undertake to give the proof of this assertion. It depends upon the fact that, if the laws of motion are to apply, the motion must be referred, not to *any* axes, but to what have been called kinetic axes, *i.e.* axes which have no absolute acceleration. See Newton, *Principia*, Scholium to the eighth definition. Contrast, in Clerk Maxwell's *Matter and Motion*, Arts. XVIII, CV.

Accordingly I found no other Ariadne thread to lead me out of this labyrinth than the calculation of forces, assuming this metaphysical principle, *that the total effect is always equal to its complete cause*" (L. 353; *Archiv*, I. p. 580).

On this question Leibniz's position, unlike Newton's, is, I think, full of confusion. On the one hand, space is wholly relational; hence motion is not a change of absolute position, but merely a change of relative situation. Now a change of relative situation is necessarily reciprocal, and hence Leibniz is led to the equality of action and reaction (N. E. 689; G. M. VI. 251—2). But in order to give any meaning to action, he has to forget the relativity of motion, and consequently to do away with the need for an equal reaction. He and Huygens agree, as against Newton, that the phenomena of circular motion give no more indication as to absolute motion than do those of rectilinear motion, though Huygens has the honesty to confess that he has not examined Newton's grounds (G. M. II. 177, 184—5, 192). The Copernican hypothesis, Leibniz says, anticipating Mach, is simpler, not truer, than the other (N. E. 685; G. M. VI. 248). But he nevertheless holds that, by means of force, some meaning may be given to the statement that, in a change of relative situation, one body has moved and not the other. "As for the difference of absolute and relative motion," he says, "I think that if the motion, or rather the motor force of bodies, is something real, as it seems that one must recognize, it is necessary that it should have a subject....... I agree that the phenomena could not furnish to us (or even to the angels) an infallible reason for determining the subject of motion or of its degree; and that each can be conceived apart as being at rest....... But you will not deny (I believe) that in truth each has a certain degree of motion, or, if you will, of force; in spite of the equivalence of hypotheses. It is true I draw from it this consequence, that there is in nature something besides what Geometry can determine in it" (G. M. II. 184). This, he says, is not the least of his reasons for recognizing force. Again he says, even more explicitly: "I find nothing in the eighth definition of the mathematical principles of nature, or in the scholium belonging to it [the scholium in which Newton explains the need of absolute space, time and motion] that proves, or can prove, the reality of space in itself. However, I grant there is a difference between an absolute true motion of a body, and a mere relative change of situation with respect to another body" (D. 269; G. VII. 404). But it must be evident that, if position is relative, absolute motion is meaningless. The two cannot possibly be reconciled. Leibniz, like Newton, rightly perceived that Dynamics requires us to distinguish, in a change of relative situation, the proportion in which accelerations are shared between two bodies. He was also right in maintaining that, on a geometrical or kinematical view, such a distinction cannot be practically effected. But Geometry does not show the distinction to be meaningless, and if it did, Dynamics could not make the distinction. Thus it would seem that Newton was right in inferring, from Dynamics, the necessity of absolute space. When I come to the theory of space, I shall maintain that even Geometry requires this, though only metaphysically, not, like Dynamics, for empirical reasons also.

As this point is important, it may be well briefly to repeat the arguments which show the relativity of motion to be inconsistent with the absoluteness of force. "As regards Physics," Leibniz says, "it is necessary to understand the nature of force, a thing entirely different from motion, which is something more relative. This force is to be measured by the quantity of its effect" (D. 39; G. II. 137). But the objection which here arises—an objection unavoidable on any relational theory of space—is, that the effect can only be measured by means of motion, and thus the pretended escape from endless relativity breaks down. A new objection applies to another statement, in which Leibniz endeavours to prove that motion is not purely relative. "If there is nothing in motion but this respective change," he says, "it follows that no reason is given in nature why motion must be ascribed to one thing rather than to others. The consequence of this will be that there is no real motion. Therefore in order that a thing may be said to be moved, we shall require not only that it change its situation in respect to others, but also that the cause of change, the force or action, be in it itself" (D. 61; G. IV. 369. Cf. also D. 269; G. VII. 404). This endeavour to establish absolute motion is, in the first place, wholly inconsistent with Leibniz's theory of space. Newton, from somewhat similar arguments, had rightly deduced the necessity of absolute position; Leibniz, who on many mathematical points was less philosophical than Newton, endeavoured to save absolute motion, while strenuously denying absolute position (cf. D. 266; G. VII. 401—2). But further, the theory is inconsistent with the nature of monads. Let us suppose two bodies A and B, which change their relative situation owing to the force in B. Since A mirrors the universe, a change will happen in A when B moves. Hence if the force resided only in B, B would cause a change in A, contrary to the theory that monads do not interact. Hence we must, in every case of a relative change of situation, place a force in both bodies, by which the change is to be effected. Thus we shall lose that power of discrimination which force was supposed to provide. This argument could only be evaded by the denial that monads have anything corresponding to position in space, a denial which Leibniz often attempted, but which, as we shall see later, would have destroyed the only ground for his monadism.

42. Leibniz's deduction of force as a means of escaping from the relativity of motion is thus fallacious. Motion, in its own nature, is or is not relative, and the introduction of force can make no difference to that nature. It remains to examine the metaphysical grounds for the notion of force. In so far as these are the same as those for activity in general, they have been already dealt with. But others are derived from the continuity of motion, and these must now be set forth.

"We have elsewhere suggested," Leibniz says (N. E. 671; G. M. VI. 235), "that there is in corporeal things something besides extension, nay, prior to extension, namely the force of nature everywhere implanted by its Author, which consists, not in the simple faculty with which the schools seem to have been content, but is provided, besides, with a tendency (*conatu*) or effort, which will have its full effect unless impeded by a contrary tendency. This effort often appears to the senses, and in my judgment is known everywhere in matter by the reason, even when it does not appear to the sense. But even if we are not to assign this force to God through a miracle, it is

certainly necessary that it be produced in the bodies themselves, nay that it constitute the inmost nature of bodies, since
to act is the mark of substances, and extension means nothing
else than the continuation or diffusion of the already presupposed...resisting substance, so far is it from being able itself to
constitute the very essence of substance. Nor is it relevant that
every corporeal action arises from motion, and motion itself
does not exist unless from motion.... For motion, like time,
never exists, if you reduce the thing to ἀκρίβεια, because it
never exists as a whole, since it has not co-existing parts. And
nothing at all is real in it, except that momentary property,
which must be constituted by a force striving for change."
This is the old argument of Zeno, suggested also in the dialogue written for Spinoza (*Archiv*, I. p. 213), and in many
other passages. Motion is change of position; but at any one
instant the position is one and only one. Hence at every
instant, and therefore always, there is no change of position and
no motion. Leibniz thought, however, what the Calculus was
likely to suggest, that the momentary increment was real in
some way in which the whole sum of increments was not real[1],
and hence force was called in to supply some reality other
than motion, out of which motion might be supposed to spring.
"Force," he says, "is something truly real, even in created
substances; but space, time and motion partake of the nature of
mental entities (*ens rationis*) and are true and real, not of themselves, but since they involve divine attributes" (N. E. p. 684;
G. M. VI. 247). And again, "Only force, and thence nascent
effort, exists in any moment, for motion never truly exists"
(N. E. p. 689; G. M. VI. 252). What Leibniz designs to effect,
by this doctrine, is, as with activity in general, the reduction of
a relation to a quality. Motion is doubly a relation—first, as
between successive moments, and secondly, as between bodies
in different places. Both relations were to be reduced by
means of force. A *state* of motion is distinguished from a
state of rest, at each instant of the motion, by the presence
of force, which, in the last analysis, is akin to desire. By
this means, not only are the difficulties of the temporal continuum supposed to be overcome (L. 351; *Archiv.* I. 577), but

---

[1] Cf. Cohen, *Infinitesimalmethode*, p. 15.

also, when two bodies change their relative situation, we can enquire whether one or both contains force, and thus assign an appropriate state of motion to each.

43. The objections to this view of force will appear more clearly from an examination of its application to the case of impact, and of the attempt to establish dynamically a plurality of causal series. We shall then find, if I am not mistaken, that the relation of Leibniz's Dynamics to his Metaphysics is hopelessly confused, and that the one cannot stand while the other is maintained. Unfortunately, the fall of the one does not involve the maintenance of the other. Leibniz has acquired much credit for the vaunted interconnection of his views in these two departments, and few seem to have perceived how false his boast really is. As a matter of fact, the want of connection is, I think, quite one of the weakest points in his system.

The problem of impact was one which pre-occupied the mathematicians of Leibniz's day far more than those of our own. It was solved only after he had acquired his mathematical equipment, and filled his mind to an extent which accounts for several curious features of his theory of matter. He appears to have quite unduly neglected impacts which are not perfectly elastic, and to have held (though he never definitely contends) that if bodies were only taken small enough, they could always be treated as perfectly elastic. Impact was ultimately, for him, the only form of dynamical interaction. He definitely rejected, as ultimately valid, the Newtonian gravitation, holding, with most moderns, that it must be explained by means of an all-pervading fluid. Perfect elasticity was ultimately required, if his law of the conservation of Vis Viva was to be preserved, since, when the coefficient of restitution is less than unity (as it always is in practice), Vis Viva is apparently lost. His reply to this objection was that it is absorbed by the small parts of bodies—transformed, in modern phraseology, from molar into molecular motion (N. E. 669—670; G. M. vi. 230—231). But if impact be the ultimate form of interaction, this answer can only serve if the smaller parts which receive the motion are themselves perfectly elastic. When pressed by Huygens on this point, Leibniz meanly evades the difficulty by denying that there are any last elements of bodies (G. M. II. 157). But a further difficulty remains, which is this. Impact is only elastic, according to Leibniz, because of a " subtle and penetrating fluid, whose motion is disturbed by the tension, or by the change of the elasticity. And as this fluid must be itself in turn composed of little solid bodies, elastic among themselves, we see that this replication of solids and fluids continues to infinity " (N. E. p. 668 ; G. M. VI. 228). He proceeds to confess that elasticity is necessary to the conservation of Vis Viva. Again he says—and this is an argument by which he often suggests the doctrine of monads :—" It is true that this conservation of force can only be obtained by putting elasticity everywhere in matter, and that a conclusion follows which will appear strange to those who do not sufficiently conceive the marvels of things: this is, that there are, so to speak, worlds in the smallest bodies, since every body, however small it may be, has elasticity, and consequently is surrounded and penetrated by a fluid as subtle, in relation to it, as that which makes the elasticity of sensible bodies can be in relation to us; and that therefore there are no first elements, since we must say as much of the smallest portion of the most subtle fluid that can be supposed " (G. III. 57). But it must be evident that, in the end, the motion of his fluid must be regulated by something other than the laws of elastic impact, since the elasticity of what is comparatively solid is only due to the presence of what is comparatively fluid. In order to develop the theory of an all-pervading fluid, Leibniz needed, what in his day did not exist, either Hydrodynamics or the modern Dynamics of the ether.

44. There are, speaking broadly, three great types of dynamical theory. There is the doctrine of hard extended atoms, for which the theory of impact is the appropriate weapon. There is the doctrine of the plenum, of an all-pervading fluid, for which the modern doctrine of the ether—the theory of Electricity, in fact—has at last partially forged the necessary weapons. And finally, there is the doctrine of unextended centres of force, with action at a distance, for which Newton supplied the required Mathematics. Leibniz failed to grasp these alternatives, and thus, from his love of a middle

position, fell between, not two, but three stools. His view of impact as the fundamental phenomenon of Dynamics should have led him to the theory of extended atoms, supported by Gassendi, and, in his own day, by Huygens. His belief in the plenum and the fluid ether should have led him to the second theory, and to the investigation of fluid motion. His relational theory of space, and his whole doctrine of monads, should have led him, as it led Boscovich, Kant[1] and Lotze, to the theory of unextended centres of force. The failure to choose between these alternatives made his Dynamics a mass of confusions. The true Leibnizian Dynamics is not his own, but that of Boscovich[2]. This theory is a simple development of the Newtonian Dynamics, in which all matter consists of material points, and all action is action at a distance. These material points are unextended like the monads, to which Boscovich appeals as analogous[3]; and in order to preserve their mutual independence, it is only necessary to regard the attraction or repulsion as due to the perception of one monad by the other, which, as a matter of fact, Leibniz actually does. Why, then, was this theory not that of Leibniz ?

There was, I think, to begin with, in later life, a personal reason. Leibniz had quarrelled with Newton concerning the Calculus, and he did not choose to admit that Newton had anything to teach him[4]. He therefore rejected gravitation as an ultimate account of things, giving as his reason that action at a distance is impossible. But this personal reason can only have operated after the publication of the *Principia* in 1687, by which date Leibniz had constructed both his philosophy and his Dynamics. It becomes necessary, therefore, to search for more objective reasons.

---

[1] That Kant's theory of space in the *Metaphysische Anfangsgründe der Naturwissenschaft* is different from that of the *Kritik*, has been often observed. See Vaihinger's *Commentar*, p. 224 ff.

[2] *Theoria Philosophiae Naturalis.* See esp. Part I, § 138 ff.

[3] Venetian edition of 1763, p. xxv. Boscovich differs from Newtonian Dynamics chiefly in assuming that, at very small distances, the force between two particles is repulsive. He differs from the Newtonian *philosophy* by regarding action at a distance as ultimate.

[4] It has even been suggested—and the suggestion appears very probably correct—that Leibniz never took the trouble to read the *Principia*. See Guhrauer, *op. cit.* Vol. I. p. 297.

Leibniz rejected atoms, the vacuum, and action at a distance. His grounds for these three rejections must be now examined.

45. (1) Against extended atoms he had, I think, fairly valid grounds. These are best set forth in his correspondence with Huygens, who maintained atoms. (See G. M. II. pp. 136, 145, 155—7). In the first place, the extended atom is composed of parts, since extension is repetition; it cannot, therefore, afford a metaphysical solution of the composition of matter. Moreover, if the laws of motion are to be preserved, the atom must be perfectly elastic, which is impossible since it must also be perfectly hard, and can contain no "subtle fluid." Again there is a breach of the law of continuity in assuming infinite hardness and absolute indivisibility to emerge suddenly when a certain stage is reached in division. And primitive rigidity is, in any case, a quality wholly without reason, and therefore inadmissible. In short, infrangible atoms would be a perpetual miracle. These arguments have been urged many times since, and are, one may suppose, on the whole valid.

46. (2) With regard to the vacuum, Leibniz relied mainly on the argument from what he called metaphysical perfection. He admitted that a vacuum is conceivable (N. E. 157; G. v. 140), but held that, wherever there is room, God might have placed matter without harm to anything else. Since, generally, the more existence the better, God would not have neglected the opportunity for creation, and therefore there is matter everywhere (D. 240, 253; G. VII. 356, 378). This principle of metaphysical perfection will be discussed later; for the present I confine myself to less theological arguments. A very weak argument, which Leibniz sometimes permits himself, is, that there could be no sufficient reason for determining the proportion of vacuum to filled space, and therefore there can be no vacuum at all (D. 253; G. II. 475; VII. 378). The only argument which attempts to be precise is one which is fatally unsound. If space be an attribute, Leibniz says, of what can empty space be an attribute (D. 248; G. VII. 372)? But space, for him, is a relation, not an attribute; his whole argument against the view that space is composed of points depends, as we shall see in Chapter IX., upon the fundamental *relation* of distance. He has, in fact, no valid arguments whatever against a vacuum. He seems to regard a belief in it as necessarily associated with a belief in extended atoms—"atoms and the void" are always spoken of together. In fact, when action at a distance is rejected, the two are necessarily connected; since unextended atoms must act at a distance, if there is to be any dynamical action at all[1].

47. (3) This brings me to Leibniz's grounds against action at a distance. I cannot discover, on this point, anything beyond vulgar prejudice. Both on this and on the previous point, his immediate followers, under the influence of Newton, abandoned the views of their master, which seem to have been mainly due to a lingering Cartesian prejudice. The spatial and temporal contiguity of cause and effect are apparently placed on a level. "A man will have an equal right to say that any-thing is the result of anything, if that which is absent in space or time can, without intermediary, operate here and now" (D. 115; G. IV. 507). With regard to time, though a difficulty arises from continuity, the maxim may be allowed; but with regard to space, it is precluded, as a metaphysical axiom, by the denial of transeunt action. For since nothing *really* acts on anything else, there seems no possible metaphysical reason why, in monads which mirror the whole universe, the perception of what is distant should not be a cause, just as much as the perception of what is near. There seems, therefore, in Leibniz's system, no metaphysical ground for the maxim; and in his time (which was that of Newton), there was certainly no dynamical ground. The denial of action at a distance must, therefore, be classed as a mere prejudice, and one, moreover, which had a most pernicious effect upon the relation of Leibniz's Dynamics to his Metaphysics.

48. I come now to another purpose which the doctrine of force was designed to fulfil. It showed, in the first place, that

---

[1] On one minor point, however, namely the possibility of motion in a plenum, Leibniz is unquestionably in the right. Locke had maintained that there must be empty space, or else there would be no room for motion. Leibniz rightly replies (N. E. pp. 53—4; L. 385; G. v. 52), that if matter be fluid, this difficulty is obviated. It should indeed be obvious, even to the non-mathematical, that motion in a closed circuit is possible for a fluid. It is a pity philosophers have allowed themselves to repeat this argument, which a week's study of Hydrodynamics would suffice to dispel. The complete answer to it is contained in what is called the equation of continuity.

actual secondary matter—as opposed to primary matter, which is a mere abstraction—is essentially active, as everything substantial must be. But it also attempted to show—what is essential to the doctrine of monads—that every piece of matter has its own force, and is the source of all its own changes. It was necessary, as we saw in Chapter IV., to maintain the plurality of independent causal series, and thus to exhibit force as *really* affecting only the body in which it was, not those upon which it apparently acted. Here Leibniz, quite unconsciously, took one side of what appears to be an antinomy, and appealed to his Dynamics as proving the thesis only, when it proved, with quite equal evidence, the antithesis also[1]. This brings us to the aspect of force in which it confers individuality[2]—an aspect which Leibniz also employs to prove the necessity of force. Without it, he says, all matter would be alike, and therefore motion, since space is a plenum, would make no difference (D. 122 ; G. iv. 512—3). This argument is certainly valid, on a relational theory of space, as against those (Cartesians or moderns) who hold to the relativity of motion, while they reduce all motion to vortices in a perfect fluid. But this is a digression, from which we must return to Dynamics and impact.

Every body, we are told, is really moved, not by other bodies, but by its own force. Thus in the successive impacts of a number of balls, " each ball repelled from the next one impinging on it, is set in motion by its *own force*, viz. its elasticity" (D. 124; G. iv. 515). The laws of motion, Leibniz thinks, compel us to admit independent causal action on the part of each particle of matter, and it is only by such action that we can free the idea of motion from a relativity which would make it wholly indeterminate. Therefore there must be, in each particle of matter, a force or activity from which its changes spring, by which we can give a meaning to a state of motion, and connect the states of a body at successive instants.

---

[1] See §§ 49, 50.

[2] This is connected with the doctrine of activity as the essence of individuality—a doctrine with which, by the way, Spinoza's dictum may be compared, that "desire is the very nature or essence of a person." *Ethics*, Pt. III. Prop. ix. Schol. and Prop. lvii.

Force is related to *materia prima* as form to matter in the Aristotelian sense. "Because of form every body always acts, and because of matter every body always endures and resists" (N. E. 673; G. M. VI. 237). In active force is the entelechy, analogous to a soul, whose nature consists in a certain perpetual law of its series of changes, which it spontaneously carries out (G. II. 171). It is this force which constitutes the identity of each piece of matter, and differentiates it from all other pieces. And Leibniz endeavours, as his metaphysics requires, to show that force only acts on the body in which it is, and never on any other body. Cases where a body *appears* to be acted upon by another are called cases of passion, but even here, the appearance is deceptive. "The passion of every body is spontaneous, or arises from internal force, though upon occasion of something external. I understand here, however, passion proper, which arises from percussion, or which remains the same, whatever hypothesis is finally assigned, or to whatever we finally ascribe absolute rest or motion. For since the percussion is the same, to whatever at length true motion belongs, it follows that the result of the percussion is distributed equally between both, and thus *both act equally in the encounter*, and thus half the result arises from the action of the one, the other half from the action of the other; and since half also of the result or passion is in one, half in the other, it is sufficient that we derive the passion which is in one from the action which is also in itself, and we need no influence of the one upon the other, although by the one an occasion is furnished to the action of the other, which is producing a change in itself" (N. E. 688; G. M. VI. 251).

49. To bring this doctrine into harmony with the facts, a further distinction was required between primitive and derivative force. The latter, which is a modification of the former, is the actual present state while tending to the future. The primitive force is persistent, and is, as it were, the law of the series, while the derived force is the determination designating a particular term of the series (G. II. 262). "Active force," Leibniz says, "......is twofold, namely *primitive*, which exists in every corporeal substance *per se* (since I think a wholly quiescent body abhorrent to the nature of things), or *derivative*, which by a limitation, as it were, of the primitive, resulting through the conflicts of bodies with each other, is variously exercised. And, indeed, the primitive force (which is nothing other than the first entelechy) corresponds to the *soul or substantial form*, but for this very reason pertains only to general causes, which cannot suffice for the explanation of phenomena. And so we agree with those who deny that forms must be employed in deducing the particular and special causes of sensible things" (N. E. 672; G. M. vi. 236). The primitive force is constant in each body throughout all time; the sum of derived forces throughout the universe is also constant, being what Leibniz calls Vis Viva, and what is still sometimes so called, which is double what is now known as kinetic energy (G. iii. 457). "Derivative force is what some call impetus, that is a *conatus* or tendency to some determinate motion, by which the primitive force, or principle of action, is modified. This (the derivative force) I have shown to be not conserved the same in the same body, but yet being distributed among many bodies, to preserve a constant sum, and to differ from motion, whose quantity is not conserved" (N. E. 702; G. iv. 396).

In this argument, it must be evident that, so far from basing Metaphysics upon Dynamics, Leibniz has inferred, on purely metaphysical grounds, a primitive force of which no dynamical use is made[1]. What was useful in Dynamics was, not the primitive force, which was constant in each separate piece of matter, but the derivative force, which was transferred from body to body. The primitive force was thus invoked for purely metaphysical reasons, and could not validly be used to show that Dynamics supported the doctrine of the independence of substances. Here again, I think, as in the case of continuity, there is an antinomy which Leibniz refused to face. The total effect on any particle is, dynamically, made up of effects caused by all other particles; thus the separate causation of separate elements seems conceded. But none of these separate effects ever happen: they are all mathematical

---

[1] Cf. G. ii. 251: "Every modification presupposes something durable. Therefore when you say, 'Let us suppose that nothing is to be found in bodies except derivative forces,' I reply that this is not a possible hypothesis." Cf. also G. ii. 270.

fictions. What really happens is the sum of effects, *i.e.* the effect of the sum or of the whole. Thus even when a thing is defined as one causal series, we can hardly escape the admission, which however is directly self-contradictory, that things do, after all, interact.

And this is, in fact, admitted practically in Leibniz's writings. Although Dynamics requires us to assign causal action to each piece of matter, it requires us, just as much, to take account of all material particles in discussing what will happen to any one. That is, we require, on a purely dynamical basis, to admit transeunt action, the action of one thing on another. This was not avoided by Leibniz: on the contrary, the purely material world remained, for him, one in which every motion affects every other, though *direct* inter-action occurs only in impact. " All is a *plenum* (and thus all matter is connected together), and in the *plenum* every motion has an effect upon distant bodies in proportion to their distance, so that each body not only is affected by those which are in contact with it, and in some way feels the effect of everything that happens to them, but also is mediately affected by bodies touching those with which it is in immediate contact. Wherefore it follows that this intercommunication of things extends to any distance, however great. And conse-quently every body feels the effect of all that takes place in the universe " (Monadology, § 61; L. 251; D. 227; G. VI. 617). He then proceeds to deduce the proposition that all substances mirror the universe from this standpoint, which is diametrically opposite to that of the independence of all material particles[1]. He explained this apparent interaction by a subjective theory, in which motions became merely representations in all monads, because all monads mirror the universe. The true account of the matter became, that representations of causes are causes of representations of effects (G. IV. 533), a kind of Berkeleian theory, which renders it absurd to deduce the ac-tivity of substance from anything whatever in Dynamics.

Moreover, if—as one must suppose—what seems to be motion is a real change in some assemblage of monads, and is therefore part of an independent causal series, its perception,

[1] Cf. G. II. 112.

the subjective motion, is also part of such a series, and there are as many independent causal series in each monad as there are monads in the world which it mirrors. This difficulty, however, may be left till we come to the pre-established harmony.

50. There remains one last and principal difficulty, a difficulty which, so far as I know, no existing theory of Dynamics can avoid. When a particle is subject to several forces, they are compounded by the parallelogram law, and the resultant is regarded as their sum. It is held that each independently produces its effect, and that the resultant effect is the sum of the partial effects. Thus "every conation is compatible with every other, since every motion can be compounded with every other to give a third motion, which can always be determined geometrically. And thus it did not appear how a conation could be naturally destroyed or withdrawn from a body" (*Archiv für Gesch. d. Phil.* I. 578). If we are to admit particular causes, each of which, independently of all others, produces its effect, we must regard the resultant motion as compounded of its components. If we do not admit such particular causes, every part of matter, and therefore all matter, is incapable of causal action, and Dynamics (unless the descriptive school is in the right) becomes impossible. But it has not been generally perceived that a sum of motions, or forces, or vectors generally, is a sum in a quite peculiar sense— its constituents are not parts of it. This is a peculiarity of all addition of vectors, or even of quantities having sign. Thus no one of the constituent causes ever really produces its effect : the only effect is one compounded, in this special sense, of the effects which *would* have resulted if the causes had acted independently. This is a fundamental difficulty concerning the nature of addition, and explaining, I think, how Leibniz came to be so confused as to the causation of particulars by particulars. So great is this confusion, that it is not unfairly expressed by Wundt in the words : " Every substance determines itself, but this self-determination is determined by another substance " (*Die physikalischen Axiome*, p. 57).

Thus the attempt to establish, on the basis of Dynamics, a plurality of independent causal series, must be pronounced a complete failure. Not only was it faulty in detail, but it was also mistaken in principle, since the result aimed at—the reduction of the whole series of dynamical phenomena to subjective series of perceptions—should have made the whole dynamical world a *single* series in each percipient monad. The confusion was due—as we shall find to be the case with most of Leibniz's confusions—to a failure to grasp the consequences, drawn boldly (except as to the thing in itself) by Kant, of the subjectivity of space. In the next two chapters, we shall have to consider a better argument, an argument from the difficulties of the continuum to the unreality of space, and the consequent non-spatial nature of the monads.

CHAPTER VIII

THE PHILOSOPHY OF MATTER (CONTINUED).

(b) As explaining continuity and extension.

51. WE now reach at last the central point of Leibniz's philosophy, the doctrine of extension and continuity. The most distinctive feature of Leibniz's thought is its pre-occupation with the "labyrinth of the continuum." To find a thread through this labyrinth was one main purpose of the doctrine of monads—a purpose which, in Leibniz's own opinion, that doctrine completely fulfilled. And the problem of continuity might very well be taken, as Mr Latta takes it (L. 21), as the starting-point for an exposition of Leibniz: "How can that which is continuous consist of indivisible elements"? To answer this question was, I think, one of the two chief aims of Leibniz's doctrine of substance and of all that is best in his philosophy. That I did not begin with this question, was due to motives of logical priority; for the abstract doctrines which we have hitherto considered, though perhaps invented largely with a view to this problem, are logically prior to it: they form an apparatus which must be mastered before Leibniz's treatment of the present question can be understood.

The present chapter may be regarded as a commentary on the first two paragraphs of the Monadology. "The Monad, of which we shall here speak," Leibniz says, "is nothing but a *simple* substance, which enters into compounds. By 'simple' is meant 'without parts.' And there must be simple substances, since there are compounds; for a compound is nothing but a collection or aggregate of simple things" (L. 217; D. 218;

G. vi. 607). Now in this statement, I should like to point out the following presuppositions : (1) that the meaning of *substance* is known, (2) that we have grounds for assuming the existence of something substantial but complex, (3) that everything substantial and complex must ultimately be composed of parts which are not complex, *i.e.* have no parts, but are themselves simple substances. Of these presuppositions, the meaning of substance has been already discussed. The assumption that matter exists has also been shown to be essential. It remains to enquire why matter is an aggregate of substances, and why it must consist of simple substances.

52. Leibniz starts, in this discussion, from the fact that matter is extended, and that extension is nothing but repetition (cf. G. ii. 261). In this assertion, extension must be carefully distinguished from space. Extension, like duration, is a property of an extended thing, a property which it carries with it from place to place. " A body can change space, but cannot leave its extension " (D. 263 ; G. vii. 398) ; everything has its own extension and duration, but not its own space and time (D. 265 ; G. vii. 399). What we are now concerned with, then, is extension, not space. As regards extension, Leibniz took up a more or less common-sense attitude; as regards space, he had a complicated and rather paradoxical theory, which can only be fully dealt with after the doctrine of extension has been developed. The great error, in Leibniz, was the idea that extension and duration are prior to space and time. His logical order, as opposed to the order of discovery, is as follows : First comes the notion of substance, secondly the existence of many substances, thirdly extension, resulting from their repetition, and fourthly space, depending on extension, but adding the further notion of order, and taking away the dependence upon *actual* substances. The order of proof or of discovery, however, is different from this. The existence of many substances is inferred from the fact of extension, by the contention that extension means repetition. That extension logically presupposes space, being in fact the property of occupying so much space, seems sufficiently evident. Leibniz, however, overlooked this fact. He began with extension, as was indeed natural to any one who regarded substance as logically prior to space. It is instructive to contrast the order of Kant's *Critique*, which begins with space and time, and only then advances to the categories, among which are substance and attribute. That this was not Leibniz's order, is the main objection to his philosophy of the continuum. He began, instead, with a common-sense theory of extension and duration, which he vainly endeavoured to patch up by a paradoxical theory of space and time.

53. In my last chapter (p. 78), I stated that one of Leibniz's arguments against the view that the essence of matter is extension was derived from the nature of extension itself. This argument we must now examine. Extension, he says, in a dialogue directed against Malebranche, is not a concrete, but the abstract of what is extended. This, he continues, is the essential difference between his theory of substance and the Cartesian theory advocated by Malebranche (G. VI. 582—4). "Besides extension," he says in another place, "there must be a subject which is extended, *i.e.* a substance to which it belongs to be repeated or continued. For extension signifies only a repetition or continual multiplication of that which is extended, a plurality, continuity and coexistence of parts; and hence extension is not sufficient to explain the nature of the extended or repeated substance itself, the notion of which is anterior to that of its repetition" (D. 44; G. IV. 467). And not only must there be a plurality of substances, but also—I suppose in order that the plurality may constitute a repetition—there must be a repeated or extended quality. Thus in milk there is a diffusion of whiteness, in the diamond a diffusion of hardness (G. VI. 584). But the diffusion of such qualities is only apparent, and is not to be found in the smallest parts. Thus the only quality which is properly extended is resistance, which is the essence of *materia prima* (N. E. p. 700; G. IV. 394). Thus the essence of *materia prima* is not extension, but is extended, and indeed is the only quality which can, strictly, be called extended: for it is the only quality which is common to all created substances, and thus repeated everywhere. Extension or primary matter, Leibniz says, is nothing but a certain repetition of things in so far as they are similar or indiscernible. But this supposes things which are repeated, and have, in addition to common qualities, others which are peculiar (D. 176; F. de C. 28—30). This theory explains two important points. First, it shows why all monads have *materia prima*; for it is in virtue of this common quality that a collection of monads is extended. Secondly, it connects the Identity of Indiscernibles with the abstract and phenomenal nature of extension. For extension is a repetition of things *in so far* as they are indiscernible; and thus, since no two things are really indiscernible, extension involves abstraction from those qualities in which they differ. Thus a collection of monads is only extended when we leave out of account everything except the *materia prima* of each monad and the general property of activity, and consider merely the repetition of these qualities.

54. But *materia prima*, as we saw in the last chapter, and as appears further from the fact that two pieces of *materia prima* are indiscernible, is a mere abstraction; the substances whose repetition results in extension must have other properties besides this pure passivity, namely the activity essential to substance, and the differences required to make them many. Now wherever there is repetition, there must be many indivisible substances. "Where there are only beings by aggregation," Leibniz says, "there are not even real beings. For every being by aggregation presupposes beings endowed with a true unity, since it only derives its reality from that of those of which it is composed, so that it will have none at all if every component is again a being by aggregation." If we admit aggregates, "we must either come to mathematical points,...or to the atoms of Epicurus,...or we must avow that there is no reality in bodies, or, finally, we must recognize in them some substances which have a true unity" (G. II. 96). The special objections to mathematical points I shall consider in connection with the continuum. The objections to atoms—and these apply also against points—are, that they are indiscernible, and that, if they are purely material, they cannot have activity. The objection to not admitting the reality of bodies seems to be, as I have already pointed out, nothing better than common sense; but this led Leibniz to prefer, if he could logically do so, the theory of "true unities" to the mere unreality of bodies. At the same time, it is remarkable that, in his early statements of the doctrine of monads, he hesitates to allow real unities to *all* bodies, and inclines to think that there may be inanimate bodies without any unities, and therefore without reality (G. II. 77 and 127)[1]. His argument may, then, be stated thus: Assuming that what appears to us as matter is something real, it is evident that it must be a plurality. Now a plurality is only real if its constituents are real, and nothing is ultimately real except substances and their states. But the plurality, in this case, since its constituents exist simultaneously, is not a mere plurality of states; therefore it is a plurality of substances, and substances are necessarily indivisible. Hence what appears to us as matter must be a collection of indivisible substances. What is not truly *one* being, is not truly a *being*; if it were of the essence of a body to have no unity, it would be of its essence to be a mere phenomenon (G. II. 97). These real unities are what Leibniz calls *entelechies* or *forms*. These terms, which he borrowed from Aristotle, denote, when accurately used, not the whole monad, but its activity, or that in it which is analogous to a soul, as opposed to its *materia prima*, which is passive, and is matter also in the Aristotelian sense, opposed to form (cf. G. II. 252).

What is the nature of these "true unities" involved in the reality of what appears as matter? This nature in general I shall discuss in Chapter XI.; for the present, I am concerned with it only in so far as it is required to explain extension. We shall have in the next chapter to investigate the abstract doctrine as to the continuous and the discrete, as to space and extension, which underlies this present argument; but it will be well to begin with the more concrete form of Leibniz's difficult doctrine of the continuum.

55. Leibniz distinguishes three kinds of points. "Atoms of matter," he says, "are contrary to reason......only atoms of substance, *i.e.* unities which are real and absolutely destitute of parts, are sources of actions and the absolute first principles of the composition of things, and, as it were, the last elements of the analysis of substances. They might be called *metaphysical points*; they possess a certain vitality and a kind of perception, and *mathematical points* are their points of view to

[1] Contrast Stein, *op. cit.* p. 167 note.

express the universe. But when corporeal substances are compressed, all their organs together form only a *physical point* to our sight. Thus physical points are only indivisible in appearance; mathematical points are exact, but they are merely modalities; only metaphysical points or those of substance (constituted by forms or souls) are exact and real, and without them there would be nothing real, for without true unities there would not be multiplicity" (D. 76; L. 310—1; G. IV. 482). The expression "metaphysical points" is not usual, and is only employed, apparently, to bring out the connection with infinite division. We may put the matter thus: Space consists of an assemblage of relations of distance; the terms of such relations, taken simply as terms, are *mathematical points*. They are thus mere modalities, being a mere aspect or quality of the actual terms, which are *metaphysical points* or monads. The *physical point*, on the contrary, is an infinitesimal extension, of the kind used in the Infinitesimal Calculus. This is not truly indivisible, since it is, after all, a small *extension*, and extension is essentially repetition. The argument, then, is briefly this: Matter as such is extended; extension is essentially plurality; therefore the elements of what is extended cannot themselves be extended. A simple substance cannot be extended, since all extension is composite (G. III. 363). Atoms of matter are contrary to reason, because they would have to be indivisibles whose essence is divisibility. Hence the constituents of matter are not material, if what is material must be extended. But the constituents cannot be mathematical points, since these are purely abstract, are not existents, and do not compose extension. The constituents of what appears as matter, therefore, are unextended, and are not mathematical points. They must be substances, endowed with activity, and differing *inter se* because of the Identity of Indiscernibles. Hence there remains nothing, among the objects of experience, which these substances can be, except something analogous to souls. Souls are concrete existents, or substances, differing *inter se*, and unextended. These, therefore, must be the constituents of what seem to be bodies. Bodies as such, *i.e.* as extended, are phenomena; but they are *phenomena bene fundata*, because they are the appearances of collections of real substances. The

nature of these is force, and they are indivisible like our minds
(D. 72; L. 301; G. IV. 479).

The argument is excellently stated in a letter to De Volder
(G. II. 267). De Volder says: Extension being necessary to a
mathematical body, it is rightly concluded that, in such a body,
no indivisible unities can be assigned. But this does not prove
the mathematical body to be destitute of reality. To this
argument Leibniz makes a very full reply. What can be
divided into several, he says, is an aggregate of several; an
aggregate is one only for the mind, and has no reality but what
is conferred by its constituents. Hence there are in things
indivisible unities, because otherwise there will be in things no
true unities, nor any reality not derived, which is absurd. For
where there is no true unity, there is no true multitude. And
where there is no reality not derived, there is no reality at all,
for this must at length be derived from some subject. Again,
he says, I conclude that in the mass of bodies indivisible
unities, or prime constituents, *can* be found. *Bodies* are always
divisible and always divided, but not so the elements which
constitute them. The *mathematical* body is not real, because
it has no such constituents; it is something mental, and designates a mere plurality of parts. As number is not substance
without things numbered, so the mathematical body, or extension, is not substance, without activity and passivity. But in
real corporeal things, the parts are not indefinite (as in space,
which is a mental thing), but actually assigned in a certain
manner, as nature institutes actual divisions and subdivisions
according to the varieties of motion; and these divisions
proceed to infinity, but none the less result in certain primary
constituents or real unities, only infinite in number. But to
speak strictly, matter is not *composed* of constitutive unities, but
results from them, for matter or extended mass is only a well-
founded phenomenon, and all reality consists of unities. Therefore phenomena can always be divided into lesser phenomena,
and there are no least phenomena. Substantial unities are not
parts, but foundations, of phenomena.

56. Many things in this argument presuppose Leibniz's
general position as to continuity, a position which, with his
theory of space, must be left to the next Chapter. To represent

fairly, however, the drift of Leibniz's argument from extension to monads, it must be remembered that he believed himself, on a purely dynamical basis, to have shown matter to be the appearance of something substantial. For force, which he regarded as equivalent to activity, is required by the laws of motion, and is required in each piece of matter. That there must be entelechies dispersed everywhere throughout matter, follows from the fact that principles of motion are thus dispersed (G. VII. 330). And from this point of view, we may give a slightly better meaning, than before appeared, to the doctrine of force. Force is more real than motion, or even matter. Motion is not a cause, but an effect of force, and is no more a real being than time. But force *is* a real being, though matter is only a well-founded phenomenon (G. II. 115; III. 457). Thus though matter and motion are only appearances, they are appearances *of* something having activity, and therefore of something substantial. If we assume, as Leibniz always does, that our perceptions of matter *correspond* to a real world outside us, then that world, on dynamical grounds, must contain forces, and therefore substances. The only difficulty is, to reconcile this view with the arbitrary and infinite divisibility of matter. This difficulty brings us to the doctrine of infinity and continuity.

CHAPTER IX

THE LABYRINTH OF THE CONTINUUM.

57. IN the last chapter, we saw that matter is a phenomenon, resulting from aggregates of real unities or monads. Extension is repetition, and the extended is therefore plural. But if what appears as matter is a plurality, it must be an infinite plurality. For whatever is extended, can be divided *ad infinitum*. Mass, says Leibniz, is discrete, *i.e.* an actual multitude, but composed of an infinity of units (G. II. 379). Here we have Leibniz's belief in the actual infinite. An actual infinite has been generally regarded as inadmissible, and Leibniz, in admitting it, is face to face with the problem of the continuum. At this point, therefore, it is necessary to examine his views about infinity, continuity, infinite number, and infinite division. These must be dealt with before we proceed any farther with the description of the true unities or monads, since Leibniz professes to deduce the existence and nature of monads largely from the need of explaining the continuum. "In this consideration" (*i.e.* of monads), he says, "there occurs no extension or composition of the continuum, and all difficulties about points vanish. And it is this that I meant to say somewhere in my *Théodicée*, namely that the difficulties of the continuum should admonish us that things are to be conceived in quite a different manner" (G. II. 451; cf. G. VI. 29). Again he says (G. II. 262): "The monad alone is a substance, body is substances, not a substance; nor can the difficulties of the composition of the continuum, and others allied to these, be otherwise evaded"; and "nothing but Geometry can furnish a thread for the labyrinth of the composition of the continuum, of maxima

and minima, and of the unassignable and the infinite, and no
one will arrive at a truly solid metaphysic who has not passed
through that labyrinth[1]." Now what are the difficulties of
the continuum, and how are they evaded? I cannot hope to
succeed in making the subject plain, both because it is nearly
the most difficult subject in philosophy, and because Leibniz's
treatment offers special difficulties to the commentator.

58. Every one who has ever heard of Leibniz knows that
he believed in the actual infinite. Few quotations from him
are more familiar than the following (D. 65; G. I. 416): "I am
so much in favour of the actual infinite, that, instead of admitting that nature abhors it, as is commonly said, I hold that
nature affects it everywhere, in order the better to mark the
perfections of its author. So I believe that there is no part of
matter which is not, I do not say divisible, but actually divided;
and consequently the least particle must be regarded as a world
full of an infinity of different creatures." Such passages, I say,
are well known, and are embodied in the common remark that
Leibniz believed in the actual infinite, *i.e.* in what a Hegelian
would call the false infinite. But this is by no means the
whole truth on the matter. To begin with, Leibniz denied
infinite *number*, and supported his denial by very solid arguments[2]. In the second place, he was familiar with the distinction, afterwards used by Hegel, between the true and false
infinite. " The true infinite," he says, " exists, strictly speaking,
only in the *Absolute,* which is anterior to all composition, and
is not formed by the addition of parts[3] "; an infinite aggregate
is not truly a whole, and therefore not truly infinite (G. II.

---

[1] Cohen, *Infinitesimalmethode,* p. 64; G. M. VII. 326.

[2] Cf. G. VI. 629; I. 338; II. 304—5; v. 144; N. E. p. 161.

[3] N. E. p. 162; G. v. 144. Cf. the following passage: "I believe with Mr
Locke that, strictly speaking, it may be said that there is no space, no time and
no number which is infinite, but that it is only true that however great may
be a space, a time, or a number, there is always another greater than it, *ad
infinitum*; and that thus the true infinite is not found in a whole made up of
parts. It is none the less, however, found elsewhere; namely, in the *absolute,*
which is without parts, and which has influence upon compound things because
they result from limitation of the absolute. Hence the *positive infinite* being
nothing else than the absolute, it may be said that there is in this sense a positive idea of the infinite, and that it is anterior to that of the finite " (D. 97;
N. E. 16—17; G. v. 17; Erdmann's edition, p. 138. G.'s text appears to be
defective).

304—5; N. E. pp. 161—3; G. v. 143—5). And these statements are not made in forgetfulness of his advocacy of the
actual infinite. On the contrary, he says in one passage:
"Arguments against actual infinity assume, that if this be
admitted, there will be an infinite number, and that all infini-
ties will be equal. But it is to be observed that an infinite
aggregate is neither one whole, or possessed of magnitude,
nor is it consistent with number" (G. II. 304). The actual
infinite is thus defended on the express ground that it does *not*
lead to infinite number. We must agree, therefore, that
Leibniz's views as to infinity are by no means so simple or so
naïve as is often supposed. To expound the theory from which
the above remarks follow, is a difficult attempt; but this
attempt I must now undertake.

I have already had occasion to mention Hegel, and I think
an analogy in other respects may serve to throw light on
Leibniz's arguments. In the first place, he often seems to
imply, as we have already seen in connection with extension,
the essentially Hegelian view that abstraction is falsification.
In the second place, his argument on the present question, and
his whole deduction of Monadism from the difficulties of the
continuum, seems to bear a close analogy to a dialectical argument. That is, to put the matter crudely, a result is accepted
as true because it can be inferred from premisses admittedly
false, and inconsistent with each other[1]. Those who admire
these two elements in Hegel's philosophy will think Leibniz's
argument the better for containing them. But in any case, a
comprehension of the argument is, if I am right in my interpretation, greatly facilitated by this analogy to a method which
has grown familiar.

[1] The argument is not strictly dialectical, but the following statement shows
its weakness. The general premiss is: Since matter has parts, there are many
reals. Now the parts of matter are extended, and owing to infinite divisibility,
the parts of the extended are always extended. But since extension means repetition, what is repeated is ultimately not extended. Hence the parts of
matter are ultimately not extended. Therefore it is self-contradictory to suppose
that matter has parts. Hence the many reals are not parts of matter. (The
argument is stated almost exactly in this form in G. VII. 552.)

It is evident that this argument, in obtaining many reals, assumes that these
are parts of matter—a premiss which it is compelled to deny in order to show
that the reals are not material.

59. In spite of the law of continuity, Leibniz's philosophy may be described as a complete denial of the continuous. Repetition is *discrete*, he says, where aggregate parts are discerned, as in number : it is *continuous* where the parts are indeterminate, and can be assumed in an infinite number of ways (N. E. p. 700; G. IV. 394). That anything actual is continuous in this sense, Leibniz denies; for though what is actual may have an infinite number of parts, these parts are not indeterminate or arbitrary, but perfectly definite (G. II. 379). Only space and time are continuous in Leibniz's sense, and these are purely ideal. In actuals, he says, the simple is prior to the aggregate ; in ideals, the whole is prior to the part (G. II. 379). Again he says that the continuum is ideal, because it involves indeterminate parts, whereas in the actual everything is determinate. The labyrinth of the continuum, he continues—and this is one of his favourite remarks—comes from looking for actual parts in the order of possibles, and indeterminate parts in the aggregate of actuals (G. II. 282. Cf. *Ib.* 379; IV. 491). This means that points and instants are not actual parts of space and time, which are ideal[1]; and that nothing extended (since the extended is indeterminate) can be a true component of an aggregate of substances, which is actual. As regards space and time, and number also, the finite whole is logically prior to the parts into which it may be divided; as regards substance, on the contrary, the aggregate is logically subsequent to the individual substances which compose it[2].

What Leibniz means, seems to be this. There are two sorts of indivisibles, namely simple ideas, and single substances. In the former sense, the number one is indivisible : it is a simple idea, logically prior to the fractions whose sum is one. These fractions presuppose it, and its simplicity is not disproved by the fact that there are an infinite number of fractions of which it may be composed. It is truer, in fact, to regard fractions as formed by dividing unity, than to regard unity as formed by compounding fractions. Similarly one half, abstractly taken, is a mere ratio, not the sum of two quarters; the latter is only true

[1] Contrast Cohen, *op. cit.* p. 63, G. M. v. 385 : "A point is an infinitely small or evanescent line." This seems only to be meant mathematically.

[2] Cf. G. M. IV. 89 ff.

of numbered things (G. IV. 491). Thus many who have philosophized about the point and unity have become confused, through not distinguishing resolution into notions and division into parts (G. III. 583). Similarly, Leibniz thinks, the abstract line is not compounded (G. IV. 491), for what is true about the line is only the relation of distance, which, quâ relation, is indivisible. Composition exists only in concretes, i.e. in the masses of which these abstract lines mark the relations. In substantial actual things, the whole is a result or assemblage of simple substances (Ib.). It is the confusion of the ideal and the actual, Leibniz says again, which has embroiled everything, and produced the labyrinth of the continuum.

60. At this point, it seems essential to consider Leibniz's theory of space. This theory is more or less involved in everything that can be said about his philosophy; I have already said something about it, and much more will follow. But here a few explicit remarks will illustrate the doctrine of the continuum.

The ideals in which, according to Leibniz, the whole is prior to the part, are numbers, space, and time. As regards numbers, it is evident that unity, and even the other integers, are prior to fractions. As regards space and time, a similar result is attained by the relational theory. In all these cases, Leibniz would have done better to say boldly, that, though numbers and distances may be greater or smaller, they have no parts. With regard to fractions, he does say this (G. IV. 491), and this is what he means to say in all such cases. Ideals, if they are numbers, are concepts applicable to possible aggregates, but are not themselves aggregates; if they are distances, they are possible relations, and must be distinguished from an extension which extends from one end of the distance to the other.

61. There are two great types of spatial theory, the one represented by Newton, the other by Leibniz. These two are brought face to face in the controversy with Clarke. Both result from emphasizing one or other of the following pair of ideas. If we take two points A and B, they have (1) a distance, which is simply a relation between the two, (2) an actual length, consisting of so much space, and stretching from

A to B. If we insist on the former as the essence of space, we get a relational theory; the terms A and B, whose distance is spatial, must themselves be non-spatial, since they are not relations. If we insist on the latter, the actual intervening length, we find it divisible into an infinite number of points each like the end points A and B. This alternative gives the Newtonian theory of absolute space, consisting, not in an assemblage of possible relations, but in an infinite collection of actual points. The objection to Newton's theory is, that it is self-contradictory; the objection to Leibniz's, that it is plainly inconsistent with the facts, and, in the end, just as self-contradictory as Newton's. A theory free from both these defects is much to be desired, as it will be something which philosophy has not hitherto known. I shall return to Leibniz's arguments in my next chapter. For the present, I only wish to point out the consequences of his relational theory—consequences also drawn by Lotze and others who have advocated this theory.

Space is an assemblage of possible relations of distance. These become actual only when the points A, B are occupied by actual substances. Distances may be greater or less, but cannot be divided into parts, since they are relations. (This consequence is not drawn by Leibniz, indeed it is expressly denied; but he uses *part* more generally than I am using it. He says, what suffices for me, that in space and time there are no divisions but such as are made by the mind [G. II. 278—9]). And the terms which are distant, since space is relational, cannot themselves be spatial or extended. The distance, moreover, should be analyzed into predicates of the distant terms A and B; this Leibniz does by representing distance as part of the manner in which A and B mirror one another. And thus a mathematical point, the *place* of A, is merely that quality of A in virtue of which, at any moment, it mirrors other things as it does. This is why mathematical points are the *points of view* of the monads, and also why they are mere modalities, and not parts of space. This view of space also explains why the whole is not composed of its parts. For the parts of a distance are merely other smaller relations of distance, and are in no way presupposed by the larger distance, which is logically independent of them. The distinction is, in fact, that between intensive and extensive quantities. Extensive quantities presuppose all the constituents whose sum they are; intensive quantities, on the contrary, do not in any way presuppose the existence of smaller quantities of the same kind. . Leibniz's position is, then, that spatial and temporal quantities are relations, and therefore intensive; while extension is an extensive quantity, and presupposes actual parts in that which is extended[1].

The distinction between the composition of what is actual, and the resolution of what is ideal, is thus of great importance. It explains what Leibniz means by saying that an instant is not a part of time (G. III. 591), nor a mathematical point a part of the spatial continuum (D. 64, 76; L. 311; G. I. 416; II. 279; IV. 482). The spatial continuum is the assemblage of all possible distances. Mathematical points are merely positions, *i.e.* possible terms for the relations of distance. Thus they are not of the same order as the possible distances which make up the spatial continuum; they are not parts of this continuum. Indeed a distance, being a relation, has properly no parts, and thus we have no reason to resolve it into indivisible parts. What is extended in space, on the contrary, is concrete; we have not merely distances, but also terms between which the distances hold. An abstract space is not plural, but a body which occupies that space must be plural. For instead of bare possibility, we now have something actual in the positions which, otherwise, are "mere modalities."

62. We may put the whole argument briefly thus. (1) Nothing is absolutely real but indivisible substances and their various states (G. II. 119). This is the outcome of the abstract logical doctrine with which I began my account of

---

[1] Thus in reply to Clarke, Leibniz says: "As for the objection that space and time are quantities, or rather things endowed with quantity, and that situation and order are not so, I answer, that order also has its quantity; there is in it that which goes before, and that which follows; there is distance or interval. Relative things have their quantity, as well as absolute ones. For instance, ratios or proportions in mathematics have their quantity, and are measured by logarithms; and yet they are relations. And therefore, though time and space consist in relations, yet they have their quantity" (D. 270; G. VII. 404). Leibniz's views on intensive quantity were, however, by no means clear.

Leibniz; it is presupposed in the argument from extension to monads, and must not be regarded as a result of that argument. (2) What appears to us as matter is real, though *quâ* matter it is phenomenal. The reality of what appears as matter is, as we saw, a mere prejudice. (3) Matter, *quâ* phenomenon, is an aggregate, in fact an aggregate of an infinite number of parts. (4) An aggregate can have no reality but what it derives from its constituents, since only substances are real, and substances are indivisible. (5) Hence, if the reality of what appears to be matter is to be saved, this must consist of an infinite plurality of indivisible substances.

63. But infinite number is self-contradictory, and we cannot be content with the assertion that there is an infinite number of monads. To evade this argument, Leibniz makes a very bold use of his principle that, in concretes, the part is prior to the whole, and that nothing is absolutely real but indivisible substances and their various states. Being and unity, he says, are convertible terms (G. ii. 304). Aggregates, not having unity, are nothing but phenomena, for except the component monads, the rest (the unity of the aggregate, I suppose) is added by perception alone, by the very fact of their being perceived at one time (G. ii. 517). This remark is of the utmost importance. It is a legitimate outcome of Leibniz's general position, and is perhaps the best alternative which that position allowed him. At the same time, its implications, as will soon be evident, completely destroy the possibility of a plurality of substances.

Leibniz's position is this: that the notion of a *whole* can only be applied to what is substantially indivisible. Whatever is real about an aggregate is *only* the reality of its constituents taken one at a time; the unity of a collection is what Leibniz calls semi-mental (G. ii. 304), and therefore the collection is phenomenal although its constituents are all real. *One* is the only number that is applicable to what is real, since any other number implies parts, and aggregates, like relations, are not "real beings." This explains how infinite number can be denied, while the actual infinite is admitted. "There is no infinite number," Leibniz says, "or line or other infinite quantity, if they are taken as veritable wholes" (N. E. p. 161;

G. V. 144). One whole must be one substance, and to what is not one whole, number cannot properly be applied. The world is only verbally a whole (G. II. 305), and even a finite aggregate of monads is not a whole *per se*. The unity is mental or semi-mental. In most passages, Leibniz only applies this doctrine against infinite aggregates, but it is evident that it must apply equally against all aggregates. This Leibniz seems to have known. Thus he says (N. E. p. 148; G. v. 132): "Perhaps a dozen or a score are only relations, and are constituted only by relation to the understanding. The units are separate, and the understanding gathers them together, however dispersed they may be." The same view is expressed at the end of the same chapter (Book II. Chap. XII.), where he says: "This unity of the idea of aggregates is very true, but at bottom, it must be confessed, this unity of collections is only a respect (*rapport*) or a relation, whose foundation is in what is found in each single substance by itself. And so these beings by aggregation have no other complete unity but that which is mental; and consequently their entity also is in some way mental or phenomenal, like that of the rainbow" (N. E. 149; G. v. 133).

Now this position is a legitimate deduction from the theory that all propositions are to be reduced to the subject-predicate form. The assertion of a plurality of substances is not of this form—it does not assign predicates to a substance. Accordingly, as in other instances of a similar kind, Leibniz takes refuge, like many later philosophers, in the mind—one might almost say, in the synthetic unity of apperception. The mind, and the mind only, synthesizes the diversity of monads; each separate monad is real apart from the perception of it, but a collection, as such, acquires only a precarious and derived reality from simultaneous perception. Thus the truth in the judgment of plurality is reduced to a judgment as to the state of every monad which perceives the plurality. It is only in such perception that a plurality forms a whole, and thus perception is defined by Leibniz as the expression of a multitude in a unity (G. III. 69).

64. This notion, that propositions derive their truth from being believed, is one which I shall criticize in dealing with

God's relation to the eternal truths. For the present, it is enough to place a dilemma before Leibniz. If the plurality lies *only* in the percipient, there cannot be many percipients, and thus the whole doctrine of monads collapses. If the plurality lies *not* only in the percipient, then there is a proposition not reducible to the subject-predicate form, the basis for the use of substance has fallen through, and the assertion of infinite aggregates, with all its contradictions, becomes quite inevitable for Leibniz. The boasted solution of the difficulties of the continuum is thus resolved into smoke, and we are left with all the problems of matter unanswered[1].

We have now seen the use which Leibniz made of his principle that in actuals the part is prior to the whole. We have seen how this enabled him to say that there is an infinite multitude of things, while at the same time denying infinite number. The multitude of things, he says, passes every finite number, or rather every number (G. vi. 629). We could only demand that some number should be applicable, if this multitude were a whole; and that it is a whole, he denies, though the assertion of a whole is involved even in calling it a multitude. It cannot be denied that this position is consistent with his principles, and is even a direct result of them. But the consistency is of that kind which shows a mistake in the principles. The dilemma in which Leibniz is placed, is a direct result of the combination of three premisses, which, as I asserted in Chapter I. (p. 4), are hopelessly inconsistent. These three premisses are (1) that all propositions have a subject and a predicate, (2) that perception gives knowledge of a world not myself or my predicates, (3) that the Ego is an ultimate logical subject.

---

[1] The general principle that all aggregates are phenomenal must not be confounded with the principle, which Leibniz also held, that infinite aggregates have no number. This latter principle is perhaps one of the best ways of escaping from the antinomy of infinite number.

CHAPTER X

THE THEORY OF SPACE AND TIME AND ITS RELATION TO MONADISM.

65. I STATED broadly, in the preceding chapter, the nature of Leibniz's theory of space and time; I wish to examine, in this chapter, what were its grounds, how far those grounds are the same as the grounds for monadism in general, and what was the relation of Leibniz's monads to space. Much of what I shall say will be applicable also to Lotze[1], and generally to all theories which advocate a plurality of things. Let us begin with the theory of space.

"I have several demonstrations," Leibniz says, "to confute the fancy of those who take space to be a substance, or at least an absolute being" (D. 243; G. VII. 363). These demonstrations, as they occur in Leibniz, proceed on the basis of the traditional logic, and have, on that basis, very great force. For the traditional logic—the logic underlying all use of substance or of the Absolute—assumes, as I have endeavoured to show, that all propositions have a subject and a predicate. If, now, space be admitted to exist *per se*, while the doctrine of substance is retained, there will be a relation between substances and the spaces they occupy. But this relation will be *sui generis*; it will not be a relation of subject and predicate, since each term of the relation exists, and may continue to exist though the relation be changed. Neither the thing nor the part of space is annihilated when the part is evacuated by the thing and reoccupied by a different thing. The relation, then, between a

[1] Although Lotze did not ultimately advocate plurality, but merged all in his M.

place and the substance occupying it, is one for which the traditional logic had no room. Accordingly, the independent existence of places was denied by careful philosophers, and admitted by Newton only because he was blind to its consequences. Clarke, to evade the consequences, made space and time parts of God's essence, a position which Leibniz easily showed to be absurd (D. 263; G. VII. 398). The contention Leibniz was really combating was, that space exists *per se*, and not as a mere attribute of anything.

We thus see why, for a philosophy of substance, it is essential to disprove the reality of space. A monist must contend that space is an attribute; a monadist, that space is an assemblage of relations. Against the former view, Leibniz is fairly strong; in favour of the latter, he is inconclusive. But let us proceed to his arguments.

"If there were no creatures," Leibniz says, " space and time would be only in the ideas of God" (D. 252; G. VII. 376—7). Against this view, Kant says: " We can never imagine that there should be no space, though we can quite well think that there should be no objects in it" (ed. Hartenstein, 1867, Vol. III. p. 59). Here we have a sharp and definite opposition: Kant has drawn the consequence which Leibniz's theory is designed to avoid[1]. "If space be an absolute reality," Leibniz says, " far from being a property or an accident opposed to substance, it will be more subsistent than substances " (D. 248; G. VII. 373). What, then, were the arguments by which Leibniz disproved the reality of space?

66. The abstract logical argument, that space must, if real, be either subject or predicate, but is evidently neither, is not, so far as I know, set forth explicitly in Leibniz, though in the controversy with Clarke he urges that space, since it has parts, cannot be an attribute of God, and that empty space cannot be an attribute of anything (D. 264, 248; G. VII. 399, 372). Against regarding space as an *attribute,* the real argument is, that the essence of matter is not extension—an argument we have already seen to be conclusive. Against regarding space as a *substance,* or independent existent, Leibniz's favourite argument is derived from the Identity of

---

[1] The Kantian subjectivity of space may be here left out of account.

Indiscernibles and the Law of Sufficient Reason; and this argument applies equally against time. Space is absolutely uniform, and one point of it is just like another. Thus not only are the points indiscernible, but various arrangements of things would be indiscernible—for example, the actual arrangement and that which would result from turning the whole universe through any angle (D. 243—4; G. VII. 364). Again, if time were real, the world might have been created sooner, and no sufficient reason could appear for creating it at one time rather than another (D. 249; G. VII. 373). And generally, the universe as a whole cannot have different absolute positions in space or time, since these positions would be indiscernible, and therefore one and the same (D. 247; G. VII. 372). Besides these arguments, there are the contradictions of the continuum, which we examined in the last chapter. Space and time, if they are real, cannot be composed otherwise than of *mathematical points*; but of these they can never be composed, since these are mere extremities; two of them are not bigger than one, any more than two perfect darknesses are darker than one (G. II. 347). And as regards time, nothing of it exists but instants, and they are not properly parts of it, and how can a thing exist, whereof no part does ever exist (D. 268; G. VII. 402)?

67. But if space and time are not real, what are they? The answer is suggested by the argument from the Identity of Indiscernibles. From that argument it follows that there is no absolute position, but only mutual relations of things, from which position is abstracted. Space is an order according to which situations are disposed, and abstract space is that order of situations, when they are conceived as being possible (D. 281; G. VII. 415). Time, again, is a being of reason exactly as much as space, but co- pre- and post-existence are something real (G. II. 183). But if space is an order of situations, what are the situations themselves? How are *they* to be explained relationally?

On this question, Leibniz is very explicit (D. 265—7; G. VII. 400—402). When the relation of situation of a body A to other bodies C, D, E etc., changes, while the mutual relations of situation of C, D, E etc., do not change, we infer that the *cause* of change is in A, and not in C, D, E etc. If now

another body B has, to C, D, E etc., a precisely similar
relation of situation to that which A formerly had, we say
that B is in the *same place* as A was. But really there
is nothing individually the same in the two cases; for in
the first case, the relations of situation were affections of A,
while now they are affections of B, and the same individual
accident cannot be in two different subjects. Thus the identity
implied in speaking of the *same place* is an illusion; there are
only precisely similar relations of situation. Leibniz's account
is rendered unnecessarily self-contradictory by the introduction
of absolute motion, which, as we saw, he deduced from force
(cf. D. 269 ; G. VII. 404). From absolute motion he ought, like
Newton, to have inferred absolute position. But his account of
situation can be freed from this inconsistency. He is anxious
to give an unambiguous meaning to *same place*, so as to be
able to say definitely that the two bodies A and B either are,
or are not, successively in the same place. But this, on his
theory, is neither necessary nor possible. He must always
specify the bodies by relation to which place is to be estimated,
and must admit, as he may without contradiction, that other
bodies of reference would, equally legitimately, bring out a
different result. His reference to the *cause* of change of
situation is due to an inconsistency, fundamental in his
Dynamics, and in all Dynamics which works with relative
position, but avoidable, in a relational theory of space, so long
as no reference to Dynamics is introduced. Thus we may
accept the following definition : " Place is that which is the
same in different moments to different existent things, when
their relations of coexistence to certain other existents......
agree entirely together." But when he adds that these other
existents " are supposed to continue fixed from one of these
moments to the other," he is making a supposition which, on a
relational theory, is wholly and absolutely devoid of meaning
(D. 266 ; G. VII. 400). It is such additions which show the
weakness of the theory. There is plainly something more than
relations about space, and those who try to deny this are
unable, owing to obvious facts, to avoid contradicting themselves. But by practice in denying the obvious, it must be
admitted, the relational theory may acquire a high degree of
internal self-consistency.

68. I come now to another closely allied topic, namely, the relation of space to the monads. Space, we have seen, is something purely ideal; it is a collection of abstract possible relations. Now relations must always be reduced to attributes of the related terms. To effect this reduction of spatial relations, the monads and their perceptions must be introduced. And here Leibniz ought to have found a great difficulty—a difficulty which besets every monadism, and generally every philosophy which, while admitting an external world, maintains the subjectivity of space.

The difficulty is this. Spatial relations do not hold between monads, but only between simultaneous objects of perception of each monad[1]. Thus space is properly subjective, as in Kant. Nevertheless, the perceptions of different monads differ, owing to the difference of the points of view; but points of view are mathematical points, and the assemblage of possible points of view is the assemblage of possible positions[2]. Thus Leibniz had two theories of space, the first subjective and Kantian, the second giving an objective counterpart, *i.e.* the various points of view of the monads. The difficulty is, that the objective counterpart cannot consist *merely* in the difference of points of view, unless the subjective space is *purely* subjective; but if it *be* purely subjective, the ground for different points of view has disappeared, since there is no reason to believe that phenomena are *bene fundata*.

The nature of this difficulty will be made clearer by examining the development of Leibniz's views on the relation of the Monads to space. We shall see that, when he was young, in accordance with his materialistic bias, he definitely regarded souls as occupying points in space, while later, after he had become persuaded of the unreality of space, he endeavoured more and more to emphasize the subjectivity of space at the expense of the objective counterpart.

69. "Many years ago," Leibniz wrote in 1709, "when my philosophy was not yet sufficiently mature, I located souls in points" (G. II. 372). From this early view he seems to have

---

[1] G. II. 444, 450—1, 378; III. 357, 623.

[2] Cf. G. II. 253, 324, 339, 438; IV. 439, 482—3 (D. 76; L. 311), 484—5 (D. 78; L. 314); VII. 303—4 (D. 102; L. 340—2).

derived many of the premisses of his doctrine, and these premisses he thereafter accepted as an established basis for further argument. Forgetting that these premisses were themselves derived from the reality of space, he was not afraid of using them to disprove that reality. Such, at least, appears to me a plausible view of his development. He would seem to have come very near to his theory of monads in 1671–2, and then, by his contact with Cartesianism, to have been led away, for a while, from his individualistic tendencies, returning to them only when he had proved the inadequacy of Cartesian Dynamics, and the falsity of the dictum that extension is the essence of matter.

He had, before his journey to Paris, already come very near to the doctrine of monads. "I can prove," he says, "from the nature of motion...that mind acts on itself...that mind consists in a point or centre, and is therefore indivisible, incorruptible, immortal.... Mind is a little world, comprised in a point, and consisting of its ideas, as a centre, though indivisible, consists of angles" (G. I. 61). And in 1671 he says that his proofs of God and immortality rest on the difficult doctrine of the point, the instant, the indivisible, and conation—precisely the same difficulties as his later theory was designed to solve. "Mind itself," he continues, "consists properly in a single point of space, whereas a body occupies a place." "If we give the mind a larger place than a point, it is already a body, and has *partes extra partes*; it is not therefore immediately present to itself." But if we posit that the mind consists in a point, it is indivisible and indestructible. The body, he says, has a kernel of substance which is always preserved, and this kernel consists in a physical point, while the soul consists in a mathematical point (G. I. 52—4).

70. In these early views there is a frank acceptance of the reality of space, and a materialism which reminds one of Karl Pearson's central telephone exchange[1]. The mind, he says, must be in the place of concourse of all motions which are impressed by objects of sense (G. I. 53). It must have been soon apparent to Leibniz that this doctrine did not solve the

---

[1] *Grammar of Science*, Chap. II. § 3.

difficulties of the point and the instant, or afford a consistent theory of substance. And so we find, in his early published accounts of the doctrine of monads, a third kind of point added to the above two, namely the metaphysical point, while the mathematical point is no longer that in which the soul consists, but only its point of view (D. 76; L. 311; G. iv. 482—3).

71. But even here space and the mathematical point retained more reality than was to be wished, and accordingly both the expression "metaphysical points," and the assertion that mathematical points are the points of view of substances, disappear after 1695[1]. After this time, he still speaks of points of view, and always explains them on the analogy of spatial points from which the world is, *as it were*, seen in perspective (G. ii. 438; iii. 357). But he insists that this is *only* an analogy, without, however, telling us to what it is analogous. He seems to have been aware of the difficulty, for in his later writings he avoids any distinct statement as to the soul's *ubeity*. Souls may have, he thinks, at least in relation to bodies, what may be called *definitive* ubeity, *i.e.* they are in a certain volume, without our being able to assign them any special point in that volume (N. E. 230—1; G. v. 205—6). In the last year of his life, he is even more negative in his remarks. "God," he says, "is not present to things by situation, but by essence; his presence is manifested by his immediate operation. The presence of the soul is of quite another nature. To say that it is diffused all over the body is to make it extended and divisible. To say it is, the whole of it, in every part of some body, is to make it divisible from itself. To fix it to a point, to diffuse it all over many points, are only abusive expressions, *idola tribus*" (D. 245—6; G. vii. 365—6). After this purely negative statement, Leibniz advances to another topic. He seems, in fact, to have nothing better to say, than that there are three kinds of *ubeity*, circumscriptive, definitive, and repletive[2], that the first belongs to bodies, the second to

---

[1] The disappearance of the former is not to be ascribed solely to the discovery of the term *monad* in 1696, for he retained other terms—entelechies, simple substances, forms etc.—in spite of the adoption of the word *monad*.

[2] An opinion which, it is true, is quoted as that of the schools, but without disapproval.

souls, and the third to God (N. E. 230; G. v. 205). The most definite statement is one in a letter to Lady Masham (G. III. 357): "The question whether (a simple substance) is somewhere or nowhere, is one of words: for its nature does not consist in extension, but it is related to the extension which it represents; and so one must place the soul in the body, where is its point of view according to which it now represents the universe. To want anything more, and to enclose souls in dimensions, is to wish to imagine souls like bodies." Here, and in all other passages known to me, Leibniz refuses to face the fact that all monads represent the same world, and that this world is always imagined by him to have something analogous to the space of our perceptions. He seems once, indeed, to have perceived that the argument from extension to plurality of substances involved an objective space, and to have accordingly repudiated this argument. "What belongs to extension," he says, "must not be assigned to souls, nor must we derive their unity or plurality from the predicament of quantity, but from the predicament of substance, *i.e.* not from points, but from the primitive force of operation" (G. II. 372). This suggests that the argument from Dynamics is more fundamental than that from extension—a view which, as we have seen, cannot be maintained. A closer investigation shows more and more hopeless confusions. He tries to give position to monads by relation to bodies. Monads, he says, though they are not extended, have a certain kind of situation, *i.e.* an ordered relation of coexistence to other things, through the machine which they dominate. "Extended things involve many things having situation; but simple things, though they have not extension, yet must have situation in extension, though this cannot be designated *punctatim* as in incomplete phenomena" (G. II. 253). Again he says that a simple substance, though it has no extension, has position, which is the foundation of extension, since extension is a simultaneous continuous repetition of position (G. II. 339). As he also insists that an infinite number of *points* do not together make an extension (*ib.* 370), we must suppose the position, in this case also, to be presence in a volume, not in a point. This view, curiously enough, is definitely put forward in the New System, the same work in which he speaks of mathe-

matical points as the points of view of souls. After explaining
the union of soul and body by means of the pre-established
harmony, he continues: "And we can hence understand how
the soul has its seat in the body by an immediate presence,
which could not be greater, since the soul is in the body as the
unit (or *unity* : the French is *unité*) is in the resultant of units,
which is the multitude[1]." This preposterous notion of immediate presence in a volume was rendered plausible by reference
to the organic body or machine; but as this in turn consisted
of monads, a new explanation would have been required for
their position. Souls, Leibniz says, are not to be considered as
in points, but we may say they are in a place by correspondence, and thus are in the whole body which they animate (G. II.
371). But as the body in turn consists of monads, the obvious
question arises: Where is the body? None of his devices, in
short, give Leibniz any escape from an objective space, prior to
the phenomenal and subjective space in each monad's perceptions; and this ought to have been obvious to him, from
the fact that there are not as many spaces as monads, but one
space, and even one only for all possible worlds[2]. The conge-
ries of relations and places which constitutes space is not only
in the perceptions of the monads, but must be actually something which is perceived in all those perceptions. The confusions into which Leibniz falls are the penalty for taking extension as prior to space, and they reveal a fundamental objection
to all monadisms. For these, since they work with substance,
must deny the reality of space; but to obtain a plurality of
coexistent substances, they must surreptitiously assume that
reality. Spinoza, we may say, had shown that the actual world
could not be explained by means of one substance; Leibniz
showed that it could not be explained by means of many substances. It became necessary, therefore, to base metaphysics
on some notion other than that of substance—a task not yet
accomplished.

[1] G. IV. 485; D. 78; L. 314. Cf. Mr Latta's note on this passage. On the
notion of presence by operation which Leibniz seems here to be thinking of, I
shall speak later, when I come to the theory of soul and body. Leibniz,
however, rejected with ridicule the view, which seems to follow from this theory,
that souls are extended. See D. 267; G. VII. 402.

[2] Cf. D. 102; L. 340—2; G. VII. 303—4; II. 379.

72. It remains to say something concerning time and change. Here we have much fewer passages to refer to, and— so far as I know—no thorough discussion after Leibniz's philosophy is mature. Time, like space, is relational and subjective (cf. D. 244; G. VII. 364; II. 183). Its subjectivity has been already discussed in Chapter IV.; I wish here to discuss only its relativity. Leibniz does not seem to have perceived clearly what is involved in this. What is involved is, that in time, as in space, we have only distances, not lengths or points. That is, we have only *before* and *after*: events are not at a certain time, but those which are not simultaneous have a distance, expressed by saying that one is before the other. This distance does not consist of points of time, so that we cannot say time has elapsed between two events. Other events may be between them—*i.e.* there may be events before one of our pair and after the other. But when two events have no event between them, they have merely a relation of before and after, without being separated by a series of moments. No event can last for any length of time, for there is no such thing as a length of time—there are only different events forming a series. Nor can we say that events last for an instant, since there are no instants. Thus there will be no such thing as a *state* of change, for this implies continuity. In motion, for example, we shall have different spatial positions occupied serially, but there will not be a passage from one to the other. It is true, Leibniz holds time to be a plenum (D. 281; G. VII. 415)—a phrase which, as in space, can only mean, on a relational theory, that the smallest distances which actually occur are infinitesimal. Or rather, since, as Leibniz confesses (N. E. 159; G. v. 142), if two events were only separated by empty time, we could never discover the amount of such time, we must mean, when we say that time is a plenum, that between any two given events there is always another. But this view leaves the *difficulties* of continuity intact.

When applied to motion, this view must not be expressed as saying that a body passes instantaneously from one place to another, and then remains there till it takes another leap. For this would imply that time elapsed between successive leaps, whereas the essence of the relational view is, that no time

elapses: presence in one position in space is separated by a
temporal distance, but not by a temporal length (*v.* p. 112), from
presence at the position next occupied. Nor must we say, that
a moving body is sometimes in motion and sometimes at rest;
in fact it can never, in the usual acceptation of the words, be
either at rest or in motion. To say that a body is at rest, can
only mean that its occupancy of a certain position in space is
simultaneous (simultaneity being an ultimate relation) with
two events which are not simultaneous with each other. And
to say that a body is in motion will mean that its occupancy
of one position and its occupancy of another are successive.
But from this we shall never arrive at a *state* of a motion, even
by taking an infinite number of spatial positions successively
occupied. Exactly the same argument will apply to change in
general, and a state of motion or change, as we have seen, is
absolutely necessary to Leibniz's doctrine of activity[1].

73. The relational theory of time is altogether more
paradoxical than that of space, and is rendered so by the fact
that the past and future do not exist in the same sense as the
present. Moreover Leibniz admits that previous time has a
priority of nature over subsequent time (G. III. 582), and that
there was probably a first event, *i.e.* the creation (D. 274;
G. VII. 408)—admissions which greatly add to the difficulty of
maintaining the relativity of temporal position. There is,
moreover, in all monadisms, an asymmetry in regard to the
relation of things to space and time, for which there is, so far
as I know, nothing to urge except the apparent persistence of
the Ego. It is held that substances persist through time, but
do not pervade space. Difference of spatial position at the
same time shows difference of substance, but difference of
temporal position at the same place does not show this. The
time-order consists of relations between predicates, the space-
order holds between substances. For this important assumption
there is, in Leibniz, no sort of argument. It is made confusedly by common sense as regards things, and seems to be
borrowed thence quite uncritically by all monadisms. That it

---

[1] Cf. G. IV. 513. I know of no discussion of the difficulties of motion except
that in the *Archiv f. Gesch. der Phil.* I. 213—4 which belongs to 1676, and
throws little light upon what Leibniz thought when his philosophy was mature.

should have been so little discussed, even by those who believed that they were treating time and space quite similarly, is a curious and unfortunate instance of the strength of psychological imagination.

74. It would thus appear that Leibniz, more or less unconsciously, had two theories of space and time, the one subjective, giving merely relations among the perceptions of each monad, the other objective, giving to the relations among perceptions that counterpart, in the *objects* of perception, which is one and the same for all monads and even for all possible worlds. This counterpart Leibniz would fain have regarded as a "purely ideal thing," a "being of reason," a "mental entity." I wish to repeat briefly the reasons which make these abusive epithets applicable only to *subjective* space and time, not to that counterpart which they must have outside perception. This will be effected by recapitulating the arguments on which the Monadology is based.

"Body is an aggregate of substances," Leibniz says, "and not properly one substance. It must be, consequently, that everywhere in body there are found indivisible substances" (D. 38; G. II. 135[1]). This argument would vanish if space were *purely* subjective, and extended body, as with Kant, a pure phenomenon. Another favourite argument for difference among monads, which, according to Leibniz, is on a level with geometrical proofs (G. II. 295), is, that if they were not different, motion in a plenum would make no difference, for each place could receive only the equivalent of what it had before (D. 219; L. 221; G. VI. 608)—again an argument involving a *place* which is not merely in the perceptions of monads. And this is to be connected with his argument, that there must be entelechies dispersed throughout matter, since principles of motion are thus dispersed (G. VII. 330). Another reason for the objectivity of space and time is, that they are orders of the possible as well as the actual, while yet, in some sense, they existed after the creation in a way different from that in which they had previously existed in the mind of God. In the origin

[1] Cf. G. II. 301: "Since monads or principles of substantial unity are everywhere in matter, it follows hence that there must be an actual infinity, since there is no part, or part of a part, which does not contain monads."

of things, we are told, a certain divine mathematics was employed to determine the greatest quantity of existence, "regard being had to the capacity of the time and of the place (or of the possible order of existence)" (D. 102; L. 341; G. VII. 304). Now this possible order, before creation, existed only in the mind of God (D. 252; G. VII. 377), but after the creation, it existed in some other way; for Leibniz definitely declares that space does not, like God, exist necessarily (G. VI. 405), though space as the mere object of God's understanding must, of course, necessarily exist. Hence we must distinguish (1) space and time in the mind of God, (2) space and time in the perceptions of each monad, (3) objective space and time, which existed after the creation, but not before. This third kind would, of course, for Leibniz, be still relational. Thus, he says (D. 209; L. 408; G. VI. 598), "There are simple substances everywhere, which are actually separated from each other by actions of their own, which continually change their relations." But the important point is, that the relations, being between monads, not between the various perceptions of one monad, would be irreducible relations, not pairs of adjectives of monads. In the case of simultaneity, this is peculiarly obvious, and seems, indeed, to be presupposed in the idea of perception. If this be the fact, to deduce simultaneity from perception is a fatally vicious circle.

CHAPTER XI

THE NATURE OF MONADS IN GENERAL.

75. I COME now to the description of the common qualities of monads. The first of these are *perception* and *appetition*. That monads must have perceptions is proved in various ways. (1) (D. 209 ; L. 407 ; G. VI. 598) Monads " cannot have shapes ; otherwise they would have parts. And consequently a monad, in itself and at a given moment, cannot be distinguished from another except by its internal qualities and actions, which cannot be other than its *perceptions* (that is to say, representations of the compound, or of what is outside, in the simple) and its *appetitions* (that is to say, its tendencies to pass from one perception to another), which are the principles of change." That is, owing to the Identity of Indiscernibles, monads must differ ; but since they have no parts, they can only differ in their internal states ; and internal states, as far as experience goes, are either perceptions or appetitions. (2) There is another argument of a more dynamical nature (D. 210; L. 409 ; G. VI. 599). " Since the world is a plenum all things are connected together, and every body acts upon every other, more or less, according to their distance, and is affected by the other through reaction. Hence it follows that each Monad is a living mirror, or a mirror endowed with inner activity, representative of the universe according to its point of view." Leibniz could not evidently employ this argument to prove that he himself has perceptions, since these, according to such a system as his, are presupposed in Dynamics. Thus the proof that all monads have perceptions presupposes that oneself has them, and this remains a premiss. What is proved is that everything else consists of similar substances with similar perceptions.

That Leibniz himself had perceptions, or, if you prefer it, that there is a world not oneself or one's predicates, was never deduced by him from any further principle. "Souls know things," he says, "because God has put in them a principle representative of things without" (D. 251; G. VII. 375. Cf. D. 275–6; G. VII. 410). "What is miraculous, or rather marvellous is that each substance represents the universe from its point of view " (G. III. 464). Perception is marvellous, because it cannot be conceived as an action of the object on the percipient, since substances never interact. Thus although it is related to the object and simultaneous with it (or approximately so), it is in no way due to the object, but only to the nature of the percipient. Occasionalism prepared the way for this view by the doctrine that the mind perceives matter, though the two cannot interact. What Leibniz did, was to extend to an infinite number of substances the theory invented for two only (D. 275–6; G. VII. 410).

As to the meaning of perception, it is " the expression of plurality in a unity (*l'expression de la multitude dans l'unité* ") (G. III. 69). As to what is meant by *expression*, Leibniz is very definite. "One thing expresses another," he says, "...when there is a constant and regular relation between what can be said about the one and the other. It is thus that a projection in perspective expresses its original. Expression is common to all forms, and is a genus of which natural perception, animal feeling, and intellectual knowledge are species. In natural perception and in feeling it suffices that what is divisible and material, and dispersed among several beings, be expressed or represented in one indivisible being, or in a substance endowed with a true unity" (G. II. 112). Again Leibniz says: "It is not necessary that what expresses be similar to the thing expressed, provided a certain analogy of conditions is preserved ......And so the fact that ideas of things are in us is nothing else than the fact that God, the author alike of things and the mind, has impressed a faculty of thought upon the mind, such that out of its own workings it can draw what perfectly corresponds to what follows from the things. And so, although the idea of the circle be not similar to the circle, yet from it truths can be drawn which in the true circle experience would no doubt have confirmed" (N. E. 716–7; G. VII. 264). Thus perception might seem to be hardly distinguishable from the pre-established harmony, and to amount only to the assertion that every state of a monad corresponds, according to some law, with the simultaneous state of every other monad : and it is thus that, as I suggested at the end of Chapter X., simultaneity is involved in the definition of perception. There is, however, one element in perception, namely the synthesis or expression of the *multitude*, which is not involved in the pre-established harmony alone ; and this element accordingly must be remembered and emphasized.

76. As regards *appetition*, there is little to say beyond what was said about the activity of substance. "Appetite is the tendency from one perception to another" (G. III. 575). It is conceived on the analogy of volition. The nature of substantial forms, Leibniz says, is force, which involves something like sensation or desire, so that they become similar to souls (D. 72 ; L. 301 ; G. IV. 479). Perceptions in the monad spring from one another according to the law of appetites, or by the final causes of good and evil (D. 210 ; L. 409 ; G. VI. 599). Only volition, however, which is confined to self-conscious monads, is definitely determined by the fact that the object of desire seems good. This point, on which Leibniz is somewhat vague, will be treated later.

77. Leibniz's theory of perception is rendered peculiar by the fact that he denies any action of outside things upon the percipient. His theory may be regarded as the antithesis of Kant's. Kant thought that things in themselves are causes (or grounds) of presentations, but cannot be known by means of presentations[1]. Leibniz, on the contrary, denied the causal relation, but admitted the knowledge. His denial of the causal relation was, of course, due to his general denial of transeunt action, which, as we saw, was due to his conception of an individual substance as eternally containing all its

---

[1] E.g. *Reine Vernunft*, ed. Hartenstein, 1867, p. 349.

predicates. "I do not believe," he says, "that any system is possible in which the monads interact, for there seems no possible way of explaining such action. Moreover, such action would be superfluous, for why should one monad give another what the other has already? For this is the very nature of substance, that the present is big with the future" (G. II. 503). His first somewhat tentative expression of the mutual independence of substances, in January 1686, is interesting as giving very clearly his grounds for this opinion. "We may say, in some manner, and with a good sense, though not according to usage, that a particular substance never acts on another particular substance, and does not suffer from it either, if we consider that what happens to each is only a consequence of its idea or complete notion quite alone, since this idea already contains all its predicates or events, and expresses the whole universe." He proceeds to explain that nothing can happen to us but thoughts and perceptions, which will be consequences of the present ones. "If I could see distinctly all that is happening to me now, I could see all that ever will happen to me, and this would happen though all were destroyed but God and me" (G. IV. 440).

This theory of perception has, no doubt, a paradoxical appearance. It seems absurd to suppose that knowledge of what is going on outside me should arise in me simultaneously with the external event, unless there is some causal connection between the two. But to the theory that external objects act on the mind and produce perceptions there are many objections. One of these is that such an explanation does not apply to the knowledge of eternal truths. We cannot suppose that the proposition " two and two are four" acts on the mind whenever the mind is aware of it. For a cause must be an event, and this proposition is not an event. We must admit, therefore, that *some* knowledge is not caused by the proposition which is known. There seems no reason, when this is admitted, to deny that all knowledge may be otherwise caused. Leibniz does not, so far as I know, expressly use this argument, but his special anxiety in the first book of the New Essays to prove that *eternal* truths are innate may be connected with some such view. For according to his theory, all knowledge is innate in the same sense as the eternal truths, *i.e.* all knowledge springs from the nature of the mind, and not from the objects of sense. The argument which Leibniz does use is a better one, namely the unintelligibility of any such causal action as is ascribed to objects of sense. " I don't assent," Leibniz says, " to the vulgar notions that the images of things are conveyed by the organs of sense to the soul. For it is not conceivable by what aperture or by what means of conveyance these images can be carried from the organ to the soul " (D. 275 ; G. VII. 410). Indeed it is only necessary to state these notions in order to see how very " vulgar " they are. But when Leibniz goes on to say, in agreement with the Cartesians, that "it cannot be explained how immaterial substance is affected by matter" (D. 276 ; G. VII. 410), he is employing an argument which doubtless greatly influenced the formation of his theory, but which, none the less, he has not the slightest right to employ. For as he holds that there are only monads, perception, if it were caused from without, would still be an action of like upon like, and not, as he suggests, an action of mere matter upon the mind. The relation of mind and body, in fact, is a relation between many monads, not between two radically different substances, mind and matter.

78. Lotze has given, in his Metaphysic (§§ 63–67), a criticism of the independence of monads, which seems to me to show a radical misconception of Leibniz's grounds. " I cannot admire," he says (§ 63), " this expression (that monads have no windows), because I find it quite unmotived, and find that it curtly excludes just what was still in question." If Lotze had remembered the array of logical arguments set forth in Chapters II.—IV. above, proving that, if there be substances at all, each must be the source of all its predicates, he could hardly have made this statement. If he had remembered his own philosophy—how, in the very next chapter (Bk. I. Chap. VI.) he has to abandon plurality of things on the explicit ground that transeunt action is unintelligible—if he had remembered that, in his own teaching, the unity of a thing is essentially the unity of one causal series—if all or any of these considerations had been in his mind, he would have spared his own glass house, and not ventured on throwing stones. And when we consider that a thing for him is a single causal series, the absurdity of allowing interaction of things becomes a direct contradiction. The antinomy of causation—that every element of the present must have its effect, while yet no effect can be affirmed without taking account of the *whole* present—this antinomy, I think, is one on which he was never clear. He contents himself with asserting first the thesis, while he is concerned with plurality, and then the antithesis, when he comes to his *M*, his unity. But to assert, as he does, that two causal series can interact, is a direct contradiction, and one which, even if it embodies a real antinomy, a man can hardly be called absurd for denying. Lotze's criticism of Leibniz, therefore, seems due rather to his own confusion of thought, than to any error in Leibniz. There is as good ground for Monadism as for Monism, and a Monadist must, with Leibniz, maintain the mutual independence of substances.

79. To explain how perceptions give knowledge of present external things, though not due to these things, Leibniz invented the crowning conception of his philosophy, the conception by which he denoted his system. He loved to call himself "the author of the system of the pre-established harmony." The pre-established harmony is that in his philosophy of which he seems to have been proudest. Like the mutual independence of substances, this was doubtless suggested by the course of Cartesian philosophy. The simile of the clocks, by which he illustrated it, is to be found in Geulincx and other contemporary occasionalists, and even in Des Cartes[1]. The relation of thought and extension in Spinoza is very similar to that of any two monads in Leibniz. The advantage which he had over occasionalism, and of which he made the most, was that by the activity of every substance he was able to preserve the harmony of all the series without the perpetual intervention of God. This advantage was already secured in Spinoza, but not in occasionalism such as that of

---

[1] See Ludwig Stein, *Zur Genesis des Occasionalismus, Archiv fur Gesch. der Phil.*, Vol. i.; esp. p. 59, note. Leibniz has been accused of stealing this illustration from Geulincx, but Stein points out that it was so common as to be obtainable from many other sources, and not to require special acknowledgment.

Malebranche.   It was there held that, since matter is essentially passive, the changes in matter corresponding to those in mind must be effected by the direct operation of God in each case. In Leibniz, on the contrary, only one original miracle was required to start all the clocks (G. III. 143)—the rest was all effected naturally.   We may suppose that Leibniz began with the Cartesian problem of the harmony of soul and body, and found in his doctrine of monads a far wider harmony by which far more was explained.   The pre-established harmony, he thinks, is proved à priori: only three explanations of the relation of soul and body are possible, and of the three his is the best (G. III. 144).   The other two are, of course, the *influxus physicus* or direct causal action, and the system of occasional causes, *i.e.* the action of God upon matter on *occasion* of every volition.   As long as the perfect passivity of matter was maintained, Leibniz's hypothesis certainly was the best. But the systems of Geulincx and Spinoza, which he leaves out of account in this connection (Geulincx, in fact, is never mentioned, and seems to have been unknown to him), have many of the advantages in this problem which he claims as peculiarly his own.   It is interesting to compare, for instance, the enunciation of Prop. XII. Part II. of Spinoza's *Ethics*: " Whatever happens in the object of the idea constituting the human mind must be perceived by the human mind, or, in other words, an idea of that thing will necessarily exist in the human mind.   That is to say, if the object of the idea constituting the human mind be a body, nothing can happen in that body which is not perceived by the mind."   From such a theory it is evident that Leibniz may have derived many suggestions for his theory of perception and pre-established harmony.   It is to be regretted, therefore, that he did not take more account of this more allied hypothesis.

The pre-established harmony is an immediate result of perception and the mutual independence of monads.   " The nature of every simple substance, soul, or true monad," Leibniz explains, " being such that its following state is a consequence of the preceding one ; here now is the cause of the harmony found out.   For God needs only to make a simple substance become once and at the beginning a representation of the universe, according to its point of view ; since from thence alone it follows that it will be so perpetually ; and that all simple substances will always have a harmony among themselves, because they always represent the same universe" (D. 278 ; G. VII. 412)[1]. Each monad always represents the whole universe, and therefore the states of all monads at every instant correspond, in that it is the same universe they represent. To this Lotze objects that some monads might run through their series of perceptions faster or slower than others (Met. § 66). To this difficulty, he says, he remembers no answer in Leibniz. He appears to have forgotten that Clarke raised precisely the same point (G. VII. 387–8) and that Leibniz replied to it (G. VII. 415 and D. 281). " If the time is greater," he says, " there will be more successive and like states interposed ; and if it be less, there will be fewer ; seeing there is no vacuum, nor condensation, nor penetration (if I may so speak) in times, any more than in places." That is to say, just as the quantity of *materia prima* is proportional to extension, so the number of events is proportional to time. Whatever may be thought of this answer, it is evident that the monads, if each of them mirrors the present state of the universe, necessarily keep pace with one another. It is better, perhaps, to start with perception, and deduce the pre-established harmony. For some arguments can be adduced, if it be admitted that *we* have perceptions of an external world, to show that this is also true of other substances ; and hence the pre-established harmony follows.

It remains to explain, in terms of monads, the relation of soul and body, and the activity and passivity of substances. This will be attempted in the next chapter.

[1] Cf. also G. I. 382—3.

CHAPTER XII

SOUL AND BODY.

80. I PASS now to an entirely new department of the doctrine of monads. Hitherto we have considered single monads as isolated units, but we must now attend to their relations. We have to consider, in fact, the same problem as that which, in a dualistic system, would be the relation of mind and matter. The special form of this problem, which is usually considered, is the relation of Soul and Body. In discussing this relation, Leibniz introduced a new idea, that of *passivity*. This idea, it is true, was already involved in *materia prima*, but there it was not, as in the theory of soul and body, relative to the *activity* of some other monad. By this relation, both activity and passivity acquire new meanings. From this point onwards, Leibniz's philosophy is less original than heretofore. Indeed he is chiefly engaged in adapting to the doctrine of monads previous theories (notably that of Spinoza), which, by means of the relation of activity and passivity, become available for him in spite of the denial of transeunt action. Thus a sharp line should, I think, be drawn between those parts of Leibniz's philosophy which we have hitherto discussed, and those which, through passivity, depend upon the apparent interaction of monads. The former seem mainly original, while the latter are borrowed in great part, though always without acknowledgment, from Spinoza.

81. The problem of the relation of Soul and Body was one which occupied much of the attention of Cartesians. Des Cartes' own position on this question, that a direct action of mind on matter is possible, by altering the *direction*, though not the quantity, of the motion of the animal spirits, was abandoned by his followers for very good reasons. They perceived that, if mind and matter are two substances, they must not be supposed capable of interaction. This led to Occasionalism on the one hand—the theory, namely, that God moves the body on occasion of our volitions—and to the theory of Spinoza on the other hand. In this latter theory, which is more akin to Leibniz's, mind and body are not different substances, but different attributes of one substance, whose modifications form two parallel series. The mind is the idea of the body, and any change in the body is accompanied, though without interaction, by a corresponding change in its idea, *i.e.* in the mind. This theory, as well as that of the Occasionalists, was rendered impossible for Leibniz by the discovery that the essence of matter is not extension, but that matter is necessarily plural. Accordingly he required a new theory of Soul and Body, and this requirement was doubtless a main motive to the doctrine of pre-established harmony[1]. The use of this doctrine in explaining the relation of Soul and Body is most ingenious. I shall now endeavour to set it forth.

82. Briefly, the doctrine is as follows. Since there is nothing real but monads, the body is the appearance of an infinite collection of monads. But monads differ in the clearness of their perceptions, and those which have clearer perceptions are more active. When a change in one monad explains a change in another, the first is said to be active, the second passive. So, in my body, that monad which is myself has clearer perceptions than any of the others, and may be said to be dominant in the body, since, in relation to the other monads, it is active while they are passive. There is no real interaction, but the appearance of it results from the pre-established harmony. Thus the soul is one, the body many, and there is no interaction between them. But in so far as the soul has clear perceptions, the reasons for what happens in the body are to be found in the soul; and in this sense the soul acts on the body and dominates it. This is the outline of the theory which must now be examined in detail.

[1] In Wolff's philosophy, the harmony of all monads has disappeared, and only that of soul and body remains.

83. There are, in the first place, three great classes in the hierarchy of monads, not sharply distinguished, but merging into each other. These are bare monads, souls and spirits. *Bare monads*, which are also called forms or entelechies, have the minimum of perception and desire; they have something analogous to souls, but nothing that could strictly be called a soul. *Souls* are distinguished from the first class by memory, feeling, and attention (D. 190—1 ; G. VII. 529; D. 220 ; L. 230 ; G. VI. 610). Animals have souls, but men have *spirits* or *rational* souls. *Spirits* include an infinite hierarchy of genii and angels superior to man, but not differing from him except in degree. They are defined by self-consciousness or apperception, by the knowledge of God and eternal truths, and by the possession of what is called *reason*. Spirits do not, like souls, mirror only the universe of creatures, but also God. They thus compose the City of God, in relation to which alone God properly possesses goodness [G. VI. 621-2 (D. 231 ; L. 267—8); contrast G. VI. 169]. *Spirits* also are immortal : they preserve moral identity, which depends on memory of self, while other monads are merely incessant, *i.e.* they remain numerically identical without knowing it.

84. In relation to clearness of perception, monads are said to be active or passive[1]. We can still popularly speak of one substance acting on another, Leibniz says, when a change in the one explains a change in the other (D. 79; L. 317; G. IV. 486). But "the domination and subordination of monads, considered in the monads themselves, consists only in the degrees of their perfections" (G. II. 451). "Modifications of one monad are ideal causes of those of another, in so far as the reasons appear in one monad which led God in the beginning to arrange for modifications in the other" (G. II. 475). And so the body depends upon the mind in this sense, that the reason of what happens in the body is to be found in the mind. In so far, Leibniz continues, as the soul is perfect, and has clear perceptions, the body is subject to it; in so far as it is imperfect, it is subject to the body (G. VI. 138)[2]. Again he says that the

---

[1] This sense of activity must not be confounded with that which is essential to substance.

[2] Of Spinoza's *Ethics*, Pt. V. Prop. X.

creature is said to *act* externally so far as it is perfect, and to *suffer* from another in so far as it is imperfect. Action is therefore attributed where perceptions are distinct, passion where they are indistinct. One creature is more perfect than another, when it contains what accounts *à priori* for what happens in the other, and in this way it is said to act on another. The influence of one monad on another is purely ideal, through God, who takes notice of the superior monad in regulating others [G. VI. 615 (D. 225; L. 245)]. Every substance which passes to a greater degree of perfection acts, and one which passes to a lesser degree of perfection suffers. In any substance which has perception, action brings joy, while passion brings pain (G. IV. 441).

The activity which is opposed to passivity is quite distinct from that which is essential to substance. "Taking action in metaphysical strictness," Leibniz says (N. E. p. 218—9; G. V. 195), "as that which takes place in a substance spontaneously and from its own nature, whatever is properly a substance only acts, for everything comes to it from itself, after God, since it is impossible that one created substance should have influence on another. But taking action as an exercise of perfection, and passion as the contrary, there is action in true substances only when their perception (for I grant it to all) is developed and becomes more distinct, as there is passion only when it becomes more confused; so that in substances capable of pleasure and of pain, all action is a step to pleasure, and all passion a step to pain."

85. In this theory, which is full of reminders of Spinoza[1], there are two elements in what is active, namely perfection, and clearness of perception. It is plain that Leibniz does not confuse these two elements, but regards them as necessarily connected. He evidently thinks, moreover, that his usage will cover the cases which are ordinarily regarded as cases of action and passion respectively. But these ideas need some explanation, as does also the phrase " accounting *à priori* for what happens in another monad." The explanation, I think, is as follows.

Only spirits are good or bad as ends in themselves: bare

[1] Cf. *e.g.* Spinoza, *Ethics*, Bk. III. Prop. I.

monads and souls are mere means to them. Now in spirits, volition is always determined by the reason of the good[1], *i.e.* we pursue what we judge to be the best possible[2]. Hence we shall always act rightly if we always judge rightly (G. VII. 92)[3]. Accordingly, since right judgment depends upon clear perception, we are more or less perfect according as we have more or less clear perceptions. In volition, where we are ordinarily said to be active, the passage to a new perception is *perceived* to be, what it always is really, determined from within, and our perception, therefore, is so far clear. But in sensation, where we are ordinarily said to be passive, the new perception falsely appears to come from without, and our perception is therefore confused. We do not perceive the connection with the previous perception, and are so far imperfect. Thus Leibniz's use of the words *active* and *passive* is not wholly disconnected from the popular use, though it would be unwise to see too close a relation.

And thus the phrase "containing what accounts *à priori* for the changes in another monad," is to be understood in relation both to perfection and to clearness of perception. Owing to the pre-established harmony, the changes in different monads are inter-related; but the changes in inferior monads exist mainly for the sake of the correlated changes in spirits[4]. Thus the explanation by sufficient reason, or by final causes, of what happens in an inferior monad, is only possible by taking account of some superior monad, in which the correlated change is good. But when this superior monad is free, and owing to confused perception chooses what is really bad, this explanation by final causes no longer holds, and the superior monad is

---

[1] G. IV. 454; v. 171 (N. E. 190–1); F. de C. 62 (D. 182).

[2] It is thus, by the way, that actual sufficient reasons of the actual are distinguished from possible sufficient reasons of the possible. All actual sufficient reasons are volitions either of God or of free creatures, and these are always determined by the (true or false) perception of the good. But it would be possible, not only for us, but also for God, to pursue evil, and then the perception of evil would be a sufficient reason. Thus *actual* sufficient reasons are final causes, and involve reference to the good. Cf. § 15, *supra*.

[3] That this view was often contradicted by Leibniz (*e.g.* implicitly, *ib.* p. 95) was only due to theological reasons. It was the only view to which he was entitled.

[4] For Leibniz's inconsistency on this point see § 124.

therefore regarded as passive, since the final reason of its
change for the worse is not in itself, but in some correlated
change elsewhere.

86. There are, in the above theory, many obvious gaps,
which I leave without comment[1]. It is more important to
explain the connection of passivity and *materia prima*. Leibniz
distinguishes in one place (G. II. 252) the following five terms:
"(1) The primitive entelechy or soul, (2) primary matter or
primitive passive power, (3) the monad composed of these two,
(4) mass or secondary matter or the organic machine, to which
innumerable subordinate monads concur, (5) the animal or
corporeal substance, which the dominant monad makes into
one machine." Moreover the connection of soul and body is
only explicable by means of *materia prima*[2]. Hence we must,
before we can understand the connection of soul and body,
examine the nature of *materia prima* as an element in each
monad, and its connection with *materia prima* in Dynamics.

Materia prima, as an element in each monad, is that whose
repetition produces the *materia prima* of Dynamics. It is also
identified with the passivity or passive force of each monad,
with confused perception, and with finitude generally. God
could deprive a monad of *materia secunda, i.e.* of the assemblage
of monads which constitutes its body; but He could not deprive
a monad of *materia prima*, without which it would be *actus
purus, i.e.* God Himself (G. II. 325). It is thus by *materia
prima* that monads are distinguished from God, and rendered
limited and finite; and this seems to be Leibniz's meaning in
saying that confused perceptions are what involve matter or
the infinite in number (G. III. 636). In writing to Arnauld,
Leibniz says: "If we understand by matter something always
essential to the same substance, we might, with some scholastics, understand by it the primitive passive power of a substance, and in this sense matter would be neither extended nor

[1] The chief of these is that there seems no reason why action in one
substance should correspond to passion rather than action in another. Leibniz
seems indeed to regard it as more or less accidental when this occurs; thus he
says (G. IV. 440): "It may happen that a change which increases the expression
of the one diminishes that of the other."

[2] G. II. 520, 248; VI. 546 (D. 169).

divisible, though it would be the principle of divisibility, or of
that, in it, that belongs to substance" (G. II. 120) (1687). This
is, I think, the first time that he introduces into the theory of
monads *materia prima* in the sense given it by "some scholastics," and it has the tentativeness of a new idea. But to this
sense he afterwards always adheres. *Materia prima*, he says,
is not extended, but is what extension presupposes. It is the
passive power which, with the entelechy or active power, com-
pletes the monad, and it adheres always to its own monad[1].
Substances have metaphysical matter or passive power in so far
as they express anything confusedly; they have active power in
so far as they express anything distinctly (N. E. 720; G. VII.
322). Monads are subject to passions, and are thus not pure
forces; they are the foundations not only of actions, but also of
resistances or passibilities, and their passions are in confused
perceptions (G. III. 636). For substance acts as much as it
can, unless it is impeded; and it is not impeded naturally
except from within. When one monad is said to be impeded
by another, this is to be understood of the representation of
that other in itself (G. II. 516). Moreover it is not absurd,
Leibniz thinks, that resistance in a substance should do nothing
but impede its own activity; we need, he says, a principle of
limitation in limited things, as of action in agents (*ib.* 257).

87. Several things are interesting and noteworthy in this
theory of *materia prima*. First, it is instructive to observe
the difference between Leibniz's account of limitation and that
of Spinoza. "That thing is called finite in its own kind,"
Spinoza says (Eth. I. Def. 2), "which can be limited by another
thing of the same nature." Thus finitude consists in a relation
to something else, and the finite is not self-subsistent. But
Leibniz's *materia prima* is nothing relative, but part of the
nature of each monad. Each monad is limited, not by something else, but by itself[2]; and thus God is not the sum of finite

---

[1] G. II. 306; cf. also G. IV. 511 (D. 120).

[2] Cf. Erdmann, *Grundriss der Geschichte der Philosophie*, 3rd ed. Berlin, 1878,
Vol. II. p. 150. In a highly interesting paper, which is very Spinozistic throughout, and belongs probably to the period between 1676 and 1680, Leibniz actually
gives Spinoza's definition of finitude as his own: "The finite involves negation
of something of its own kind" (G. VII. 196). He proceeds to remark, however,
that this definition seems inapplicable to discreta.

monads, but something radically different in his nature. Connected with this point is the way in which passivity involves matter and the infinite in number (G. III. 636). There is only one way of perceiving the world clearly, namely the way in which God perceived it, *i.e.* as it really is. But there is an infinite number of ways of perceiving it confusedly. Thus the Identity of Indiscernibles allows only one God, and is only compatible with many other substances if these all have perceptions which are more or less confused. And as matter is the confused perception of an infinite plurality of monads, matter doubly presupposes *materia prima*, namely as the source of the plurality, and again as the reason why the plurality is perceived as matter. And this brings us to the relation of the *materia prima* in each monad to the *materia prima* in Dynamics. The two elements in the dynamical¨ definition— impenetrability and inertia—correspond respectively, I think (though this is only an inference), to the fact that monads differ as to their point of view, and the fact that passivity causes a resistance to a new perception in the monad. Both these are included under confused perception. God, who alone sees quite clearly, has no point of view—space, to him, is as it is in Geometry, without any *here* or *there*. All points are alike in their relation to God (G. IV. 439; II. 438), and the same must be true of the parts of time. Thus the point of view is a part of confused perception, and therefore of *materia prima;* and the difference of points of view is the source of impenetrability. Similarly, owing to passivity or indistinctness of perception, a given perception does not give rise to the perception which would result if the same thing were more clearly perceived; and this, we may suppose, is the source of inertia. There is, however, a difference between the dynamical use of *materia prima* and the use in the theory of monads, namely that, in Dynamics, the word is usually applied to a finite extension, resulting from an infinite number of monads, whereas in the theory of monads it is applied to the corresponding quality of each monad, *i.e.* to that quality whose repetition is required to produce extension.

88. The connection of confused perception with the point of view explains also some rather difficult dicta on the interconnection of monads. "If there were only spirits," Leibniz says, "they would be without the required connection, without the order of times and places. This order demands matter and motion and its laws" (G. VI. 172). God alone is above all matter; creatures free from matter would be deserters from the general order, and detached from the universal concatenation (D. 169; G. VI. 546). Again Leibniz pronounces against the view that angels are disembodied spirits. To remove them from bodies and from place, he says, is to remove them from the universal connection and order of the world, which is made by relations to time and place (G. II. 324). All these sayings seem explained by the fact that places result from points of view, and points of view involve confused perception or *materia prima*. And this, again, is intimately connected with the doctrine of unconscious perception, which Leibniz urged with such success against Locke. To maintain that we mirror the whole universe was only possible by a large use of this doctrine. And Leibniz did, in fact, carry the doctrine so far as to maintain that every perception of which we are sensible is composed of an infinite number of insensible perceptions (N. E. 116—8: G. V. 105—7). He once even deduces the infinite number of monads from this consideration alone. In our perceptions, he says, however distinct they may be, there are confused ones to any degree of smallness, and to these, as to the greater and more distinct ones, monads will correspond (G. II. 460—1).

89. We can now endeavour to understand the connection of soul and body. There are here, I think, two inconsistent theories, both contained in Leibniz. This has led to a division among commentators, some insisting on the one as the only theory, others on the other. As I have found no way of reconciling all Leibniz's statements on the matter, I shall first set forth the theory which seems to me consistent with the rest of his philosophy, and shall then proceed to the second theory, showing why it cannot be reconciled with his other views, and how he seems to have been led to it. The first theory has been supported by Erdmann, the second by Kuno Fischer, in whose histories the arguments will be found at length.

90. We must, to begin with, distinguish an organic body from a mere mass. An organic body has one dominant monad, by relation to which it acquires a certain unity. It is as regards the nature and degree of this unity that the two theories differ. An inorganic body has no such single dominant monad, but is a mere aggregate[1]. But every monad belongs to *some* organic body, either as dominant or as subordinate monad[2]. Every organic body is composed of an infinite number of smaller organic bodies, the smallest organic bodies occupying only a physical point. A natural machine, Leibniz says, is a machine even in its smallest perceptible parts [G. VI. 599 (D. 209; L. 408); G. II. 100; IV. 492]. In the first theory, the dominant monad dominates in the sense that it represents more clearly what the other monads represent very confusedly. In accordance with the affections of the body, the dominant monad represents, as a centre, the things outside itself [G. VI. 598 (D. 209; L. 407)]. Leibniz is not very definite as to the meaning of domination, but the following seems to be his meaning. Every monad perceives more clearly what happens in its neighbourhood than what happens at a distance [G. II. 74; G. VI. 599 (D. 210; L. 409)]. If, then, in a certain volume, there is one monad with much clearer perceptions than the rest, this monad may perceive all that happens within that volume more clearly than do any of the others within that volume. And in this sense it may be dominant over all the monads in its immediate neighbourhood.

But we must not suppose that the monads composing the organic body are always the same. There is not a portion of matter, *i.e.* of inferior living beings, appropriated to the soul for ever, for bodies are in perpetual flux. The soul changes its body, but always gradually [G. VI. 619 (D. 229; L. 258)]. Thus we cannot be certain that the smallest particle of matter (*i.e.* secondary matter) received by us at birth, remains in our body. But the same animal or machine subsists in a sense [G. VI. 543 (D. 167)]; it persists, as Leibniz puts it, specifically but not individually [G. V. 214 (N. E. 240)]. Certain organs remain, at least by the substitution of an equivalent, as a river remains the same though its matter changes (G. IV. 529). This is merely the ordinary scientific view, according to which

---

[1] G. VI. 539 (D. 163); G. V. 309 (N. E. 362); G. II. 75, 100.
[2] G. II. 118, 135; III. 356; VII. 502.

the body remains of the same kind, though not composed of the same matter. Thus the body consists merely of those inferior monads whose points of view, at any given time, are so near that of the dominant monad that they perceive *everything* less clearly than it does, since every monad perceives most clearly what is in its own neighbourhood. Body and soul do not together form one substance (G. VI. 595), and do not even interact. "Bodies act as if (what is impossible) there were no souls, and souls act as if there were no bodies, and both act as if the one influenced the other" [G. VI. 621 (D. 230; L. 264)]. The organized mass, within which is the point of view of the soul, is ready to act of itself, at the moment when the soul wills it. This, Leibniz says, produces the so-called union of soul and body [G. IV. 484 (D. 78; L. 314)]. Soul and body do not interact, but only agree, the one acting freely, according to the rules of final causes, the other acting mechanically, according to the laws of efficient causes. But this does not derogate from the liberty of the soul. For every agent which acts according to final causes is free. God, foreseeing what the free cause would do, regulated the machine to agree with it [G. VII. 412 (D. 278)].

This, then, is the first theory of soul and body. An organic body is a collection of changing monads, which acquires unity by being always subject to one and the same dominant monad. This subjection consists both in the clearer perceptions of the dominant monad, and in the fact that the final causes, which govern all events, have reference, so far as the body is concerned, either to the dominant monad, or to some monad outside the body, or to "metaphysical perfection" and the "order of things." A body dominated by a spirit consists of innumerable smaller organic bodies, but does not itself, apparently, form part of any larger organic body. Secondary matter, or mass, consists of a collection of organic bodies not unified by one dominant monad. There are, however, many things in Leibniz inconsistent with this simple theory. To these we must now turn our attention.

91. Though everything in the above theory, as I set it forth, is to be found in Leibniz, there are many other passages, concerning which I said nothing, which lead to a totally different theory. This theory is to be rejected, I think, because it is wholly inconsistent with Leibniz's general philosophy. But it is necessary to say something about it, particularly as it has been supported, with constant appeal to the sources, by a recent commentator, Dillmann[1].

In this other theory, mind and body together make one substance, having a true unity. The mind makes the body into a *unum per se*, instead of a mere aggregate. *Against* this view, we have perfectly definite assertions, such as the following (D. 177; F. de C. pp. 32, 34): "Corporeal substance has a soul and an organic body, that is, a mass made up of other substances. It is true that the same substance thinks, and has an extended mass joined to it, but it does not consist of this mass, since all this can be taken away from it without altering the substance." Nevertheless, in other places, Leibniz speaks as if the soul and the body make one substance.

"The entelechy," he says, "is either a soul, or something analogous to a soul, and always naturally actuates some organic body, which taken by itself, apart from the soul, is not one substance, but an aggregate of several, in a word, a natural machine" (G. IV. 395—6; N. E. 701) (1702). Again he says: "Every created monad is endowed with some organic body" (G. VII. 502), "principles of life belong only to organic bodies" [G. VI. 539 (D. 163)], and again: "There are as many entelechies as organic bodies" (G. II. 368). It is evident that not *every* monad can have an organic body, if this consists of other subordinate monads. And there are many more direct reasons for the view that body and soul together make one substance. "Bodies which are a *unum per se*, like man," Leibniz says, "are substances, and have substantial forms" (G. IV. 459) (Jan. 1686). And Leibniz always speaks as if the presence of the soul prevented the body from being a *mere* aggregate: he suggests that the body *without* the soul *is* a mere aggregate, but *with* it, acquires a true unity. "The number of simple substances," he says, "in any mass, however small, is infinite; for beside the soul, which makes the real unity of the animal, the body of the sheep, for example, is actually divided, *i.e.* is an assemblage of invisible animals or plants, similarly composite except for what makes *their* real unity; and though this goes to infinity,

---

[1] *Eine neue Darstellung der Leibnizischen Monadenlehre auf Grund der Quellen.* Leipzig, 1891.

it is plain that all in the end depends on these unities, the rest, or the results, being only well-grounded phenomena " (G. IV. 492). This tendency is carried farthest in a theory which has given commentators much trouble, but is really no more inconsistent with Leibniz's system than many other passages—I mean the doctrine of the *vinculum substantiale*.

92. This doctrine is developed in the letters to Des Bosses, and springs from Leibniz's endeavour to reconcile his philosophy with the dogma of transubstantiation. It is necessary to find some sense in which the Body of Christ is one substance. Leibniz first admits " a certain real metaphysical union of soul and organic body " (G. II. 371), an admission he had already made to Tournemine (G. VI. 595), but Des Bosses persuades him that this is not sufficient for Catholic orthodoxy. He then suggests, as a view which he does not accept, but which might be helpful to a good Catholic, the hypothesis of a *substantial bond* (G. II. 435). " If corporeal substance," he says, "is something real beside monads, as a line is held to be something beside its points, we shall have to say, that corporeal substance consists in a certain union, or rather in some real thing which unites, and is added by God to the monads; that from a certain union of the passive power of monads *materia prima* results, that is, what is required by extension and antitypia, or diffusion and resistance; but that, from the union of the entelechies of monads, a substantial form arises, but one which can thus be born and extinguished, and is extinguished when that union ceases, unless God miraculously preserves it. But such a form will not be a soul, which is a simple and indivisible substance[1]." This *vinculum substantiale* is only asserted to be useful " if faith leads us to corporeal substances " (*ib.*). And later he says (*ib.* p. 458): " And this seems what should be said by people of your way of thinking (*secundum vestros*), of the change of the whole substance of one body into the whole substance of another body, which yet retains its former nature." The *vinculum substantiale* differs from the real union of soul and body—which Leibniz also admits elsewhere—by the fact that the monads are not added as wholes to form a sum having a true unity, but are split

[1] Cf. the schedule of all entities, G. II. 506.

up into *materia prima* and entelechy before addition. Thus
the sum of constituent elements of *materia prima* gives an
extended passive mass, while the sum of the entelechies gives
a substantial form animating the mass. There is one *vinculum
substantiale* for each organic body, *i.e.* one corresponding to each
dominant monad (G. II. 481, 486, 496). Leibniz is afterwards
led by Des Bosses to admit that this substantial bond must, if
it is to be theologically serviceable, be imperishable like the
individual soul (G. II. 481). In later letters, the doctrine is
usually presupposed as the basis of discussion, and is employed
to establish real matter and a real continuum. But nowhere
does Leibniz himself assert that he believes it. He was ex-
tremely anxious to persuade Catholics that they might, without
heresy, believe in his doctrine of monads. Thus the *vinculum
substantiale* is rather the concession of a diplomatist than the
creed of a philosopher (cf. G. II. 499).

93. It seems not impossible that others of Leibniz's remarks, in so far as they are inconsistent with the first theory
of body, are also due to theological influences. The problem
of the Real Presence occupied Leibniz from the time when
he was in the service of the Archbishop of Mainz, and formed
one of his grounds for denying that the essence of matter is
extension. In his earliest accounts of his system, designed for
the zealous and proselytising Arnauld, similar suggestions are
to be found. "The body by itself," Leibniz says, "apart from
the soul, has only a unity of aggregation" (G. II. 100); and
this seems to imply that *with* the soul the body has a real
unity. Again he says that the body, *apart* from the soul, is
not properly a substance, but an aggregate, like a heap of
stones (*ib.* 75). And when Arnauld objects to the new philosophy, that the soul joined to matter does not make one,
since it gives only an extrinsic denomination, Leibniz replies
that the matter belongs to the animated substance, which is
veritably one being; and matter taken only as mass is merely a
well-founded phenomenon, like space and time (*ib.* 118). This
might be understood as referring, in the first part, to *materia
prima*, but the following passage is more difficult. "Those
who will not admit," he says, " that there are souls in beasts,
and substantial forms elsewhere, can nevertheless approve the

way in which I explain the union of mind and body, and all
that I say about true substance; but it remains to them to
save, as they best may, without such forms, and without anything which has a true unity, either by points, or, if it seems
good to them, by atoms, the reality of matter and of corporeal
substances" (G. II. 127). Again he says that if there are no
corporeal substances such as he wants, then bodies are merely
true phenomena, like the rainbow. For, since matter is actually
infinitely divided, we shall never reach a true being, save when
we find animated machines, whose soul or substantial form
makes a substantial unity independent of mere contiguity.
And if there are none such, he concludes, then man is the
only substantial thing in the visible world (G. II. 77). All
these statements imply that soul and body together are veritably one, though the body alone, in so far as it is real, is
many. In the letters to Arnauld, this might be attributed
merely to the crudity of a new philosophy, but, as we have
seen, there are many later expressions of a similar kind. And
the doctrine which, in discussing the relation of monads to
space (§ 71), we found inevitable, namely that the soul is present
in a volume, not in a mere point, is to be associated with
this view. The soul by its presence informs the whole body
and makes it one, though other subordinate souls are present
in various parts of the body, and make each such part one[1].
Again space, for Leibniz, is a plenum, but is not composed of
mathematical points. Hence we must suppose every monad
to occupy at least a physical point. Such a physical point
might be called an organic body, and might explain how all
monads come to have an organic body. The organic body of
a monad which does not dominate would, by itself, be a *pure*
phenomenon, and in no sense an aggregate. It is impossible,
however, to free this view from inconsistencies. To these two
causes may have contributed, the one the theological desire
to save the reality of bodies[2], the other an occasional confusion

---

[1] Cf. the following (G. II. 474): "It is asked whether the soul of a worm
existing in the body of a man is a substantial part of the human body, or rather,
as I should prefer to say, a bare requisite, and something not metaphysically
necessary, but which is only required in the course of nature."

[2] Thus in one passage Leibniz clinches his arguments by the remark:
"Moreover the last Lateran Council declares that the soul is veritably the
substantial form of our body" (G. II. 75).

of primary matter, as an element in each monad, either with primary matter as extended, or even with secondary matter. The latter may have been a partial cause in the letters to Arnauld ; in the letters to Des Bosses, the former must have operated alone, for the distinctions of the various kinds of matter are there more clearly drawn than anywhere else[1].

There may be a theory which accounts better for these apparent inconsistencies, but I have been unable to find one. My theory is substantially that of Erdmann, to whom I may refer for further discussion.

94. A few words seem necessary about Preformation, the theory by which Leibniz explained generation. As every monad is eternal, the monad which is myself must have previously existed. Leibniz holds that it formed one of the monads composing the body either of father or mother (G. III. 565). Before conception, he thinks, it was either a mere sensitive monad, or had at any rate only an elementary reason. The latter view has the advantage that it enables us to do without miracles. On the former view, since a sensitive monad cannot naturally become rational, we must suppose generation to involve a miracle. Leibniz cannot decide between these alternatives, indeed both are to be found in the *Théodicée*[2] (G. VI. 152, 352). It would seem that the miraculous alternative is the best, because Leibniz wishes to maintain that human beings cannot naturally, after death, sink to the level of mere sensitive monads; but if monads can naturally *become* rational, there seems no reason why they should not naturally cease to be so. Leibniz supported his theory of preformation by reference to the microscopic embryology of his day. It is, however, sufficiently evident that he could not account for the equal influence of both parents. When this is taken into account, we lose the simplicity of the one dominant monad, but we get a theory uncommonly like Weissmann's continuity of the germ-plasm. A few years ago, therefore, we might have referred to Leibniz as anticipating the latest results of modern science; but since the fall of Weissmann, we must deny ourselves this pleasure.

---

[1] See *e.g.* G. II. 368, 370, 371.

[2] A fact which, by the way, supports Stein's contention that the parts were written at very different times: v. *Leibniz und Spinoza*, Berlin, 1890, p. 275 ff.

CHAPTER XIII

CONFUSED AND UNCONSCIOUS PERCEPTION.

95. THERE are, we have seen, two respects in which monads differ. They differ as to *point of view*, and they differ as to *clearness of perception*. The first of these is continually changing: the reality underlying the phenomenon of motion is change of point of view. This seems to me, at least, the only possible interpretation, though Leibniz nowhere definitely makes this statement. In this way we should be able to interpret the difference between absolute and relative motion. The monad which changes its point of view has absolute motion, while another which perceives this change has only a relative change of situation[1]. This view again involves the objective counterpart to space, which we have seen throughout to be unavoidable.

The point of view, as we have seen, depends upon confused perception, but not upon different degrees of confusion. As regards the degree of confusion, also, we must suppose change possible. Leaving aside the possibly miraculous change in conception, Leibniz could hardly maintain that babies have as clear perceptions as grown-up people. And he says that death, though it cannot entirely destroy memory, does render our perceptions confused [G. VII. 531 ; (D. 193)]. This is also his explanation of sleep. He maintains, against Locke, that the soul always thinks, but he confesses that it is not always conscious of thought. We are never without perceptions, he says, but often without apperceptions, namely when we have no distinct perceptions (N. E. p. 166 ; G. v. 148). Thought is

---

[1] Compare, on this subject, G. II. 92 and IV. 513.

the proper activity of the soul, and a substance once in action will be so always (G. v. 101 ; N. E. 111). If its activity ceased, the substance too, as we have seen, would cease, and on waking we should not be numerically the same as when we went to sleep.

96. This brings us to a very important advance which Leibniz made in Psychology. Locke thought there could be nothing in the mind of which the mind was not conscious. Leibniz pointed out the absolute necessity of unconscious mental states. He distinguished between perception, which consists merely in being conscious of something, and apperception, which consists in self-consciousness, *i.e.* in being aware of perception [G. v. 46 (N. E. 47 ; L. 370); G. vi. 600 (D. 211 ; L. 411)]. An unconscious perception *is* a state of consciousness, but is unconscious in the sense that we are not aware *of* it, though in it we are aware of something else. How important these unconscious perceptions are, appears from the Introduction to the New Essays. It is in consequence of these that " the present is big with the future and laden with the past, that all things conspire, and that, in the least of substances, eyes as penetrating as those of God could read the whole course of the things in the universe " (N. E. 48 ; L. 373 ; G. v. 48). They also preserve the identity of the individual, and explain the pre-established harmony ; they prevent an indifference of equilibrium (*ib.*), and it is in virtue of them that no two things are perfectly alike (G. v. 49; N. E. 51; L. 377).

In favour of unconscious mental states Leibniz has several arguments, some quite cogent, others, I think, depending upon confusions. Locke's argument, he says, that we cannot know anything which we are not aware of knowing, proves too much, for then we know nothing that we are not actually thinking of (G. v. 80; N. E. 84). Again, and this is the most conclusive argument, " it is impossible for us always to reflect expressly upon all our thoughts ; otherwise the mind would reflect upon each reflection to infinity, without ever being able to pass to a new thought. For example, in perceiving some present feeling, I should always have to think that I think of it, and again think that I think of thinking of it, and so on to infinity "

(G. v. 108; N. E. 118—9). Another less conclusive argument is, that all impressions have their effect, and the perceptible must be composed of imperceptible parts [G. v. 24, 105, 107 (N. E. 25, 116, 118)]; whence it is supposed to follow that finite perceptions, like their objects, must be infinitely divisible, and therefore composed of parts of which we are not conscious. Leibniz, in fact, identified four apparently different things, namely (1) unconscious perception, (2) confused perception, (3) minute perception, and (4) psychical disposition. Of these four, the first is proved by the endless regress resulting from self-consciousness, and is required for maintaining that we always think and always mirror the whole universe. The second is required for explaining sense-perception, and, as we have seen, for the differences between different monads. The third follows from the argument that a perception, which is supposed finite, has as many parts as its object, and since its object may be the whole universe, the number of its parts may be infinite. The fourth is required to explain the sense in which truths are innate—a sense, by the way, very like that in which Kant's *à priori* is in the mind. All four appear to have been equally denied by Locke and asserted by Leibniz. It is worth while, therefore, to enquire into their connections.

97. It seems evident that unconscious perception is the most fundamental, and that the others follow if this be admitted. A confused perception, we may say, is such that we are not separately conscious of all its parts. Knowledge is confused, in Leibniz's phraseology, when I cannot enumerate separately the marks required to distinguish the thing known from other things (G. IV. 422; D. 27). And so, in confused perception, though I may be conscious of *some* elements of my perception, I am not conscious of *all* (*e.g.* G. v. 109; N. E. 120); for the perception is supposed to be as complex as its object, and therefore, if I were conscious of all the elements in my perception, I could wholly distinguish the object from other different objects. The parts which I do not distinguish are minute[1].

---

[1] Cf. G. IV. 574: "At bottom confused thoughts are nothing but a multitude of thoughts which in themselves are like those that are distinct, but are so small that each separately does not excite our attention, and does not cause us to distinguish it."

Again, as regards minute perceptions, Leibniz holds, with modern psycophysics, that a perception must reach a certain magnitude before we become aware of it, and thus sufficiently minute perceptions are necessarily unconscious. Psychical dispositions, finally, are a *name* for something which must be assumed by anyone who holds that every mind has a definite nature, and is not Locke's *tabula rasa*; but the name *per se* is not an explanation, which Leibniz's theory is intended to be. Locke had denied that any truth is innate, because whatever we know has been *learnt*. Leibniz, in reply, does not, like Shelley on Magdalen Bridge, show astonishment that babies should forget so soon. But he says that innate truths are always in the mind, but are only elicited, *i.e.* made objects of *apperception,* by experience and education. The senses, he says, give the material for reflection; we should not think of thought, if we did not think of something else, *i.e.* of the particular things which the senses furnish (G. v. 197; N. E. 220). There may, he confesses, be innate truths in the soul, which the soul never knows; but until it knows them, it cannot know they were always there (G. v. 75; N. E. 80). That is to say, the mind perceives these truths, but is not conscious of perceiving them. This is an explanation of the vague idea of psychical dispositions **by** means of unconscious perception. Leibniz explains that **when** he says truths are innate, he does not mean simply that **the** mind has the faculty of knowing them, but that it has the faculty of finding them in itself (G. v. 70; N. E. 74—5)[1]. Everything we know is developed out of our own nature, that is, it is obtained by reflection, by rendering conscious the perceptions which before were unconscious. Thus all in the end depends upon unconscious perception, whose possibility was denied by Locke, and whose necessity was demonstrated by Leibniz.

At the same time, it would appear that minute and unconscious perceptions are, after all, very nearly synonymous, and that confused perceptions are such as contain parts which

---

[1] It cannot be denied, however, that both in the remainder of this passage, and elsewhere, he falls back into the explanation of truths as psychical dispositions [*e.g.* G. v. 79, 97 (N. E. 84, 105)].

are minute or unconscious. To begin with, not all cognitions are confused. The knowledge of a necessary truth is distinct and indivisible—if we have it at all, it is not confused. And in any given complex perception, if any part be distinctly known, that part may be separated from the remainder, which alone is properly confused. Since our perceptions are always partially correct, the part which is correct may be abstracted as distinct perception, and only the remainder will be confused. For example, in the perception of matter, since there really is plurality, it is not in the plurality that our conception is confused. The confusion lies in the apparent continuity of parts, and this is due to their minuteness. And in all Leibniz's favourite illustrations of confused perception—*e.g.* the roar of the sea, which is composed of noises made by separate waves—he always insists on the minuteness of the constituents. Thus it seems that we may identify minute and unconscious perception. This, however, would create a difficulty in the explanation of innate truths of which we are unconscious, unless we suppose that our perception of such truths may grow intensively greater and less, without being divisible into parts. On this point there is, to my knowledge, nothing definite in Leibniz. He does not seem to have perceived that confused perception, if it gives any true knowledge, must be partly distinct; and this, I think, prevented him from a clear perception of the relation between confusion and minuteness. The use which he made of these will appear further in the next chapter, where we shall have to examine his theory of knowledge.

CHAPTER XIV

LEIBNIZ'S THEORY OF KNOWLEDGE.

98. BEFORE I begin an account of Leibniz's theory of knowledge, I may as well point out that what I am going to discuss is not exactly Epistemology, but a subject which belongs in the main to Psychology. The logical discussions of Chapters II.—V. dealt with that part, in what is commonly called Epistemology, which seems to me not psychological. The problem we are now concerned with is of a different kind; it is not the problem : What are the general conditions of truth? or, What is the nature of propositions? It is the entirely subsequent problem, How do we and other people come to know any truth? What is the origin of cognitions as events in time? And this question evidently belongs mainly to Psychology, and, as Leibniz says, is not preliminary in philosophy [G. v. 15 (N. E. 15; D. 95)]. The two questions have been confused—at any rate since Des Cartes—because people have supposed that truth would not be true if no one knew it, but becomes true by being known. Leibniz, as we shall see in discussing God, made this confusion, and Locke might seem to have made it, since he disclaims a merely psychological purpose[1]. But that is no reason for our making it, and in what follows I shall try to avoid it. At the same time Locke is in one sense justified. The problem is not a *purely* psychological one, since it discusses knowledge rather than belief. From the strict standpoint of Psychology, no distinction can be made between true and false belief, between knowledge and error. As a psychical phenomenon, a belief

---

[1] *Essay*, Introduction, § 2.

may be distinguished by its content, but not by the truth or
falsity of that content. Thus in discussing knowledge, *i.e.* the
belief in a true proposition, we presuppose both truth and
belief. The inquiry is thus hybrid, and subsequent both to the
philosophical discussion of truth, and to the psychological
discussion of belief.

99. I explained briefly in my last chapter the sense in
which Leibniz held to innate ideas and truths. They are in
the mind always, but only become properly known by becoming conscious objects of apperception. Leibniz only
endeavours, in the New Essays, to show the innateness of
necessary truths, though he is bound to hold, owing to the
independence of monads, that all the truths that ever come to
be known are innate. He finds it easier, however, to prove
the impossibility of learning necessary truths by experience,
and trusts, I suppose, that this will afford a presumption
against Locke's whole theory of knowledge. He uses the
expression *innate truth* in the New Essays, to denote a truth
in which all the ideas are innate, *i.e.* not derived from sense ;
but he explains that there is a different use of the word
[G. v. 66 (N. E. 70)]. In the sense in which he uses it, "the
sweet is not the bitter" is not innate, because *sweet* and
bitter come from the external senses. But "the square is not
the circle" is innate, because *square* and *circle* are ideas
furnished by the understanding itself [G. v. 79 (N. E. 84)].
Now the question arises : How does Leibniz distinguish ideas
of sense from other ideas ? For he cannot hold, as other
philosophers might, that ideas of sense are impressed from
without. Nor can he hold that they are such as alone are
capable of representing external things, for they are one and all
confused, and would be absent in a true knowledge of the
world [G. v. 77, 109 (N. E. 82, 120)]. Sense-ideas must, therefore, be distinguished by their own nature, and not by a
reference to external causes. On this point, Leibniz, so far
as I know, says nothing quite definite. The nearest approach
to a definite explanation is in the *Discours de Métaphysique*
(G. IV. 452). He speaks of the action of objects of sense
upon us, he says, in the same way as a Copernican may
speak of sunrise. There is a sense in which substances may

be said to act upon each other, "and in this same sense it may be said that we receive knowledge from without, by the ministration of the senses, because some external things contain or express more particularly the reasons which determine our soul to certain thoughts." Thus sense-ideas are those in which we are passive in the sense explained in Chapter XII. Again sense-ideas are confused and express the external world. "Distinct ideas are a representation of God, confused ideas are a representation of the universe" [G. v. 99 (N. E. 109)]. He does, as a matter of fact, denote as sense-ideas all those which presuppose extension or spatial externality, though space itself is not an idea of sense. "The ideas which are said to come from more than one sense," he explains, "like those of space, figure, motion, rest, are rather from common-sense, that is from the mind itself, for they are ideas of the pure understanding, but they are related to the external, and the senses make us perceive them" [G. v. 116 (N. E. 129)]. Thus the qualities which appear as external are ideas of sense, but all that is involved in externality itself is not sensational. And the qualities that appear as external are confused, since they cannot, as they appear, be states of monads. Ideas derived from reflection, on the contrary, are not necessarily confused (cf. G. II. 265), for if they truly describe our own states of mind, they describe something actual and not a mere phenomenon. Besides this reason, there is also the fact that by reflection we discover the categories (or predicaments, as Leibniz calls them). There is, indeed, much that reminds one of Kant in Leibniz's theory of knowledge. Existence, he says, cannot be found in sensible objects but by the aid of reason, and hence the idea of existence is derived from reflection [G. v. 117 (N. E. 130)]. To the maxim that there is nothing in the intellect but what comes from the senses, Leibniz adds, *except the intellect itself* (G. v. 100 ; N. E. 111). "It is very true," he says, "that our perceptions of ideas come either from the external senses, or from the internal sense, which may be called reflection; but this reflection is not limited to the mere operations of the mind, as is stated (by Locke); it extends even to the mind itself, and it is in perceiving the mind that we perceive substance" [G. v. 23 (N. E.

24)]. The soul, he says, is innate to itself, and therefore contains certain ideas essentially [G. III. 479; G. v. 93 (N. E. 100)]. Thus it comprises being, unity, substance, identity, cause, perception, reason, and many other notions which the senses cannot give [G. v. 100 (N. E. 111)] ; and these ideas are presupposed in any knowledge that can be derived from the senses. And necessary truths, Leibniz points out, are certainly known, though the senses cannot show them to be necessary [G. v. 77 (N. E. 81)]. It follows that such truths are developed from the nature of the mind. It may be surmised that Leibniz dwelt on necessary truths because, in their case, knowledge cannot be supposed due to a causal action of what is known upon the mind. For what is known, in this case, is not in time, and therefore cannot be the cause of our knowledge. This made it easier to suppose that knowledge is never caused by what is known, but arises independently from the nature of the mind.

100. The doctrine of innate truths, as developed in the New Essays, is more like Kant's doctrine than it has any right to be. Space and time and the categories are innate, while the qualities which appear in space are not innate. To the general theory that all truths which are known are innate, which Leibniz should have adopted, there is no answer but one which attacks the whole doctrine of monads. But to the theory of the New Essays, which adopts the common-sense view that sense-perceptions are caused by their objects, while innate truths are incapable of such a cause, there are, I think, answers which apply equally against Kant's doctrine that the à *priori* is subjective. The argument for subjectivity seems to be simply this : When what we know is the existence of something now, our knowledge may be supposed caused by that existence, since there is a temporal relation between them. But when what we know is an eternal truth, there can be no such temporal relation. Hence the knowledge is not caused by what is known. But nothing else, it is held, could have caused it unless the knowledge had been already obscurely in the mind. Hence such knowledge must be, in some sense, innate. It is difficult to state this argument in a form which shall be at all convincing. It seems to depend upon the radically vicious disjunction that knowledge must be either caused by what is known or wholly uncaused. In Leibniz, who rejected a causal action of the objects of perception, this argument, as a means of distinguishing different kinds of knowledge, is peculiarly scandalous. But leaving aside this special doctrine, and admitting that objects cause our perceptions, does it follow that necessary truths must be innate ? All who hold this view are compelled, like Leibniz, to admit that innate knowledge is only virtual [G. v. 71 (N. E. 76)], while all *conscious* knowledge is acquired, and has its definite causes. Now if the knowledge can be rendered conscious by causes other than what is known, why cannot it be wholly due to such causes ? All that we can say is, that the mind must have had a *disposition* towards such knowledge—a vague phrase which explains nothing. Moreover, the same argument applies to sense-perception. If the mind were not capable of sense-knowledge, objects could not cause such knowledge. Sensations of colours, sounds, smells, etc., must be equally innate on this view. There is, in fact, just the same difficulty in admitting *conscious* knowledge of a necessary truth to be caused, as in admitting *any* knowledge of it to be caused. The difficulty, in each case, is manufactured by supposing that knowledge can only be caused by what is known. This supposition would have disappeared if people had asked themselves what really *is* known. It is supposed that in *à priori* knowledge we know a proposition, while in perception we know an existent. This is false. We know a proposition equally in both cases. In perception we know the proposition that something exists. It is evident that we do not merely know the something, whatever it be, for this is equally present in mere imagination. What distinguishes perception is the knowledge that the something exists. And indeed whatever can be known must be true, and must therefore be a proposition. Perception, we may say, is the knowledge of an existential proposition, not consciously inferred from any other proposition, and referring to the same or nearly the same time as that in which the knowledge exists. If this had been duly realized—if people had reflected that what is known is always a proposition—they would have been less ready to suppose that knowledge could be caused by what is known. To say knowledge is caused in perception

by what exists, not by the fact that it exists, is at once to admit
that such knowledge is not caused by what is known. Thus
perception and intellectual knowledge become much more akin
than is generally supposed. We must either hold all knowledge
to be always in the mind, in which case its emergence into
consciousness becomes a problem, or we must admit that all
knowledge is acquired, but is never caused by the proposition
which is known. What its causes are, in any particular case,
becomes a purely empirical problem, which may be left wholly
to Psychology.

101. There is, moreover, a great difficulty as to what
Leibniz meant by ideas which are innate. This question is
dealt with in the New Essays, at the beginning of Book II
[G. v. 99 (N. E. 109)]. "Is it not true," Locke is made to ask,
"that the idea is the object of thought?" "I admit it,"
Leibniz replies, "provided you add that it is an immediate
internal object, and that this object is an expression of the
nature or the qualities of things. If the idea were the *form*
of thought, it would spring up and cease with the actual
thoughts which correspond to it ; but being the *object*, it may
be before and after the thoughts[1]." Thus an idea, though it
is in the mind, is neither knowledge nor desire; it is not a
thought, but what a thought thinks about. This passage
makes it clear that the only reason Leibniz had for saying ideas
exist in the mind is that they evidently do not exist outside of
it. He seems never to have asked himself why they should be
supposed to exist at all, nor to have considered the difficulty in
making them merely mental existents. Consider, for example,
the idea 2. This is not, Leibniz confesses, my thought of 2,
but something which my thought is about. But this something exists in my mind, and is therefore not the same as the
2 which some one else thinks of. Hence we cannot say that
there is one definite number 2, which different people think of;
there are as many numbers 2 as there are minds. These, it
will be said, all have something in common. But this something can be nothing but another idea which will, therefore, in
turn, consist of as many different ideas as there are minds.
Thus we are led to an endless regress. Not only can no two

[1] Cf. also G. iii. 659 (D. 236); iv. 451.

people think of the *same* idea, but they cannot even think of ideas that have anything in common, unless there are ideas which are not essentially constituents of any mind. With Locke's definition, that an idea is the object of thought, we may agree; but we must not seek to evade the consequence that an idea is not merely something in the mind, nor must we seek to give every idea an existence somewhere else. Precisely the same criticism applies to the statement that knowledge, ideas and truths "are only natural habits, *i.e.* active and passive dispositions and aptitudes" (N. E. 105 ; G. v. 97).

102. Sense-knowledge in Leibniz is not properly distinguished from intellectual knowledge by its *genesis*, but by its nature. It differs in that the qualities with which it deals are spatially extended, and are one and all confused. From their confusion it follows that those which seem simple are in reality complex, though we are unable to make the analysis. Thus green, though it appears simple, is, Leibniz thinks, really a mixture of insensible portions of blue and yellow [G. v. 275 (N. E. 320)]. But how blue and yellow would appear, if they were distinctly perceived, he does not inform us. He seems to think, however, as was natural to one who believed in analytic judgments, that the nature of our *evidence* for necessary and for sensational truths is different. The first truth of reason, he says, is the law of contradiction, whilst the first truths of fact are as many as the immediate perceptions. That I think is no *more* immediate than that various things are thought by me, and this is urged as a criticism of Des Cartes' *cogito* [G. iv. 357 (D. 48)]. That is to say, the law of contradiction is the sole ultimate premiss for necessary truths, but for contingent truths there are as many ultimate premisses as there are experiences. Nothing, he says, should be taken as primitive principles, except experiences and the law of identity or contradiction, without which last there would be no difference between truth and falsehood [G. v. 14 (D. 94; N. E. 13)]. Thus many truths of fact have no evidence except self-evidence, but this is only the case, among necessary truths, as regards the law of contradiction. The self-evident truths of fact, however, are all psychological : they concern our own thoughts. To this extent Leibniz is at one with Des Cartes and with Berkeley.

Where he is more philosophical than either is in perceiving
that truths of fact presuppose necessary truths, and that our
own existence is not therefore an ultimate and fundamental
premiss for all truths. My own existence is an axiom, he says,
in the sense of being indemonstrable, not in the sense of
being necessary [G. v. 391 (N. E. 469)]. Like all finite existence, it is contingent, but it is just as *certain* as necessary
truths (N. E. 499; G. v. 415). Thus Leibniz agrees with Locke
that we have an intuitive knowledge of our own existence, a
demonstrative knowledge of God's existence, and a sensitive
knowledge of that of other things (*ib.*). But the sensitive
knowledge may be doubted, and cannot be accepted without
some general ground for the existence of other things [G. v. 117
(N. E. 130)]. In this theory which, in its general outlines, is
more or less Cartesian, there are, as I have already pointed out,
two distinct advances upon Des Cartes. The first is that my
own existence is not taken as the premiss for necessary truths ;
the second is that the existence of my various thoughts is as
certain as the existence of myself. Leibniz did not discover,
what seems equally true, that the existence of external things
is just as certain and immediate as that of my own thoughts,
and thus he was unable, as we saw, to justify his belief in
an external world.

103. I come now to another respect in which Leibniz
refined upon Des Cartes, namely in the doctrine known as the
quality of ideas. This is developed in the "Thoughts on
Knowledge, Truth and Ideas" (D. 27—32 ; G. iv. 422—6)
(1684). Des Cartes held that whatever is clearly and distinctly conceived is true. This maxim, Leibniz points out,
is useless without criteria of clearness and distinctness [G. iv.
425 (D. 31)]. He therefore lays down the following definitions. Knowledge is either *obscure* or *clear*. Clear knowledge
is *confused* or *distinct*. Distinct knowledge is *adequate* or
inadequate, and is also either *symbolical* or *intuitive*. Perfect
knowledge is both adequate and intuitive.

As to the meanings of these terms, a notion is *obscure* when
it does not enable me to recognize the thing represented, or
distinguish it from other similar things ; it is *clear* when it does
enable me to recognize the thing represented. Clear knowledge

is *confused* when I cannot enumerate separately the *marks*
required to distinguish the thing known from other things,
although there are such marks. Instances of this are colours
and smells, which though we cannot analyze them, are certainly
complex, as may be seen by considering their causes. (We
must remember that Leibniz believed perception to have
always the same degree of complexity as its object, and since
green can be produced by mixing blue and yellow, a green
object is complex, and therefore our perception of green is also
complex.) Clear knowledge is *distinct*, either when we can
separately enumerate the marks of what is known—*i.e.* when
there is a nominal definition—or where what is known is
indefinable but primitive, *i.e.* an ultimate simple notion. Thus
a composite notion, such as gold, is distinct when all its marks
are known *clearly* ; it is *adequate*, if all the marks are also
known *distinctly* ; if they are not known *distinctly*, the knowledge is *inadequate*. Leibniz is not certain whether there is
any perfect example of adequate knowledge, but Arithmetic,
he thinks, approaches it very nearly. Distinct knowledge is
also divided according as it is symbolical or intuitive. It is
symbolical or blind, when we do not perceive the whole nature
of the object at one time, but substitute signs or symbols, as in
Mathematics, whose meaning we can recall when we will.
When we embrace in thought at once all the elementary
notions which compose an idea, our thought is *intuitive*. Thus
our knowledge of distinct primitive ideas, if we have it, must be
intuitive, while our knowledge of complex notions is, in general,
only symbolical.

104. This doctrine has important bearings on definition.
A *real* definition, as opposed to one which is merely nominal,
shows the possibility of the thing defined, and though this may
be done *à posteriori*, by showing the thing actually existing, it
may also be done *à priori*, wherever our knowledge is
adequate. For in this case, a complete analysis has been
effected without discovering any contradiction ; and where
there is no contradiction, that which is defined is necessarily
possible [G. IV. 424—5 (D. 30)]. On definition generally,
Leibniz makes many important observations. A definition is
only the distinct exposition of an idea [G. V. 92 (N. E. 99)],

but it may be either real or nominal. It is nominal when it merely enumerates marks, without showing them to be compatible. It is real when all the marks are shown to be compatible, so that what is defined is possible. The idea defined is then real, even if nothing ever exists of which it can be predicated [G. v. 279 (N. E. 325)]. Simple terms cannot have a nominal definition; but when they are only simple with regard to us, like green, they can have a real definition explaining their cause, as when we say green is a mixture of blue and yellow [G. v. 275 (N. E. 319)]. The continuity of forms gives him some trouble in regard to definition, and compels him to admit that we may be in doubt whether some babies are human or not. But he points out, against Locke, that though we may be unable to decide the question, there always is only one true answer. If the creature is rational, it is human, otherwise it is not human; and it always is either rational or not rational, though we may be in doubt as to the alternative to be chosen [G. v. 290 (N. E. p. 339)]. There is, however, a real difficulty in all cases of continuity, that an infinitesimal change in the object may make a finite change in the idea; as the loss of one more hair may just make a man bald. In such cases, Leibniz thinks that nature has not precisely determined the notion [G. v. 281 (N. E. 328)]; but this seems an inadequate reply.

105. Connected with Leibniz's notion of definitions, and of the reduction of all axioms to such as are identical, or immediate consequences of definitions [G. v. 92 (N. E. 99)], is his idea of a *Characteristica Universalis*, or Universal Mathematics. This was an idea which he cherished throughout his life, and on which he already wrote at the age of 20[1]. He seems to have thought that the symbolic method, in which formal rules obviate the necessity of thinking, could produce everywhere the same fruitful results as it has produced in the sciences of number and quantity. "Telescopes and microscopes," he says, "have not been so useful to the eye as this instrument would be in adding to the capacity of thought" (G. VII. 14). "If we had it, we should be able to reason in metaphysics and morals in much the same way as

---

[1] In the *Dissertatio de Arte Combinatoria*, G. IV. 27—102.

in geometry and analysis" (G. VII. 21). "If controversies were to arise, there would be no more need of disputation between two philosophers than between two accountants. For it would suffice to take their pencils in their hands, to sit down to their slates, and to say to each other (with a friend as witness, if they liked): Let us calculate" (G. VII. 200). By establishing the premisses in any *à priori* science, the rest, he thought, could be effected by mere rules of inference; and to establish the right premisses, it was only necessary to analyze all the notions employed until simple notions were reached, when all the axioms would at once follow as identical propositions. He urged that this method should be employed in regard to Euclid's axioms, which he held to be capable of proof [G. v. 92 (N. E. 99)]. The Universal Characteristic seems to have been something very like the syllogism. The syllogism, he says, is one of the most fruitful of human inventions, a kind of universal Mathematics [G. v. 460 (N. E. 559)]. What he desired was evidently akin to the modern science of Symbolic Logic[1], which is definitely a branch of Mathematics, and was developed by Boole under the impression that he was dealing with the "Laws of Thought." As a mathematical idea— as a Universal Algebra, embracing Formal Logic, ordinary Algebra, and Geometry as special cases—Leibniz's conception has shown itself in the highest degree useful. But as a method of pursuing philosophy, it had the formalist defect which results from a belief in analytic propositions, and which led Spinoza to employ a geometrical method. For the business of philosophy is just the discovery of those simple notions, and those primitive axioms, upon which any calculus or science must be based. The belief that the primitive axioms are identical leads to an emphasis on *results*, rather than premisses, which is radically opposed to the true philosophic method. There can be neither difficulty nor interest in the premisses, if these are of such a kind as "A is A" or "AB is not non-A." And thus Leibniz supposed that the great requisite was a convenient method of deduction. Whereas,

---

[1] Cf. G. VII. 214—15, 230, where several of the rules of the Calculus of Symbolic Logic are given.

in fact, the problems of philosophy should be anterior to deduction. An idea which can be defined, or a proposition which can be proved, is of only subordinate philosophical interest. The emphasis should be laid on the indefinable and indemonstrable, and here no method is available save intuition. The Universal Characteristic, therefore, though in Mathematics it was an idea of the highest importance, showed, in philosophy, a radical misconception, encouraged by the syllogism, and based upon the belief in the analytic nature of necessary truths[1].

---

[1] For an account of Leibniz's views on this matter see Guhrauer, *op. cit.* Vol. I. p. 320 ff. For a full treatment, see Couturat, *La Logique de Leibnitz*, Paris, 1900 (in the press).

172

CHAPTER XV

PROOFS OF THE EXISTENCE OF GOD.

106. I COME now to the weakest part in Leibniz's philosophy, the part most full of inconsistencies. Whatever, in the doctrine we have examined, seemed arbitrary, or in need of further explanation, was easily explained by the lazy device of reference to an Omnipotent Creator. And not only unavoidable difficulties, but others which might have been avoided, were left, because they reinforced the arguments upon which Leibniz's orthodoxy loved to dwell. A philosophy of substance, we may say generally, should be either a monism or a monadism. A monism is necessarily pantheistic, and a monadism, when it is logical, is as necessarily atheistic. Leibniz, however, felt any philosophy to be worthless which did not establish the existence of God, and it cannot be denied that certain gaps in his system were patched up by a reference to the Divine Power, Goodness and Wisdom. Let us now examine what the arguments were by which this result was attained.

There are four distinct arguments, in Leibniz, which attempt to prove the existence of God. Only one of these, so far as I know, was invented by him, and that was the worst of the four. They are: The Ontological Argument, the Cosmological Argument, the Argument from the Eternal Truths, and the Argument from the Pre-established Harmony.

107. The Ontological Argument, which Des Cartes had adapted from Anselm, is not much used by Leibniz, and is, in the Cartesian form, severely criticized by him. At the same time, it and the argument from the eternal truths alone start from necessary premisses, and alone, therefore, are formally capable of bringing out a necessary result. And it is, of course, quite essential to show that God's existence is a necessary truth. Moreover, if this be true, the Ontological Argument must be substantially correct. For if it is self-contradictory to suppose that God does not exist, it follows that his existence is of his essence, and consequently, that his existence can be inferred from his essence. And this is precisely what the Ontological Argument attempts. Accordingly Leibniz is careful not wholly to reject it.

The Ontological Argument may be put in many ways. In its original form, it states that God has all perfections, and existence is among perfections—that is, the good is better if it exists than if it does not exist. Consequently existence is of God's essence; to suppose that the most perfect Being does not exist, is self-contradictory. Again God may be defined, without reference to the Good, as the most real Being, or the sum of all reality, and then equally it follows from his essence that he exists. To these arguments Leibniz objected that they do not prove the idea of God to be a *possible* idea. They prove, he admits, what is true only of God, that if he be possible he exists [*e.g.* G. v. 419 (N. E. 504); G. vi. 614 (D. 224; L. 242)]. This objection had been already made to Des Cartes, and replied to in the answers to the second objections to his Meditations[1]. Leibniz showed, without difficulty, that the idea of God is possible. His possibility follows *à posteriori* from the existence of contingent things; for necessary being is being of itself, and if this were not possible, no being would be possible [G. iv. 406 (D. 137)]. But this line of argument belongs rather to the cosmological proof. God's possibility follows *à priori* from his having no limitations, no negation, and therefore no contradiction [G. vi. 614 (D. 224; L. 242)]. This argument is well stated in the paper which Leibniz submitted to Spinoza at the Hague in 1676, with the title, "That the most perfect Being exists[2]." The contents of this paper, in spite of its early date, are in complete harmony with his later

---

[1] See *Oeuvres de Des Cartes*, ed. Cousin, Vol. i. pp. 407, 440 ff.

[2] G. vii. 261 (N. E. 714). Also Stein, *Leibniz u. Spinoza*, Beilage i. Cf. Beilage vii., Jan. 1678.

philosophy. He undertakes to prove, from premisses which he always accepted, that God is *possible*, and then uses the Ontological Argument to show that God is actual. Thus he prefaces the Ontological Argument by exactly the reasoning which he always held to be required.

108. The argument is as follows. Every quality which is simple or absolute, positive and indefinable, and expresses its object without limits, is a *perfection*. All such qualities can be predicates of one and the same subject. For let us assume that two of them, A and B, are incompatible. Their incompatibility, Leibniz says, cannot be proved without resolving them, otherwise their nature would not enter into the reasoning. But both are irresolvable. Nor can their incompatibility, Leibniz thinks, be known *per se*. Hence, A and B are not incompatible, and such a subject is possible. And since existence is a perfection, such a subject exists.

This reasoning is certainly valid, in so far as it proves that God, so defined, is not self-contradictory; and with the analytic theory of necessary judgments, this is all that is required to prove him possible. The interesting point, however, is the Ontological Argument itself, which is involved in saying that since existence is a perfection, God exists. This depends upon regarding existence as a predicate, which Leibniz does [G. v. 339 (N. E. 401)]. But he recognizes, as regards finite things, a great difference between existence and all other predicates. Existential judgments alone are not analytic. In any proposition in which the predicate is *not* existence, the predicate is contained in the subject; but when the predicate *is* existence, it is not so contained, except in the one case of God. Leibniz would have admitted, what Kant urged, that a hundred thalers which I merely imagine are exactly like a hundred thalers which really exist; for this is involved in the synthetic nature of assertions of existence. If this were not the case, the notion of a hundred actual thalers would be different from that of a hundred possible thalers; existence would be contained in the notion, and the existential judgment would be analytic. But Leibniz ought not to have held existence to be a predicate at all, since two subjects, one of which has a given predicate, while the other does not have it, cannot possibly be exactly

alike. He ought, therefore, to have arrived at Kant's position,
that existence is not a predicate, and that God's non-existence
cannot be self-contradictory[1]. He endeavoured, instead, to
bridge the gulf between contingent and necessary truths, *i.e.*
between such as are existential and such as are not so, by
means of the necessary existence of God. This attempt is at
the bottom of all his arguments, and is especially obvious in the
case of the cosmological argument, which we must now examine.

109. The cosmological argument is, at first sight, more
plausible than the ontological argument, but it is less philosophical, and derives its superior plausibility only from conceal-
ing its implications. It has a formal vice, in that it starts from
finite existence as its datum, and admitting this to be contingent, it proceeds to infer an existent which is not contingent.
But as the premiss is contingent, the conclusion also must be
contingent. This is only to be avoided by pointing out that
the argument is analytic, that it proceeds from a complex
proposition to one which is logically presupposed in it, and that
necessary truths may be involved in those that are contingent.
But such a procedure is not properly a proof of the presupposition. If a judgment A presupposes another B, then, no doubt,
if A is true, B is true. But it is impossible that there should
be valid grounds for admitting A, which are not also grounds
for admitting B. In Euclid, for example, if you admit the
propositions, you must admit the axioms; but it would be
absurd to give this as a reason for admitting the axioms. Such
an argument is at best *ad hominem*, when your opponent is a
poor reasoner. If people are willing to admit finite existence,
then you force them to admit God's existence; but if they ask
a reason why they should admit finite existence, the only
grounds, if the cosmological argument be valid, are such as
lead first to the existence of God; such grounds, however, if
they exist, are only to be found in the ontological argument;
and this Leibniz virtually admits by calling this proof an argument *à posteriori* [G. VI. 614 (D. 224; L. 242)].

[1] "Being is evidently not a real predicate, *i.e.* a conception of something,
which could be added to the conception of a thing. It is merely the positing of
a thing, or of certain determinations, in itself" (*Reine Vernunft*, ed. Hart.
p. 409).

The cosmological argument, as Leibniz states it, is briefly as follows. The present world is necessary hypothetically, but not absolutely. Since it is what it is, it follows that it will be what it will be. But causality, which connects one state of the world with the next, never shows why there is any world at all. Even if we suppose the eternity of the world, we cannot escape the necessity for some reason of the whole series; though each state follows from the preceding, we never get a sufficient reason why there are any states at all. Hence there must be some extramundane reason of things. The whole collection of finite existents is contingent, and therefore demands a sufficient reason; but this cannot be found within the series, since every term is contingent, and itself requires a sufficient reason. Hence the sufficient reason of all contingents must be itself not contingent, but metaphysically necessary. Moreover the reason of the existing can only be derived from the existing. Hence the metaphysically necessary sufficient reason of all contingents must be a necessary existent, *i.e.* a Being whose essence involves existence; and this can only be God [G. VII. 302 (D. 100; L. 337)].

110. This argument is open to attack on the ground that, if the reason of an existent can only be some other existent, then the ontological argument cannot be valid. "For in eternal things it must be understood that, even if there were no cause, there is a reason, which, in perduring things, is necessity itself or essence" (*Ib.*). Thus it is only the reason of a *contingent* existent that must be an existent. But this can only be on the ground that the reason of the contingent must be one that inclines, but does not necessitate, which is, indeed, of the very essence of contingency. Accordingly, when God's necessary existence has been obtained, the world of contingents must not follow from it necessarily. It follows that God's volitions must be contingent, for they necessarily attain their effects, and if these effects are to be contingent it can only be, therefore, because the volitions are contingent. The volitions themselves, therefore, require a sufficient reason, which inclines but does not necessitate. This is found in God's goodness. It is held that God is free to do evil, but does not do so [G. VI. 386 (D. 203); G. VII. 409 (D. 274)]. But God's goodness itself must be supposed necessary (cf. p. 39 *supra*). Thus the contingency of existential propositions rests ultimately upon the assertion that God does not necessarily do good (G. IV. 438). God's good actions, in fact, have to be conceived as a collection of particular existents, each having a sufficient reason in his goodness. Or else we may place their sufficient reason in his wisdom, namely in his knowledge of the good, which is a knowledge of necessary propositions. God's goodness, Leibniz says, led him to desire to create the good, his wisdom showed him the best possible, and his power enabled him to create it (G. VI. 167).

But to return to the cosmological argument. By saying that the whole world of contingents is still contingent, and must have a reason in some metaphysically necessary Being other than itself, Leibniz endeavours to exclude the pantheism which lurks in all arguments for God. He might equally well have said that every finite existent is conditioned by some other existent, but the whole series of existents cannot be conditioned by any existent. It would follow that its sufficient reason was not an existent, and therefore that the sum total of existence is metaphysically necessary. This form of argument would, however, have landed him in Spinozism. It is very analogous to the form used by Mr Bradley, and it really underlies Leibniz's argument. Its validity is indisputable if the existential theory of judgment be admitted. To maintain that there is no truth is self-contradictory, for if our contention were itself true, there would be truth. If, then, all truth consists in propositions about what exists, it is self-contradictory to maintain that nothing exists. Thus the existence of something is metaphysically necessary. This argument, which is set forth at length in Book I., Chaps. II.—IV. of Mr Bradley's *Logic*, partakes of both the Ontological and Cosmological arguments. It also suggests Leibniz's proof from the Eternal Truths, from which we shall discover the sense in which he held the existential theory of judgments.

111. We have seen that Leibniz held the eternal truths to be one and all hypothetical. They do not assert the existence of their subjects. The possible is wider than the actual, and all the possible worlds can only be described by eternal truths. But this view, which seems to me thoroughly sound, alarms Leibniz. It may be objected, he thinks, that possibilities or essences prior to existence are fictions. To this he replies, that they are not fictions, but must be sought in the mind of God, along with the eternal truths. The existence of the actual series of things, he continues, shows his assertion to be not gratuitous; for the reason of the series is not to be found within it, but must be sought in metaphysical necessities or eternal truths, while at the same time the reason of a contingent existent must itself exist. Therefore the eternal truths must have their existence in an absolutely or metaphysically necessary Being, *i.e.* in God [G. VII. 305 (D. 103; L. 343)]. Thus confused ideas are those which represent the universe, while distinct ideas, from which necessary truths are derived, are a representation of God (N. E. 109; G. v. 99). And God's understanding is described as the region of the eternal truths (G. VI. 115; G. VII. 311). In God those things which otherwise would be imaginary are realized [G. VII. 305 (D. 103; L. 343)]. Thus relations derive their reality from the supreme reason (G. v. 210; N. E. 235), *i.e.* from the fact that they exist in the divine mind. God, according to Leibniz, sees not only individual monads and their various states, but also the relations between monads, and in this consists the reality of relations[1]. Thus in the case of relations, and of eternal truths generally, *esse* is *percipi*. But the perception must be God's perception, and this, after all, has an object, though an internal one [G. VI. 614 (D. 225; L. 243)]. Thus our knowledge of the eternal truths becomes a knowledge of God, since these truths are part of God's nature. And this is why rational spirits, which know eternal truths, are said to mirror not only the universe of creatures, but also God.

112. This argument I can only describe as scandalous. In the first place it confuses God's knowledge with the truths which God knows—a confusion which, in other places, Leibniz quite clearly exposes. " Essences," he says, " can, in a certain way, be conceived of without God.......And the very essence of God embraces all other essences to such a degree that God cannot be perfectly conceived without them" (D. 175; F. de C.

---

[1] G. II. 438. Cf. also *Monadology*, § 43.

24). And again: "It can no more be said that God and the things known by God are one and the same thing, than that the mind and the things perceived by the mind are the same" (D. 177; F. de C. 34). This last passage is an argument against Spinoza, and doubtless has only existents in view. But if truths can be the same as the knowledge of them, why may not this be so when the truths are existential? And the former passage cannot be thus disposed of, since it deals explicitly with essences, and points out the true argument, namely that God cannot be conceived of without essences. Moreover, as I have already suggested, God's existence itself, since it is proved, has a ground; and this ground cannot be identified with God's knowledge of it. The eternal truths, Leibniz strongly urges, do not depend, as Des Cartes had held, upon God's will. For this there are many reasons. In the first place, God's will depends upon a sufficient reason, which must always be his perception of the good. But this can only be a motive to God's choice, if the good itself is independent of such choice. God could have no motive in deciding what was to be decreed good, unless one possible decree was better than another, and thus we get into a vicious circle[1]. Moreover God's existence is among eternal truths, and who would dare, Leibniz asks triumphantly, to declare that God's existence is due to his will (G. VII. 310—1)? But who would dare, we may retort, to say that God's existence depends upon his understanding? Would any one maintain that the *reason* of God's existence is his knowledge of it? If this were the case, proofs of the existence of God ought first to prove that God knows of it, and thence deduce that what he knows, *i.e.* his own existence, is true. But it must be obvious that his existence does not depend upon his knowledge of it. Nor can it be maintained that the two are identical, for his knowledge comprises many other propositions, and he contains, besides knowledge, the attributes of Goodness and Power. Thus his existence cannot be synonymous with his knowledge of it. And the same is evident, on reflection, concerning all other truths. Leibniz maintains that God's view is veritable, that what he knows is true (*e.g.* G. IV. 439); and he evidently regards this statement as not tautological. But if truth *means*

---

[1] G. VII. 365 (D. 244), 379; IV. 344.

what God knows, the statement that God's view is veritable is equivalent to the statement that he knows what he knows. Moreover, God's existence is deduced from the Law of Contradiction, to which it is therefore subsequent. Hence we cannot, without a vicious circle, maintain that this law is only due to God's knowledge of it. Again, without the law of identity or contradiction, as Leibniz truly says [G. v. 14 (D. 94; N. E. 14)], there would be no difference between truth and falsehood. Therefore, without this law, it could not be true, rather than false, that God exists. Hence, though God's existence may depend upon the law of contradiction, this law cannot in turn depend upon God's existence. Finally, consider the very meaning of the word *proposition*. Leibniz has to maintain that eternal truths *exist* in the mind of God [G. vi. 230; vii. 305 (D. 103; L. 343)]. Thus we cannot say that God is *subjected* to eternal truths, for they form part of his very nature, to wit his understanding. But again Leibniz speaks of them as the internal *object* of his understanding [G. vi. 614 (D. 225; L. 243)], thus suggesting by the word *object*, what the word *internal* is intended to deny, that the truths are something different from the knowledge of them. And this, if we consider, is obvious. For how can an eternal truth exist? The Law of Contradiction, or the proposition that two and two are four, or the truths of Geometry—these, we are told, *exist* in the mind of God. But it must surely be evident, if we consider the matter, that these truths are wholly incapable of existence, and that what exists is only the knowledge of them. It can scarcely be maintained that in studying Euclid we are studying God's Psychology. If, to mend matters, we were to say that truths actually constitute God's understanding, and if this is what makes them true, then, since we must always distinguish between a proposition and the knowledge of it, the impious consequence follows that God can have no knowledge. Truths *are* God's states of mind, and *we* know these truths; but God cannot know them, since knowledge is distinct from what is known[1].

---

[1] This objection is urged by Leibniz himself, in a paper written probably about 1680, against Des Cartes. "The God of Des Cartes," he says, "has neither will nor understanding, since, according to Des Cartes, he has not the good for the object of his will, nor the true for the object of his understanding" (G. iv. 299).

And generally if a truth be something existing in some mind, then that mind, and another which knows the truth, cannot be aware of the *same* truth. If we once admit that there is one and only one Law of Contradiction, which is the same whoever knows it, then the law itself is something distinct from all knowledge, and cannot logically depend upon God's mind. Unless truth be distinct from God's knowledge, there is nothing for God to know. God's understanding is constituted by knowledge of the eternal truths, and if these in turn are constituted by his knowledge, there is no way for his knowledge to begin, and no reason why it should know the propositions it does know rather than other propositions. Thus the eternal truths must be true apart from God's knowledge, and cannot therefore be used to prove his existence. Leibniz seems, in fact, never to have made up his mind as to whether God's understanding is a collection of truths, or the knowledge of this collection. The former alternative would have led to a God almost exactly like Spinoza's, but would have left no place for God's will. The latter should have left the truth of what God knows independent of his knowledge, and therefore not a ground for inferring the existence of the knowledge or of the Knower.

113. We have now seen the fallacies involved in Leibniz's deduction of God from the eternal truths. I wish to reinforce the above arguments by some general remarks on truth and knowledge, suggested by that proof.

It is a view commonly held that, as Leibniz puts it, the eternal truths would not subsist if there were no understanding, not even God's (G. VI. 226. Cf. Spinoza, *Ethics*, II. 7, Schol.). This view has been encouraged by Kant's notion that *à priori* truths are in some way the work of the mind, and has been exalted by Hegelianism into a first principle. Since it is self-contradictory to deny all truth, it has thus become self-contradictory to deny all knowledge. And since, on this view, nothing can be true without being known, it has become necessary to postulate either a personal God, or a kind of pantheistic universal Mind from whose nature truths perpetually flow or emanate. What I wish to point out is, that Leibniz's proof of God is merely a theological form of this argument, and that everything that I urged against Leibniz applies equally against all who make truth dependent upon knowledge. It is to be remembered, in this connection, that knowledge is a complex conception, compounded of truth and belief. Belief, as a psychical phenomenon, is just the same when the proposition believed is false as when it is true. The first difficulty encountered by the view I am discussing is, therefore, the distinction between true and false belief, between knowledge and error. The second difficulty is analogous to the difficulty of supposing the truth that God exists to be dependent upon God's knowledge of this truth. Is the proposition, that truth depends upon knowledge, itself true or false? If false, the position collapses. If true, how can it be itself dependent upon knowledge? To make it thus dependent is to incur a vicious circle; to make it not dependent, is again to abandon the position. A third difficulty is, that knowledge is not a simple idea, and the propositions defining it must be prior to the proposition that knowledge exists.

The position rests on the same basis as the cosmological argument. This depends upon the existential theory of judgment, the theory, namely, that all truth consists in describing what exists. The dependence of truth upon knowledge is really a particular case of the existential theory of propositions, and like that theory, involves the gross assumption that what does not exist is nothing, or even meaningless. For truth is evidently something, and must, on this theory, be connected with existence. Now knowledge (perhaps) exists, and therefore it is convenient to make truth a property of knowledge. Thus the proposition, that a given proposition is true, is reduced to the proposition that it is known, and thus becomes existential. Hence Leibniz is right in connecting very closely the cosmological argument and the argument from the eternal truths [e.g. G. VII. 302—5 (D. 100—103; L. 337—343)]. But he is mistaken, at least so it seems to me, in holding that truth depends upon existence. And for one who held the possible to be wider than the actual, this theory is quite peculiarly untenable.

The inconsistencies, in which Leibniz is involved by the belief in God, are so many and various that it would take long to develop them all. The one which I have just mentioned is,

however, among the most important. The view that the actual
is not coextensive with the possible is, as we have seen, quite
essential to Leibniz's doctrine of contingency and freedom, as
well as to his solution of the problem of evil. This view is
denied by the existential theory of judgments, upon which two
of Leibniz's proofs of God depend. If every proposition ascribes
a predicate to some existent, then we cannot maintain, as an
ultimate truth, that the non-existent is possible. We can only
mean by this that God, or some one else, believes it to be
possible, and we must hold, if we are logical, that this belief is
erroneous. Thus Leibniz falls, by his introduction of God, into
a Spinozistic necessity: only the actual is possible, the non-
existent is impossible, and the ground for contingency has
disappeared.

Another aspect of Spinozism is also inevitable, if God be
conceived as having any influence on the monads. This is the
belief in only one substance. Before developing this inconsistency, however, it will be well to examine the proof which was
Leibniz's favourite, the proof which he himself invented, that,
namely, from the pre-established harmony.

114. The proof from the pre-established harmony is a
particular form of the so-called physico-theological proof, otherwise known as the argument from design. This is the argument
of the Bridgewater Treatises, and of popular theology generally.
Being more palpably inadequate than any of the others, it has
acquired a popularity which they have never enjoyed. The
world is so well constructed, we are told, that it must have had
a highly skilful Architect. In Leibniz's form, the argument
states that the harmony of all the monads can only have arisen
from a common cause [*e.g.* G. IV. 486 (D. 79; L. 316)]. That
they should all exactly synchronize, can only be explained by a
Creator who pre-determined their synchronism. Let us see
what this theory involves.

There are, roughly speaking, two functions which a Christian God has to fulfil. He has to be a Providence and a
Creator. Leibniz merged the first of these functions in the
second[1], though he often denied that he had done so. God, he

---

[1] See Arnauld's objections, G. II. 15.

says, is the soul's immediate external object, and is able to act
directly on the soul, though apparently he very seldom does so
[G. v. 99 (N. E. 109)]. This is a sense in which Leibniz agrees
to Malebranche's doctrine, that we see all things in God [G. vi.
578 (D. 189)]. But it is better to do away entirely with the
immediate operation of God on the world, which is plainly
inconsistent with Leibniz's logic. All the grounds against the
interaction of substances are, as we saw, grounds giving metaphysical necessity, and therefore applying equally against God's
action on the world. We will therefore suppose that God is
the Creator, and that his Providence is shown only in creating
the best possible world.

Whenever Leibniz is not thinking of theological objections,
he regards God's action on the world as entirely limited to
creation. God's goodness, he says, led him to desire to create
the good, his wisdom showed him the best possible, and his
power enabled him to create it (G. vi. 167). God's wisdom and
goodness correspond, roughly speaking, to knowledge and volition in us, but his power is a peculiar attribute, to which creatures have nothing parallel[1]. God's wisdom consists of his
knowledge of all truths, necessary and contingent alike. In so
far as truths are necessary, his knowledge of them, which constitutes his understanding, is prior to his volitions; for his
volitions are determined by his knowledge of the good, and all
true propositions about the good are necessary truths. Leibniz
perceived (*e.g.* G. iv. 344) that God's volitions could not signifi-
cantly be called good, unless the good was independent of them,
though he did not see that God's thoughts could not be signifi-
cantly called *wise*, unless the truth was independent of them.
Thus wisdom and goodness concur in creating a good world,
since wisdom is required to know that it is good. But power
is required for the creation of it, not for determining its nature.
And here Leibniz seems to be guarded against inconsistency by
the theory of contingent judgments. Every existential proposition not concerned with God is contingent, and thus, though
God cannot, without positive contradiction, be supposed to
affect the *nature* of any one substance, yet he may, without

---

[1] *E.g.* G. vi. 615 (D. 225; L. 244—5). But contrast G. iv. 515 (D. 125).

contradiction, be supposed to cause the *existence* of that substance. This is the sense in which the pre-established harmony is due to God. God chose to create monads which harmonized, and though the harmony arises from their natures, the *existence* of monads having such natures is due to God's power.

115. Concerning this argument, we may observe that, if the cosmological proof be sound, the present proof is superfluous. If God's existence can be inferred from *any* finite existence, the particular nature of what exists is irrelevant, or is useful at most, for a subsequent empirical proof that God is good. Moreover, with Leibniz's conception of substance, there is much difficulty in the idea of *creating* a substance. Here he falls into inconsistency with the ontological argument, to which I must now return.

If existence can be of God's essence—and it is necessary to the ontological proof that it should be so—then existence is a predicate of God. But if existence is a predicate of God, then it is a predicate. Hence, when we say anything exists, existence is a predicate of this existent. So far, Leibniz would admit the argument [G. v. 339 (N. E. p. 401)]. But if existence be a predicate, then it is part of the nature of a substance, and a substance, by being created, acquires a new predicate. Hence the special position of existence, as a contingent and synthetic predicate, falls to the ground. If all substances always contain all their predicates, then all substances always contain or do not contain the predicate existence, and God must be as powerless over this predicate as over any other. To add the predicate *existence* must be metaphysically impossible. Thus either creation is self-contradictory, or, if existence is not a predicate, the ontological argument is unsound. But the other arguments, as Kant pointed out, all depend upon this argument[1]. Hence if we accept it, we must regard God as the only substance, as an immanent pantheistic God incapable of creation ; or, if we reject it, we must admit that all monads exist necessarily, and are not dependent upon any outside cause. This is why I said (§ 106) that monism must be pantheistic, and monadism must be atheistic. And so it happens that Leibniz,

---

[1] *Reine Vernunft*, ed. Hartenstein, 1867, pp. 414, 427.

whenever he treats God at all seriously, falls involuntarily into a Spinozistic pantheism.

116. Some of these pantheistic consequences are worth noting. "Everything is in God," Leibniz says, " as place is in that which is placed" (I). 178 ; F. de C. 38). Now place, in his system, is a mere attribute of what is placed; therefore things should be mere attributes of God. " God alone," we are told in the Monadology, "is......the original simple substance, of which all created or derivative monads are products, born, so to speak, from moment to moment by continual fulgurations of the Deity" [G. VI. 614 (D. 225 ; L. 243)]. The following passage of the *Discours de Métaphysique* might almost have been written by Spinoza. " Created substances depend on God, who conserves them, and even produces them continually by a kind of emanation, as we produce our thoughts. For God......views all aspects of the world in all possible ways; the result of each view of the universe, as if seen from a certain place, is a substance expressing the universe conformably to this point of view, if God sees fit to make his thought effective and produce this substance. And since God's view is always veritable, our perceptions are so too; it is our judgments, which are from us, that deceive us " (G. IV. 439). One wonders what change is made when God "makes his thought effective[1]." It would seem that the sum of all substances must be indiscernible from God, and therefore identical with him—the very creed of pantheism[2]. Leibniz once approaches very near to the doctrine that all determination is negation, though he seems unaware that this ought to lead him to Spinozism. The

---

[1] Contrast the following passage in the same work (G. IV. 453): "I am not, however, of the opinion of some able philosophers, who seem to maintain that our ideas themselves are in God, and not at all in us. This comes, in my opinion, from their not yet having sufficiently considered what we have just explained here concerning substances, nor all the extent and independence of our soul, which causes it to contain all that happens to it, and to express God and with him all possible and actual beings, as an effect expresses its cause. Also it is an inconceivable thing that I should think by the ideas of another."

[2] It is true Leibniz assures us on the next page that God sees the universe not only as created substances see it, but also quite differently. But this still leaves all created substances indiscernible from a *part* of God—a view no less pantheistic than the other.

argument is as to the necessity of a primitive force in each monad, of which the derivative force is a modification. Without primitive entelechies, he says, " there would be modifications without anything substantial to be modified; for what is merely passive could not have active modifications; since *modification, far from adding any perfection, can only be a variable restriction or limitation,* and consequently cannot exceed the perfection of the subject" (G. III. 67). (My italics). Leibniz even confesses (G. II. 232) that his assertion of many substances is rather arbitrary. "If the notion of substance in its generic definition," he says, " is only applicable to the simplest or primitive substance, this alone will be substance. And it is in your power," he continues, " so to take the word substance, that God alone shall be substance, and other substances shall be called otherwise. But I prefer to seek a notion which fits other things, and agrees with common usage, according to which you, he, and I are deemed substances. You will not deny that this is legitimate, and, if it succeeds, useful."

It is thus evident how wide a gulf, when God is being considered, there is between God, the primitive substance, and the monads or created substances. But when Leibniz is occupied with the monads, God has to be debased from the high position which pantheism gives him, and twice, at least, he is spoken of as one among monads (G. III. 636; VII. 502). These two passages should, I think, be regarded as slips. The usual expressions for God are simple primitive substance, or primitive unity. In the two passages where God is called a monad, this does not occur very directly. In one, we are told that "monads, except the primitive one, are subject to passions" (G. III. 636). The other is more direct. "The monad or simple substance contains in its generic definition perception and appetition, and is either the primitive one or God, in which is the ultimate reason of things, or is derivative, *i.e.* a created monad" (G. VII. 502). That these two passages are to be regarded as slips seems likely if only because (so far as I know) there are no others. This is rendered still more probable by the fact that the traditional expression *monas monadum,* so far as I can discover, occurs nowhere. It was used by Bruno, from whom it used to be thought that Leibniz got the word *monad.*

This fact seems to have led Hegel[1] to suppose that Leibniz also used the phrase, and subsequent writers, with the exception of Erdmann (v. *Geschichte,* Vol. II. 2, p. 62), seem to have rashly assumed that Hegel had some authority for the supposition. Thus it is better not to regard Leibniz's God as one among monads, especially as the monads form a continuous series, and evidently there cannot be one differing infinitely little from God.

We may now sum up the inconsistencies into which Leibniz is led by his theology. The ontological argument, which is alone capable of proving that God's existence is a necessary truth, is incompatible with the unique position which, where finite things are concerned, is assigned to existence. Leibniz's philosophy of the finite and the contingent, if it be valid, involves Kant's position, that existence adds nothing to the nature of what exists, *i.e.* that existence is not merely one among predicates. If this be so, existence cannot form part of any essence, and the ontological argument falls. The cosmological argument depends upon the existential theory of judgment, which is inconsistent with Leibniz's separation of the possible and the actual. For his theory of contingency, it is essential that something non-existent should be possible; and this is not an existential judgment. The proof by means of the eternal truths supposes that the truth of propositions results from their being believed—a view which is in itself wholly false, and which, further, renders it quite arbitrary what propositions God is to believe. It also depends upon the existential theory of judgment, since its basis is, that truth, being as such non-existent, is nothing *per se,* but must be a mere property of true beliefs—a view whose circularity is self-evident. The argument from the pre-established harmony, again, involves a Creator, and the creation of substances is only possible if existence be not a predicate. But in that case, God's existence cannot be an analytic proposition, and must, on Leibniz's logic, be contingent. The ontological argument will be unsound, and

---

[1] *E.g.* in his history of philosophy, *Werke,* Vol. XVI. pp. 418, 422. Also in the smaller Logic, *Werke,* Vol. V. p. 365; Wallace's *Translation,* p. 334. Leibniz in all probability derived the word *monad* from his friend van Helmont. See Stein, *Leibniz und Spinoza.*

God's existence itself, being contingent, must have a sufficient reason which inclines without necessitating. But if this be required, we might just as well admit the preestablished harmony as an ultimate fact, since the assumption of God's existence is insufficient for its explanation.

117. A few words seem needed as to God's goodness. Most philosophers seem to suppose that, if they can establish God's existence, his goodness necessarily follows. Accordingly, though Leibniz does, in certain passages, give some argument for what, in a metaphysical sense, may be called God's *perfection*, he nowhere takes the trouble to prove his goodness. In the argument submitted to Spinoza, we saw that a perfection is defined as any quality which is simple and absolute, positive and indefinable, and expresses its object without limits (G. VII. 261). Leibniz seems to have adhered to this definition of a perfection. Thus he says in the Monadology [§§ 40, 41 ; G. VI. 613 (D. 223 ; L. 239)]: "We may judge also that this supreme substance, which is unique, universal and necessary, having nothing outside of itself which is independent of it, and being a simple consequence of possible being, must be incapable of limits, and must contain just as much reality as possible. Whence it follows, that God is absolutely perfect, perfection being nothing but the magnitude of positive reality strictly understood, setting aside the limits or boundaries in things which have them. And where there are no boundaries, that is to say, in God, perfection is absolutely infinite[1]." But perfection understood in this sense, though it does appear to involve God's infinite goodness, involves equally, except on a purely privative view of evil, his infinite badness. To escape this, Leibniz, like most optimists, asserts that evil is a limitation. God, he says, is infinite, the Devil is limited; good advances *ad infinitum*, evil has bounds [G. VI. 378 (D. 196)]. Thus God's perfection involves infinite goodness, but not infinite badness. If Leibniz

---

[1] This seems also Leibniz's ethical sense of perfection. Cf. G. VII. 303 (D. 101 ; L. 340): "Among the infinite combinations of possibles and possible series, that one exists by which the most of essence or of possibility is brought into existence." Also G. VII. 305 (D. 103; L. 342). But the two are distinguished on the next page, where moral perfection appears as a species of metaphysical perfection.

had admitted badness to be a positive predicate, he could not have retained his definition of God, or his doctrine of analytic judgments. For good and bad would then have been not mutually contradictory, but yet obviously incompatible as predicates of God. Accordingly he asserted—though without arguments of any kind—that badness is essentially finite. But this brings me to his Ethics, with the discussion of which this work will come to an end.

CHAPTER XVI

LEIBNIZ'S ETHICS.

118. In the last chapter we saw that God's goodness is the metaphysically necessary sufficient reason of God's good acts, which are contingent, and indeed the ultimate contingents from which all others flow. This brought us to the threshold of Leibniz's Ethics, in which, more even than in his doctrine of God, all the difficulties and inconsistencies of his system culminate. By the emphasis which he laid on final causes, he gave Ethics very great importance in his philosophy. And yet he appears to have bestowed but the smallest part of his thought on the meaning and nature of the good. His Ethics is a mass of inconsistencies, due partly to indifference, partly to deference for Christian moralists. Though I shall treat the subject briefly, I shall give it quite as large a space, proportionally, as it seems to have occupied in Leibniz's meditations.

There are three separate questions, which I shall have to treat of. The first two are psychological, and the last only is properly ethical. These are (1) the doctrine of freedom and determination, (2) the psychology of volition, (3) the nature of the good.

(1) The doctrine, by which Leibniz sought to reconcile free will with his thorough-going determinism, depends wholly upon contingency and the activity of substances. Freedom, as Leibniz points out, is a very ambiguous term.

"Freedom of will," he says, "is...understood in two different senses. The first is when it is opposed to the imperfection or slavery of the spirit, which is a coercion or constraint, but internal like that arising from the passions. The other sense is used when freedom is opposed to necessity." In the first sense, " God alone is perfectly free, and created spirits are so, only in proportion as they are superior to their passions. And this freedom properly concerns our understanding. But the freedom of spirit, opposed to necessity, concerns the bare will, and in so far as it is distinguished from the understanding. This is what is called *free-will*, and it consists in this, that we hold that the strongest reasons or impressions, which the understanding presents to the will, do not prevent the act of the will from being contingent, and do not give it a necessity which is absolute, and so to speak, metaphysical[1]."

Of these two senses, the first corresponds to the distinction of activity and passivity. The will is free in so far as we are active, *i.e.* determined by distinct ideas; God alone, who has only distinct ideas, is perfectly free. And thus this sense is connected with the understanding[2]. The other is the sense which is relevant in the free-will controversy, and the one which must be examined now.

Leibniz recognized—as every careful philosopher should—that all psychical events have their causes, just as physical events have, and that prediction is as possible, theoretically, in the one case as in the other. To this he was committed by his whole philosophy, and especially by the pre-established harmony. He points out that the future must be determined, since any proposition about it must be already true or false (G. vi. 123). And with this, if he had not been resolved to rescue free will, he might have been content. The whole doctrine of contingency might have been dropped with advantage. But that would have led to a Spinozistic necessity, and have contradicted Christian dogma. Accordingly he held —as the connection of the analytic and the necessary also led him to hold—that all existential propositions and all causal connections are contingent, and that consequently, though volitions have invariable causes, they do not follow necessarily from those causes[3]. He rejected entirely the liberty of

---

[1] N. E. pp. 179—180; G. v. 160—1, Bk. ii. Chap. xxi.
[2] Cf. G. vii. 109—110, for further developments as to freedom in this sense.
[3] Cf. G. v. 163—4 (N. E. 183).

indifference—the doctrine that the will may be uncaused—and even held this to be self-contradictory[1]. For it is necessary that every event should have a cause, though it is contingent that the cause should produce its effect. He held also that the indifference of equilibrium would destroy moral good and evil. For it would imply a choice without reason, and therefore without a good or a bad reason. But it is in the goodness or badness of the reason that moral good and evil consist (G. VI. 411). He rejected also the pretended introspective proof of freedom, by our supposed sense of it; for, as he rightly says, we may be determined by insensible perceptions (G. VI. 130). Freedom in the present sense is equally attributed to God; his volitions, though always determined by the motive of the best, are none the less contingent (G. VII. 408—9; D. 273—4). It may be asked why beasts and even bare monads are not free. For this there is, I think, no adequate ground. Beasts, Leibniz confesses, have spontaneity (G. VII. 109), but not liberty (G. VI. 421). Spontaneity, he says, is contingency without constraint, and a thing is constrained when its principle comes from without (G. VII. 110). By the principle of a thing, I imagine Leibniz must mean the sufficient reason of its changes. This, then, in an animal, should be internal. The only sense, accordingly, in which an animal is not free, would seem to be that its volitions are not determined by knowledge of the good[2].

---

[1] Cf. G. II. 420; III. 401 (D. 171); V. 164 (N. E. 183); VII. 379.

[2] Leibniz's views on this point are collected in a short paper, given by Gerhardt both in French and Latin (G. VII. 108—111). I translate from the French.

"Liberty is spontaneity joined to intelligence.

"Thus what is called spontaneity in beasts and in other substances destitute of intelligence, is raised in man to a higher degree of perfection, and is called liberty.

"Spontaneity is contingency without compulsion; in other words, we call spontaneous what is neither necessary nor constrained.

"We call contingent what is not necessary, or (what is the same thing) that whose opposite is possible, implying no contradiction.

"Constrained is that whose principle comes from without. (Cf. Pollock's *Spinoza*, 2nd ed. p. 193. Spinoza has only the opposition *free* or *constrained*, not Leibniz's further distinctions.)

"There is indifference, when there is no more reason for one than for the

119. (2) This brings me to the psychology of volition and pleasure. Leibniz holds that pleasure is a sense of perfection, and that what Locke calls *uneasiness* is essential to the happiness of created beings, which never consists in com-other. Otherwise, there would be determination. (The Latin has: And the determined is opposed to it.)

"All the actions of single substances are contingent. For it can be shown that, if things happened otherwise, there would be no contradiction on that account.

"All actions are determined, and never indifferent. For there is always a reason inclining us to one rather than the other, since nothing happens without a reason. It is true that these inclining reasons are not necessitating, and destroy neither contingency nor liberty.

"A liberty of indifference is impossible. So that it cannot be found anywhere, not even in God. For God is determined by himself to do always the best. And creatures are always determined by internal or external reasons.

"The more substances are determined by themselves, and removed from indifference, the more perfect they are. For, being always determined, they will have the determination either from themselves, and will be by so much the more powerful and perfect, or they will have it from without, and then they will be proportionally obliged to serve external things.

"The more we act according to reason the more we are free, and there is the more servitude the more we act by the passions. For the more we act according to reason, the more we act conformably to the perfections of our own nature, and in proportion as we allow ourselves to be carried away by passions, we are slaves of external things which make us suffer.

"To sum up: All actions are contingent, or without necessity. But also everything is determined or regular, and there is no indifference. We may even say that substances are freer in proportion as they are further removed from indifference and more self-determined. And that the less they have need of external determination, the nearer they approach to the divine perfection. For God, being the freest and most perfect substance, is also the most completely determined by himself to do the most perfect. So that Nothing (*le Rien*), which is the most imperfect and the furthest removed from God, is also the most indifferent and the least determined. Now in so far as we have lights, and act according to reason, we shall be determined by the perfections of our own nature, and consequently we shall be freer in proportion as we are less embarrassed as to our choice. It is true that all our perfections, and those of all nature, come from God, but this, far from being contrary to liberty, is rather the very reason why we are free, because God has communicated to us a certain degree of his perfection and of his liberty. Let us, then, content ourselves with a liberty which is desirable, and approaches that of God, which makes us the most disposed to choose well and act well; and let us not pretend to that harmful, not to say chimerical liberty, of being in uncertainty and perpetual embarrassment, like that Ass of Buridan, famous in the schools, who, being placed at an equal distance between two sacks of wheat, and having nothing that determined him to go to one rather than the other, allowed himself to die of hunger."

plete possession [G. v. 175 (N. E. 194); VII. 73 (D. 130)]. Action, he says, brings joy, while passion brings pain; and action and passion consist in passing to a greater or less degree of perfection (G. IV. 441)[1]. Thus when Leibniz agrees with Locke, that the good is what produces pleasure [G. v. 149 (N. E. 167)], he is not accepting Utilitarianism, but asserting a psychological connection between the attainment of good and the feeling of pleasure. In the same way he may be freed from the appearance of psychological hedonism, to which he approaches dangerously near (New Essays, Bk. I. Chap. II.). There are, Leibniz thinks, innate instincts, from which innate *truths* may be derived. "Although we may say truly that morals have indemonstrable principles, and that one of the first and most practical is, that we must pursue joy and shun sorrow, we must add that this is not a truth which is known purely by reason, since it is founded on internal experience, or on confused knowledge, for we do not feel what joy and sorrow are" [G. v. 81 (N. E. 86)]. "This maxim," he continues, "is not known by reason, but, so to speak, by an instinct" (*ib.*). But reason should lead us rather to seek *felicity*, which "is only a lasting joy. Our instinct, however, does not tend to felicity proper, but to joy, *i.e.* to the present; it is reason which prompts to the future and the enduring. Now the inclination, expressed by the understanding, passes into a *precept* or practical truth; and if the instinct is innate, the truth is innate also" [G. v. 82 (N. E. 87)][2]. Leibniz seems, in this passage, to suggest that he thinks joy good because it is desired, and reason only useful in showing that, if joy be good, more joy is better than less[3]. But this cannot

---

[1] Cf. Spinoza, *Ethics*, Part III. Prop. XI. Scholium: "By *pleasure* I shall, therefore, hereafter understand an affection whereby the mind passes to a greater perfection; and by *pain* an affection whereby it passes to a less perfection." Cf. also *ib.* Prop. LIX. Schol.: "Pleasure is the passage of a man from less to greater perfection. Pain is the passage of a man from greater to less perfection." Cf. Hobbes, *Human Nature*, Chap. VII. (ed. Molesworth, Vol. IV.).

[2] He proceeds to explain that the instincts are not necessarily practical, but furnish similarly the principles of the sciences and of reasoning, which are employed unconsciously.

[3] Cf. Spinoza, *Ethics*, Part III. Prop. IX. Scholium: "We have not endeavour, will, appetite or desire for anything because we deem it good, but

be his true meaning. For, as we saw, he holds that joy is a
sense of perfection, and therefore perfection must be distinct
from joy. Moreover, it is a contingent truth that volition is
determined by the good (G. II. 38 ; IV. 438). But if volition
is always necessarily determined by desire, as Leibniz seems
to hold, and if the good *means* what is desired, then volition
would be *necessarily* determined by the good. We must
suppose, therefore, that Leibniz considers it a synthetic and
contingent proposition that we desire the good, and does not
commit the fallacy of supposing that the good *means* the
desired. This appears also from a passage where Leibniz
points out that God's will could not have the good for its
effect, unless it had it for its object, and that the good is
therefore independent of God's will (G. IV. 344) ; or from the
explanation that God's goodness made him desire to create
the good, while his wisdom showed him the best possible
(G. VI. 167).

120. The question of sin is one which is very inconvenient
for Leibniz's theory of volition. Virtue, he says, is an unchangeable disposition to do what we believe to be good.
Since our will is not led to pursue anything, except as the
understanding presents it as good, we shall always act rightly
if we always judge rightly (G. VII. 92). We pursue the greatest
good we perceive, but our thoughts are for the most part *surd*,
i.e. mere empty symbols; and such knowledge cannot move us
[G. V. 171 (N. E. 191)]. And similarly vice is not the force of
action, but an impediment to it, such as ignorance (G. II. 317).
In fact, original sin and *materia prima* are almost indis-
tinguishable. From this basis he sets about manufacturing
immorality. It is evident that, had he been consistent, he
would have said boldly, all sin is due wholly to ignorance.
Instead of this, what he does say is that we must make a
rule to follow reason, though perceived only by surd thoughts
[G. V. 173 (N. E. 193)] ; that it depends upon us to take pre-
cautions against surprises by a firm determination to reflect,
and only to act, in certain junctures, after having thoroughly

contrariwise deem a thing good because we have an endeavour, will, appetite,
or desire for it." Cf. also *ib.* Prop. XXXIX. Schol. It seems probable that
Leibniz was confused in his own mind as regards this alternative.

deliberated (G. IV. 454); that the chief rule of life is, always to do, not what the passions (*Bewegungen*), but what the understanding indicates as the most useful, and when we have done it, to account ourselves happy however it turns out (G. VII. 99). All these remarks are discreditable subterfuges to conceal the fact that *all* sin, for Leibniz, is original sin, the inherent finitude of any created monad, the confusedness of its perceptions of the good, whence it is led, in honest and unavoidable delusion, to pursue the worse in place of the better. We cannot make a rule to follow reason, unless we perceive that this rule is good; and if we do perceive this, we certainly shall make the rule. His determinism has gone too far for morality and immorality, though it in no way interferes with goodness and badness.

121. (3) This brings me to the nature and meaning of good and evil themselves in Leibniz. He distinguishes three kinds of good and evil, metaphysical, moral and physical. The theory of metaphysical good and evil is clear and consistent, and harmonizes with the rest of his system; but there is no obvious ethical meaning in it. The other two seem less fundamental, and are sometimes treated as mere consequences of metaphysical good and evil. Thus Leibniz's Ethics, like many other ethical systems, suffers from non-existence. Something other than good is taken as fundamental, and the deductions from this are taken as having an ethical import[1].

"Evil," we are told, "may be taken metaphysically, physically, and morally. Metaphysical evil consists in simple imperfection, physical evil in suffering, and moral evil in sin. Now although physical and moral evil are not necessary, it is enough that, in virtue of the eternal truths, they are possible. And as this immense region of Truths contains all possibilities[2], there

---

[1] The theory of metaphysical good and evil was derived from Spinoza, and was earlier than the rest of Leibniz's Ethics. It was capable of purely logical development, and did not involve the appeal to final causes which, after 1680, Leibniz perpetually supported by an allusion to Plato's *Phaedo* (*v.* Stein, *op. cit.* p. 118 ff.). The clearest statement of the principle of metaphysical perfection occurs in an undated paper (G. VII. 194—7), written probably about the year 1677 (*v.* G. VII. 41—2), though agreeing exactly in this respect with *The ultimate Origination of things, e.g.* G. VII. 303 (L. 340; D. 101). See Appendix, § 121.

[2] This passage proves, what might otherwise be doubtful, that Leibniz realized that propositions about *possible* contingents are necessary. See p. 26 *supra*.

must be an infinity of possible worlds, evil must enter into several of them, and even the best of all must contain evil; this is what has determined God to permit evil" (G. VI. 115). This gives Leibniz's solution of the problem of evil, and it is plain that metaphysical evil is the source of the whole. The following passage leaves this beyond doubt. "We ask first, whence comes evil? If God is, whence the evil? if he is not, whence the good? The ancients attributed the cause of evil to matter, which they believed increate and independent of God; but we, who derive all things from God, where shall we find the source of evil? The answer is, that it must be sought in the ideal nature of the creature, inasmuch as this nature is contained among eternal truths, which are in the understanding of God, independently of His will. For we must consider that there is an *original imperfection in the creature*, anterior to sin, because the creature is essentially limited; whence it comes that the creature cannot know everything, and can be mistaken and commit other faults" (G. VI. 114—5). And hence Leibniz rejects Des Cartes' principle, that errors depend more on the will than on the intellect [G. IV. 361 (D. 52)].

122. Thus metaphysical evil, or limitation — though Leibniz hesitates to declare this openly—is the source of sin and pain. And this is sufficiently evident. For if we always judged rightly, we should always act rightly; but our misjudgment comes from confused perception, or *materia prima*, or limitation. And pain accompanies passage to a lower perfection, which results from wrong action. Thus physical and moral evil both depend upon metaphysical evil, *i.e.* upon imperfection or limitation. Leibniz does not usually speak of the opposite of this as metaphysical good, but as metaphysical perfection. Many of his arguments, however, involve the assumption that metaphysical perfection is good, as when he argues against a vacuum[1], or when he urges that "among the infinite combinations of possibles and possible series, that one exists by which most of essence or of possibility is brought into existence[2]." The same view seems implied in a passage

[1] *E.g.* G. VII. 377 (D. 253); but contrast G. II. 475.
[2] G. VII. 303 (D. 101; L. 340). See also the preceding sentence.

which incidentally defines metaphysical perfection. "As possibility," he says, "is the principle of essence, so perfection, or the degree of essence (by which as many things as possible are compossible), is the principle of existence." And in the preceding sentence he has used imperfection and moral absurdity as synonyms [G. VII. 304 (D. 103; L. 342)]. And on the next page, where he endeavours to distinguish metaphysical and moral perfection, he only succeeds in making the latter a species of the former. "And in order," he explains, "that no one should think that we here confound moral perfection, or goodness, with metaphysical perfection, or greatness, and should admit the latter while denying the former, it must be known that it follows from what has been said that the world is the most perfect, not only physically, or, if you prefer it, metaphysically, because that series of things has been produced in which the most reality is actualized, but also morally, because, in truth, moral perfection is physical perfection for minds themselves" [G. VII. 306 (D. 104; L. 345)]. That is to say, moral perfection is right action, and this depends upon physical perfection for minds, *i.e.* upon clear perception[1].

On the relation of metaphysical and moral perfection, Leibniz can with difficulty be cleared of dishonesty. He uses the dependance of the latter on the former to solve the problem of evil, and to show that evil is a mere limitation. This last is essential, as we saw in the preceding chapter, to his proof of God's goodness, and to his whole connection of evil with *materia prima* and finitude. But he endeavours to make moral evil independent, as soon as he thinks of sin, punishment, and responsibility, of Heaven and Hell, and the whole machinery of Christian moralists. If anything is to be made of his Ethics, we must boldly accept the supremacy of metaphysical perfection and imperfection, and draw the consequences.

Metaphysical perfection is only the quantity of essence [G. VII. 303 (D. 101; L. 340)], or the magnitude of positive

---

[1] Cf. also the following passage (G. III. 32): "Metaphysical good and evil is perfection or imperfection in the universe, but is specially understood of those good and evil things which happen to creatures that are unintelligent, or so to speak unintelligent."

reality [G. VI. 613 (D. 224; L. 240)]. This means the possession of all possible simple predicates in the highest possible degree. Leibniz asserts, against Spinoza, that one thing may have more reality than another by merely having more of one attribute, just as well as by having more attributes. For instance, he says, a circle has more extension than the inscribed square [G. I. 144 (D. 17)]. But in another place he asserts that things not capable of a highest degree, such as numbers and figures, are not perfections (G. IV. 427). As he also asserts that God is infinite, while the Devil is finite, that good advances *ad infinitum*, while evil has its bounds [G. VI. 378 (D. 196)], numbers and figures are evidently excluded because they are not true predicates, and because, as we saw in discussing the continuum, infinite *number* is self-contradictory, though the actual infinite is permissible. Thus metaphysical perfection consists in having as many predicates as possible in as high a degree as possible, and no true predicates are excluded from this definition[1].

From this it follows, of course, that imperfection is something merely negative, namely, the mere absence of perfection. Thus monads differ from God only as less and more; they have the same perfections as God has, but in a lower degree (G. II. 125)[2]. The Devil, on this view, should be the lowest of bare monads—a view which theologians would scarcely accept, since they always suppose him capable of knowledge. There is one passage where Leibniz endeavours directly to connect perfection with good. "It being once posited," he says, "that being is better than not-being, or that there is a reason why something should be rather than nothing, or that we must pass from possibility to actuality, it follows that, even in the absence of every other determination, the quantity of existence is as great as possible" [G. VII. 304 (D. 102; L. 341)]. Thus he seems to admit that goodness *means* something different from quantity of existence, and to regard the connection of the two as significant.

---

[1] Cf. also G. V. 15 (D. 95; N. E. 15).

[2] Cf. Spinoza, *Ethics*, Part II. Prop. XLIX. Scholium: "We are partakers of the Divine Nature in proportion as our actions become more and more perfect, and we more and more understand God." Also *Monadology*, § 42.

123. The Ethics to which this view leads is a common one. Goodness and Reality are held to go hand in hand, if not to be synonymous[1]. Hence it easily follows that Reality is good; and this consequence is, so far as I can discover, the sole recommendation of such an Ethics. For Leibniz especially, who admits the existence of evil [G. VI. 376 (D. 194)], such a view is absurd. For if evil be a mere limitation, all that exists is good in different degrees, and never evil in any degree at all. If any existent, such as pain, be pronounced evil, it follows that evil is a positive predicate, like good[2]. Hence it will be included in metaphysical perfection. The doctrine of analytic judgments must have contributed to the view that evil is a mere negation. For it is obvious that good and bad are incompatible predicates, and if both are positive, this is a synthetic judgment. Hence evil was regarded as the mere negation of good, though it would have been equally logical to regard good as the mere negation of evil. When once it is recognized that evil is a positive predicate, the whole privative theory of evil falls, and with it the connection of metaphysical and ethical perfection, as also the definition of God as having all positive predicates.

124. There remains one minor inconsistency which must be noticed. Leibniz speaks often as if final causes had exclusive reference to spirits [G. IV. 480 (D. 73; L. 304)], but at other times definitely denies this (e.g. G. VI. 168). He seems to hold that only spirits, among monads, are ends in themselves; other ends are not individual monads, but metaphysical good, the order and beauty of nature. The first principle of the physical world, he says, is to give it as much perfection as possible, and of the moral world, or City of God, to give it the greatest possible felicity (G. IV. 462). This leads to a harmony between the kingdoms of Nature and of Grace, between God as Architect and God as Monarch (G. VI. 605 (D. 215; L. 421)]. In the first, he seeks only order and metaphysical

---

[1] Cf. Spinoza, *Ethics*, Part II. Def. VI.: "By reality and perfection I understand the same thing."

[2] Even in 1677, when Leibniz was as near as at any time to Spinozism, he urges against a Cartesian that "both pleasure and pain are something positive" (G. I. 214). Cf. Stein, *op. cit.* pp. 90, 91.

perfection; in the second, he seeks the happiness of spirits. But so well is the world contrived, that the two ends lead to the same series of events, and in this again we have a pre-established harmony.

In Leibniz's philosophy everything, from the Law of Sufficient Reason onwards, depends, through the introduction of final causes, upon Ethics. But Ethics, being a subject on which theology is very definite, could not be dealt with by Leibniz in a free spirit. The Ethics to which he was entitled was very similar to Spinoza's; it had the same fallacies, and similar consequences. But being the champion of orthodoxy against the decried atheist, Leibniz shrank from the consequences of his views, and took refuge in the perpetual iteration of edifying phrases. The whole tendency of his temperament, as of his philosophy, was to exalt enlightenment, education, and learning, at the expense of ignorant good intentions. This tendency might have found a logical expression in his Ethics. But he preferred to support Sin and Hell, and to remain, in what concerned the Church, the champion of ignorance and obscurantism. This is the reason why the best parts of his philosophy are the most abstract, and the worst those which most nearly concern human life.

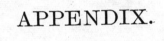

APPENDIX.

EXTRACTS FROM LEIBNIZ

CLASSIFIED ACCORDING TO SUBJECTS.

II. § 8. *Outline of Leibniz's logical argument.*

G. II. 46 (1686). In consulting the notion which I have of every true proposition, I find that every predicate, necessary or contingent, past, present, or future, is comprised in the notion of the subject, and I ask no more.......The proposition in question is of great importance, and deserves to be well established, for it follows that every soul is as a world apart, independent of everything else except God; that it is not only immortal and so to speak impassible, but that it keeps in its substance traces of all that happens to it. It follows also in what consists the intercourse of substances, and particularly the union of soul and body. This intercourse does not happen according to the ordinary hypothesis of the physical influence of one on the other, for each present state of a substance comes to it spontaneously, and is only a consequence of its previous state. It does not happen either according to the hypothesis of occasional causes,......but it happens according to the hypothesis of concomitance, which appears to me demonstrative. That is to say, each substance expresses the whole sequence of the universe according to the view or respect which is proper to it, whence it happens that they perfectly agree together.

II. § 10. *Are all propositions reducible to the subject-predicate form?*

G. II. 240. There is no denomination so extrinsic as not to have an intrinsic one for its foundation.

G. II. 250. Things which differ in place must express their place, *i.e.* the surrounding things, and thus be distinguished not only by place, or by a mere extrinsic denomination, as such things are commonly conceived.

G. V. 129 (N. E. 144). In my view, relation is more general than comparison. For relations are either of comparison or concurrence (*concours*). The former concern agreement (*convenance*) or disagreement (I take these terms in a less wide sense), which comprehends resemblance, equality, inequality, etc. The second class involve some connection, as of cause and effect, whole and parts, situation and order, etc.

G. V. 210 (N. E. 235). Relations and orders partake of the nature of rational entities (*ont quelque chose de l'être de raison*), although they have their foundation in things; for it may be said that their reality, like that of eternal truths and of possibilities, comes from the supreme reason.

G. V. 377 (N. E. 451). It is better to place truths in the relation between the objects of ideas, which causes one to be comprised or not comprised in the other.

G. V. 378 (N. E. 452). Let us be content to seek truth in the correspondence of the propositions, which are in the mind, with the things concerned.

G. II. 233. For my part, I do not think it possible that there should be an A and a B having no common predicate. It does not follow, however, if two predicates concurring to form the concept of C are separable, that there is not some one concept of C. *E.g.* a square is an equilateral rectangle, but the rectangle can be separated from the equilateral..., and the equilateral from the rectangle..., and yet a square is one figure and has one concept.

G. II. 486. You will not, I believe, admit an accident which is in two subjects at once. Thus I hold, as regards relations, that paternity in David is one thing, and filiation in Solomon is another, but the relation common to both is a merely mental thing, of which the modifications of singulars are the foundation.

II. § 11. *Analytic and synthetic propositions.*

G. V. 92 (N. E. 99). Far from approving the acceptance of doubtful principles, I would have people seek even the demonstration of the axioms of Euclid.... And when I am asked the means of knowing and examining innate principles, I reply......that, except instincts whose reason is unknown, we must try to reduce them to first principles, *i.e.* to axioms which are identical or immediate by means of definitions, which are nothing but a distinct exposition of ideas.

G. V. 342 (N. E. 403). It is not the figures which make the proof with geometers...It is the universal propositions, *i.e.* the definitions, the axioms, and the theorems already proved, which make the reasoning, and would maintain it even if there were no figure.

G. V. 343 (N. E. 404). The primitive truths, which are known by intuition, are, like the derivative, of two kinds. They are among the truths of reason or the truths of fact. Truths of reason are necessary, and those of fact are contingent. The primitive truths of reason are those which I call by the general name of *identicals*, because it seems that they only repeat the same thing, without teaching us anything. Those which are affirmative are such as the following : *everything is what it is*, and in as many examples as we may desire, A is A, B is B.......The equilateral rectangle is a rectangle.......If the regular four-sided figure is an equilateral rectangle, this figure is a rectangle.......If A is not-B, it follows that A is not-B.......I come now to the *negative* identicals, which depend either upon the principle of contradiction or upon that of disparates. The principle of contradiction is in general : A proposition is either true or false.

G. V. 347 (N. E. 410). As for the proposition that three is equal to two and one,...it is only the definition of the term *three*.... It is true there is in this a hidden enunciation,...namely, that these ideas [of numbers] are possible ; and this is here known intuitively, so that we may say intuitive knowledge is contained in definitions when their possibility is immediately evident.

G. VI. 323. The triple number of dimensions is determined [in matter], not by the reason of the best, but by a geometrical necessity ; it is because geometers have been able to show that there are only three mutually perpendicular straight lines which can intersect in the same point. Nothing could be chosen more appropriate for showing the difference there is between moral necessity, which governs the choice of the sage, and the brute necessity of Strato and the Spinozists,...than to cause people to consider the difference between the reason of the laws of motion, and the reason of the triple number of dimensions : the first consisting in the choice of the best, the second in a geometric and blind necessity.

G. IV. 357 (D. 48). The first of the truths of reason is the principle of contradiction, or, what comes to the same thing, that of identity.

G. VI. 612 (D. 223 ; L. 236). Truths of reasoning are necessary and their opposite is impossible : truths of fact are contingent and their opposite is possible. When a truth is necessary, its reason can be found by analysis, resolving it into simpler ideas and truths, until we come to those that are primary. ....Primary principles...cannot be proved, and indeed have no need of proof; and these are identical enunciations, whose opposite involves an express contradiction.

G. VII. 355 (D. 239). The great foundation of mathematics is the principle of contradiction. ....And this principle alone suffices for proving all Arithmetic and all Geometry, *i.e.* all mathematical principles. But in order to proceed from mathematics to natural philosophy another principle is requisite... : I mean the principle of a sufficient reason.

G. III. 400 (D. 170). A truth is necessary when the opposite implies contradiction; and when it is not necessary it is called contingent. That God exists, that all right angles are equal to each other, are necessary truths; but it is a contingent truth that I exist, or that there are bodies which show an actual right angle.

G. I. 384. In order to be assured that what I conclude from a definition is true, I must know that this notion is possible. For if it implies a contradiction, we may at the same time draw opposite conclusions from it. ...This is why our ideas involve a judgment.

G. V. 21 (N. E. 21). Ideas and truths can be divided into such as are primitive and such as are derivative; the knowledge of those that are primitive does not need to be formed, but only to be distinguished.

G. III. 443. Definitions are not arbitrary, as Hobbes believed, and we cannot form ideas as we like, though it seems that the Cartesians are of this opinion. For it is necessary that these ideas which we undertake to form should be veritable, *i.e.* possible, and that the ingredients which we put into them should be compatible *inter se*.

III. § 13.   *The range of contingent judgments in Leibniz.*

G. V. 428 (N. E. 515). As for the eternal truths, it is to be observed that at bottom they are all hypothetical, and say in fact: Such a thing being posited, such another thing is.

G. III. 400 (D. 171). Although all the facts of the universe are now certain in relation to God, or (what comes to the same thing) determined in themselves and even interconnected, it does not follow that their connection is always truly necessary, *i.e.* that the truth, which pronounces that one fact follows from another, is necessary. And this must be especially applied to voluntary actions.

G. VI. 123. Philosophers agree now-a-days that the truth of future contingents is determined, *i.e.* that future contingents are future, or that they will be. ...Thus the contingent, though future, is none the less contingent ; and determination, which would be called certainty if it were known, is not incompatible with contingency.

G. II. 39 (1686). The notion of a species involves only eternal or necessary truths, but the notion of an individual involves, *sub ratione possibilitatis*, what is of fact, or related to the existence of things and to time, and consequently depends upon certain free decrees of God considered as possible ; for truths of fact or of existence depend upon the decrees of God.

G. II. 40 (1686). I believe there are only a few free primitive decrees, which regulate the consequences of things, which, joined to the free decree creating Adam, decide the result.

G. IV. 437 (1686). Connection or consecution is of two sorts : the one is absolutely necessary, so that its contrary implies contradiction, and this deduction occurs in eternal truths, such as are those of geometry ; the other is only necessary *ex hypothesi*, and so to speak by accident, and it is contingent in itself, when the contrary does not imply contradiction.

G. III. 54 (D. 35). The true Physics must really be derived from the source of the Divine perfections....Far from excluding final causes, and the consideration of a Being acting with wisdom, it is hence that everything in Physics must be deduced.

G. III. 645. [Dynamics] is to a great extent the foundation of my system ; for we there learn the difference between truths whose necessity is brute and geometric, and truths which have their source in fitness and final causes.

G. VI. 319. The laws of motion which actually occur in nature, and are verified by experiments, are not in truth absolutely demonstrable, as a geometrical proposition would be : but also it is not necessary that they should be so. They do not spring entirely from the principle of necessity, but they spring from the principle of perfection and order ; they are an effect of the choice and wisdom of God.

III. § 14. *Meaning of the principle of sufficient reason.*

G. VII. 309. There are two first principles of all reasonings, the principle of contradiction...and the principle that a reason must be given, *i.e.* that every true proposition, which is not known *per se*, has an à *priori* proof, or that a reason can be given for every truth, or, as is commonly said, that nothing happens without a cause. Arithmetic and Geometry do not need this principle, but Physics and Mechanics do, and Archimedes employed it. [In a marginal note Leibniz remarks :] The true cause, why certain things exist rather than others, is to be derived from the free decrees of the divine will, the first of which is, to will to do all things in the best possible way.

G. VII. 374 (D. 250). When two things which cannot both be together, are equally good ; and neither in themselves, nor by their combination with other things, has the one any advantage over the other ; God will produce neither of them.

G. IV. 438 (1686). This demonstration of this predicate of Caesar [that he resolved to cross the Rubicon] is not as absolute as those of numbers or of Geometry, but presupposes the series of things which God has chosen freely, and which is founded on the first free decree of God, namely, to do always what is most perfect, and on the decree which God has made (in consequence of the first), in regard to human nature, which is that man will always do (though freely) what appears best. Now every truth which is founded on decrees of this kind is contingent, although it is certain. ...All contingent propositions have reasons for being as they are rather than otherwise, or (what is the same thing) they have à *priori* proofs of their truth, which render them certain, and show that the connection of subject and predicate in these propositions has its foundation in the nature of the one and the other ; but they do not have demonstrations of necessity, since these reasons are only founded on the principle of contingency, or of the existence of things, *i.e.* on what is or appears the best among several equally possible things.

G. II. 40 (1686). As there are an infinity of possible worlds, there are also an infinity of laws, some proper to one, others to another, and each possible individual of any world contains in its notion the laws of its world.

G. VII. 199. In demonstration I use two principles, of which one is that what implies contradiction is false, the other is that a reason can be given for every truth (which is not identical or immediate), *i.e.* that the notion of the predicate is always expressly or implicitly contained in the notion of its subject, and that this holds good no less in extrinsic than in intrinsic denominations, no less in contingent than in necessary truths.

III. § 15. *Its relation to the law of contradiction.*

G. VII. 419 (D. 285). Is this [the principle of sufficient reason] a principle that wants to be *proved* ?

G. VII. 364 (D. 244). It appears from what I have said, that my axiom has not been well understood; and that the author [Clarke] denies it, though he seems to grant it. *'Tis true*, says he, *that there is nothing without a sufficient reason*...but he adds, that *this sufficient reason* is often *the simple or mere will of God*....But this is plainly maintaining that God wills something, without any sufficient reason for his will : against the axiom, or general rule of whatever happens. This is falling back into the loose indifference, which I have confuted at large, and showed to be absolutely chimerical, even in creatures, and contrary to the wisdom of God, as if he could operate without acting by reason.

G. II. 56 (1686). If we were absolutely to reject pure possibles, we should destroy contingency and liberty ; for if there were nothing possible but what God actually creates, what God creates would be necessary, and if God wished to create something, he could only create that, without liberty of choice.

G. II. 423. When any one has chosen in one way, it would not imply a contradiction if he had chosen otherwise, because the determining reasons do not necessitate (the action).

G. II. 181. I think you will concede that not everything possible exists....But when this is admitted, it follows that it is not from absolute necessity, but from some other reason (as good, order, perfection) that some possibles obtain existence rather than others.

G. II. 49 (1686). Notions of individual substances, which are complete and capable of wholly distinguishing their subject, and involve consequently contingent truths or truths of fact, and individual circumstances of time, place, etc., must also involve in their notion, taken as possible, the free decrees of God, also taken as possible, because these free decrees are the principal sources of existents or facts ; whereas essences are in the Divine understanding before the consideration of the will.

G. IV. 344. In maintaining that the eternal truths of geometry and morals, and consequently also the rules of justice, goodness, and beauty, are the effect of a free or arbitrary choice of the will of God, it seems that he is deprived of his wisdom and justice, or rather of his understanding and will, having left only a certain unmeasured power from which all emanates, which deserves rather the name of nature than that of God ; for how is it possible that his understanding (whose object is the truths of the ideas contained in his essence) can depend upon his will? And how can he have a will which has the idea of the good, not for its object, but for its effect?

G. II. 424. In my opinion, if there were no best possible series, God would have certainly created nothing, since he cannot act without a reason, or prefer the less perfect to the more perfect.

## IV. § 16.	*Cartesian and Spinozistic views on substance.*

G. VI. 581. [Dialogue between Philarète (Leibniz) and Ariste (Malebranche).] *Ariste.* All that can be conceived alone, and without thinking of anything else, or without our idea of it representing something else, or what can be conceived alone as existing independently of anything else, is a *substance*. ...

G. VI. 582. *Philarète.* This definition of substance is not free from difficulties. At bottom there is nothing but God that can be conceived as independent of other things. Shall we say then, with a certain innovator who is but too well known, that God is the only substance, of whom creatures are mere modifications? If you restrict your definition, by adding that substance is what can be conceived independently of every other creature, we shall perhaps find things which, without being substances, have as much independence as extension. For example, the force of action, life, antitypia, are something at once essential and primitive, and we can conceive them independently of other notions, and even of their subjects, by means of abstractions. On the contrary, subjects are conceived by means of such attributes. ...

Ariste. ...Let us say that the definition must be only understood of concretes ; thus substance will be a concrete independent of every other created concrete.

G. VI. 585. *Philarète.* ...There is nothing but monads, *i.e.* simple or indivisible substances, which are truly independent of every other created concrete thing. [Contrast G. IV. 364, quoted in Appendix, IV. § 17.]

G. II. 249. I do not at all approve the doctrine of attributes which people form now-a-days, according to which some one simple absolute predicate, which they call an attribute, constitutes a substance; for I find among notions no predicates wholly absolute, or not involving connection with others. Certainly thought and extension, which are commonly alleged as examples, are nothing less than such attributes, as I have often shown. Nor is the predicate, unless taken in the concrete, identical with the subject; and thus a mind coincides (though not formally) with the thinker, but not with thought. For it belongs to the subject to involve, besides the present, future and past thoughts also.

IV. § 17. *The meaning of substance in Leibniz.*

G. II. 12 (1686). Since the individual notion of each person involves, once for all, what will happen to him for ever, we see here the *à priori* proofs or reasons of the truth of each event, or why one has happened rather than the other. But these truths, though certain, are none the less contingent, being founded on the free will of God and of creatures. It is true that their choice always has reasons, but they incline without necessitating.

G. II. 37 (1686). Mons. Arnaud finds strange what it seems that I maintain, namely, that all human events follow with hypothetical necessity from the sole supposition that God chose to create Adam; to which I have two answers to give, the one, that my supposition is not merely that God chose to create an Adam, whose notion was vague and incomplete, but that God chose to create such and such an Adam, sufficiently determined for an individual. And this individual complete notion, according to me, involves relations to the whole series of things....The other reply is, that the consequence, in virtue of which the events follow from the hypothesis, is indeed always certain, but is not always necessary with a metaphysical necessity, as is that which is found in M. Arnaud's example (that God, in resolving to create me, could not fail to create a nature capable of thought), but that often the consequence is only physical, and presupposes certain free decrees of God, as do consequences depending on the laws of motion, or on this principle of morals, that every spirit will pursue what seems to it the best.

G. IV. 432 (1686). It is rather difficult to distinguish the actions of God from those of creatures; for there are some who believe that God does everything, while others imagine that he only preserves the force which he has given to creatures: the sequel will show how both may be said. Now since actions and passions belong properly to individual substances (*actiones sunt suppositorum*), it would be necessary to explain what such a substance is. It is true, indeed, that when several predicates can be attributed to the same subject, and this subject can no longer be attributed to any other, we call it an individual substance; but that is not enough, and such an explanation is only nominal. We must therefore consider what it is to be truly attributed to a certain subject. Now it is certain that every true predication has some foundation in the nature of things, and when a proposition is not identical, *i.e.* when the predicate is not expressly contained in the subject, it must be contained in it virtually, and this is what philosophers call *in-esse*, by saying that the predicate *is in* the subject. Thus the subject-term must always contain the predicate-term, so that one who perfectly understood the notion of the subject would judge also that the predicate belongs to it. This being so, we may say that the nature of an individual substance, or complete being, is to have a notion so completed that it suffices to comprehend, and to render deducible from it, all the predicates of the subject to which this notion is attributed. Thus the quality of king, which belongs to Alexander the Great, abstracting from the subject, is not sufficiently determined for an individual, and does not involve the other qualities of the same subject, nor all that the notion of this Prince contains, whereas God, seeing the individual notion or hecceity of Alexander, sees in it at the same time the foundation and the reason of all the predicates which can truly be attributed to him, as *e.g.* whether he would conquer Darius and Porus, even to knowing *à priori* (and not by experience) whether he died a natural death or by poison, which we can only know by history.

G. II. 54 (1686). There would be several Adams disjunctively possible...whatever finite number of predicates incapable of determining all the rest we may take, but what determines a certain Adam must involve absolutely all his predicates, and it is this complete notion which determines the general into the individual (*rationem generalitatis ad individuum*).

G. V. 96 (N. E. 105). I am of opinion that reflection suffices for finding the idea of substance in ourselves, who are substances.

G. V. 137 (N. E. 154). I believe that the consideration of substance is one of the most important and fruitful points in philosophy.

G. V. 274 (N. E. 316). I am not of your opinion that in this [as regards real and nominal definitions] there is a difference between the ideas of substances and the ideas of predicates, as if the definitions of predicates...were always real and nominal at the same time, while those of substances were nominal only....We have a knowledge of true substances or unities (as God and the soul) as intimate as we have of most of the modes. Moreover there are predicates as little known as the contexture of bodies.

G. IV. 364 (D. 55). I know not whether the definition of substance as that which needs the concurrence of God only for its existence, is appropriate to any created substance known to us, unless interpreted in a somewhat unusual sense. For we need not only other substances, but also, much more, our accidents. Since, therefore, substance and accident mutually require each other, there will be need of other criteria for distinguishing substance from accident, among which this may be one, that a substance, though it does need some accident, yet often has no need of one determinate accident, but when this is taken away, is content with the substitution of another ; whereas an accident does not need merely some substance in general, but also that one of its own in which it once inheres, so as not to change it. There remain, however, other things to be said elsewhere of the nature of substance, which are of greater moment and require a more profound discussion.

G. IV. 469 (D. 69). The notion of substance, which I assign, is so fruitful that from it follow primary truths, even those concerning God and minds and the nature of bodies.

G. VI. 493 (D. 151). Since I conceive that other beings have also the right to say *I*, or that it may be said for them, it is by this means that I conceive what is called substance in general.

G. VI. 350. What does not act, does not deserve the name of substance.

G. II. 45 (1686). In order to judge of the notion of an individual substance, it is well to consult that which I have of myself, as we must consult the specific notion of the sphere to judge of its properties.

G. III. 247. I believe that we have a clear but not a distinct idea of substance, which comes in my opinion from the fact that we have the internal feeling of it in ourselves, who are substances.

G. II. 43 (1686). Let ABC be a line representing a certain time. And let there be a certain individual substance, for example myself, which lasts or subsists during this time. Let us then take first me who subsist during the time AB, and also me who subsist during the time BC. Since then we suppose that it is the same individual substance which endures, or that it is I who subsist during the time AB and am then at Paris, and also I who subsist during the time BC and am then in Germany, there must necessarily be a reason which makes it true to say that we last, *i.e.* that I, who have been in Paris, am now in Germany. For if there were none, we should have just as much right to say that it is another. It is true that my internal experience has convinced me *à posteriori* of this identity, but there must also be an *à priori* reason. Now it is impossible to find any other, except that my attributes of the earlier time and state, as well as my attributes of the later time and state, are predicates of the same subject, *insunt eidem subjecto*. But what is meant by saying that the predicate is in the subject, if not that the notion of the predicate is found in some way contained in the notion of the subject? And since, from the moment that I began to be, it could be truly said of me that this or that would happen to me, we must admit that these predicates were laws contained in the subject, or in the complete notion of me, which makes what is called *I*, which is the foundation of the connection of all my different states, and which God knew perfectly from all eternity. After this, I believe, all doubts must disappear, for in saying that the individual notion of Adam involves all that will ever happen to him, I mean nothing else but what all philosophers mean when they say that *the predicate is in the subject of a true proposition.*

G. II. 76 (1686)   Substantial unity demands a complete, indivisible, and naturally indestructible being, since its notion involves all that is ever to happen to it.

G. II. 77 (1686).   The notion of individual substance in general, which I have given, is as clear as that of truth.

G. II. 457.   For the nature of an accident, it does not suffice that it should be dependent on a substance, for composite substance also depends on simple ones or Monads ; but it must be added that it depends on a substance as its subject, and moreover as its ultimate subject; for an accident may be an affection of another accident, *e.g.* magnitude [may be an affection] of heat or of impetus, so that the impetus is the subject, and its magnitude inheres in it as the abstract of a predicate, when the impetus is said to become great, or so great. But the heat or impetus is in a body as its subject ; and the ultimate subject is always a substance.

G. II. 458.   I do not see how we can distinguish the abstract from the concrete, or from the subject in which it is, or explain intelligibly what it is to be or inhere in a subject, unless by considering the inherent as a mode or state of the subject.

G. II. 271.   If the principle of action were external to all, internal to none, it would be nowhere at all, but we should have to recur, with the occasionalists, to God as the sole agent. Therefore it is, in truth, internal to all simple substances, since there is no reason why it should be in one rather than another; and it consists in the progression of perceptions of each Monad.

IV. § 18. *The meaning of activity.*

G. V. 46 (N. E. 47; L. 369). I maintain that, naturally, a substance cannot be without action, and indeed that there is never a body without motion.

G. V. 100 (N. E. 110). Faculties without some act, in a word the pure powers of the school, are mere fictions, unknown to nature, and obtained only by making abstractions.

G. V. 200 (N. E. 224). If *power* is taken as the source of action, it means something more than an aptitude or facility...for it involves tendency also.... This is why, in this sense, I am accustomed to apply to it the term *entelechy*, which is either *primitive*, and corresponds to the soul taken as something abstract, or *derivative*, such as is conceived in conation, and in vigour and impetuosity.

G. IV. 469 (D. 69). The notion of force or power..., for the explanation of which I have designed the special subject of Dynamics, brings very much light for the understanding of the true notion of substance.

G. IV. 479 (D. 73; L. 302). As all simple substances which have a genuine unity can have a beginning and an end only by miracle, it follows that they can come into being only by creation and come to an end only by annihilation. Thus I was obliged to recognize that (with the exception of the souls which God still intends specially to create) the constitutive forms of substances must have been created with the world and subsist always.

G. II. 264. "That changes happen," you say, "experience teaches; but we are not inquiring what experience teaches, but what follows from the very nature of things." But do you then suppose that I am either able or desirous to prove anything in nature, unless changes are presupposed?

G. IV. 507 (D. 115). Since this past decree [by which God created the world] does not exist at present, it can produce nothing now unless it then left after it some perduring effect, which now

still continues and operates. And he who thinks otherwise re-
nounces, if I judge rightly, all distinct explanation of things, and
will have an equal right to say that anything is the result of anything, if that which is absent in space or time can, without intermediary, operate here and now....But if, on the contrary, the law
decreed by God [at the creation] left some trace of itself impressed
on things; if things were so formed by the mandate as to render
them fit to accomplish the will of the legislator, then it must be
admitted that a certain efficacy, form, or force,...was impressed on
things, whence proceeded the series of phenomena, according to the
prescription of the first command. This indwelling force, however,
may indeed be distinctly conceived, but not explained by images
(*imaginabiliter*); nor indeed ought it to be so explained, any more
than the nature of the soul, for force is one of those things which
are not to be grasped by the imagination, but by the intellect....

G. IV. 508 (D. 117). The very substance of things consists in
the force of action and passion; whence it follows that even durable
things could not be produced at all, unless a force of some perma-
nence can be imprinted upon them by the divine power. In that
case it would follow that no created substance, no soul, would
remain numerically the same; that nothing would be preserved
by God, and consequently that all things would be only certain
passing and evanescent modifications and apparitions, so to speak,
of one permanent divine substance.

G. IV. 509 (D. 117). Another question is whether we must
say that creatures properly and truly act. This question is included
in the first, if we once understand that the nature given to them
does not differ from the force of action and passion.

G. II. 169. The system of things might have been constituted
in innumerable ways, but that which had the strongest reason on
its side prevailed. The activity of substance, however, is rather of
metaphysical necessity, and would have had a place, if I am not
mistaken, in any system whatever.

IV. § 19. *Connection between activity and sufficient reason.*

G. I. 372 (ca. 1676). This variety of thoughts cannot come
from what thinks, since a single thing cannot be the cause of the
changes in itself. For everything remains in the state in which it
is, if there is nothing to change it; and not having been determined
of itself to have certain changes rather than others, we could not

begin attributing any variety to it, without saying something for which there is confessedly no reason, which is absurd.

G. II. 263. From universals follow eternal things, from singulars follow also temporal things, unless you think that temporal things have no cause. "Nor do I see," you [De Volder] say, "how any succession can follow from the nature of a thing regarded in itself." No more it can, if we assume a nature which is not singular. ......But all singular things are successive, or subject to succession. ...Nor is there, for me, anything permanent in them, except the law itself, which involves continued succession, agreeing in singulars with that which is in the universe as a whole.

IV. § 22. *Relation of time to Leibniz's notion of substance.*

G. IV. 582. The essential and the natural are always distinguished. ...Properties are essential and eternal, but modifications may be natural though changing.

G. II. 258. I distinguish between properties, which are perpetual, and modifications, which are transitory. What follows from the nature of a thing may follow perpetually, or for a time. ...From the nature of a body moving in a given straight line, with given velocity, it follows, if nothing extrinsic be assumed, that after a given time has elapsed it will reach a given point in the straight line. But will it therefore reach this point always and perpetually?

V. § 23. *Meaning of the identity of indiscernibles.*

G. VII. 372 (D. 247). Those great principles, of a sufficient reason, and of the identity of indiscernibles, change the state of metaphysics. That science becomes real and demonstrative by means of these principles; whereas before it did generally consist in empty words.

G. V. 100 (N. E. 110). According to the proofs which I believe I possess, every substantial thing, whether soul or body, has its own proper relation to each of the others; and one must always differ from the other by intrinsic denominations.

G. VII. 393 (D. 258). I infer from that principle [of sufficient reason], among other consequences, that there are not in nature two real, absolute beings, indiscernible from each other; because if there were, God and nature would act without reason, in ordering the one otherwise than the other.

G. VII. 407 (D. 273). God...will never choose among indiscernibles.

G. V. 213 (N. E. 238). It is always necessary that, besides the difference of time and place, there should be an internal principle of distinction, and though there be several things of the same species, it is none the less true that there are none perfectly similar : thus, though time and place (*i.e.* relation to the external) help us to distinguish things which by themselves we do not well distinguish, things are none the less distinguishable in themselves. Thus the essence (*le précis*) of identity and diversity consists not in time and place, though it is true that the diversity of things is accompanied by that of time and place, because they bring with them different impressions on the thing.

G. II. 131. Can it be denied that everything (whether genus, species or individual) has a complete notion, according to which it is conceived by God, who conceives everything perfectly—*i.e.* a notion containing or comprehending all that can be said about the thing : and can it be denied that God can form such an individual notion of Adam or Alexander, which comprehends all the attributes, affections, accidents, and generally all the predicates of this subject.

G. II. 249. Things which are different must differ in some way, or have in themselves some assignable diversity ; and it is wonderful that this most manifest axiom has not been employed by men along with so many others.

V. § 25. *Is Leibniz's proof of the principle valid ?*

G. V. 202 (N. E. 225). We know that it is abstractions which give rise, when we wish to scrutinize them, to the greatest number of difficulties,...... of which the thorniest fall at once if we agree to banish abstract beings, and resolve to speak ordinarily only in concretes, admitting no other terms in the demonstrations of science but such as represent substantial subjects. ...When we distinguish two things in substance, the attributes or predicates and the common subject of these predicates, it is no wonder if nothing particular can be conceived in this subject. This is necessary, since we have already separated all the attributes, in which we could conceive some detail. Thus to demand, in this pure subject in general, anything beyond what is required to conceive that it is the same thing (*e.g.* which understands and wills, imagines and reasons), is to demand the impossible, and to contravene our own supposition, which we made in abstracting and conceiving separately the subject and its qualities or accidents.

V. § 26. *Every substance has an infinite number of predicates. Connection of this with contingency and with the identity of indiscernibles.*

G. III. 582. There is a difference between analysis of the necessary and analysis of the contingent : the analysis of the necessary, which is that of essences, going from the posterior by nature to the prior by nature, ends in primitive notions, and it is thus that numbers are resolved into units. But in contingents or existents, this analysis from the subsequent by nature to the prior by nature goes to infinity, without a reduction to primitive elements being ever possible.

G. V. 268 (N. E. 309). Paradoxical as it appears, it is impossible for us to have knowledge of individuals, and to find the means of determining exactly the individuality of any thing, unless we keep it [the thing?] itself ; for all the circumstances may recur ; the smallest differences are insensible to us ; the place and the time, far from determining [things] of themselves, need to be themselves determined by the things they contain. What is most noteworthy in this is, that individuality involves infinity, and only he who is capable of understanding it [infinity] can have knowledge of the principle of individuation of such or such a thing; which comes from the influence (rightly understood) of all the things in the universe on one another. It is true that the matter would be otherwise if there were atoms of Democritus ; but also there would then be no *difference* between two *different* individuals of the same shape and size.

F. de C. 24 (D. 175). Individuals cannot be distinctly conceived. Hence they have no necessary connection with God, but are produced freely.

G. VII. 309. It is essential to discriminate between necessary or eternal truths, and contingent truths or truths of fact ; and these differ from each other almost as rational numbers and surds. For necessary truths can be resolved into such as are identical, as commensurable quantities can be brought to a common measure ; but in contingent truths, as in surd numbers, the resolution proceeds to infinity without ever terminating. And thus the certainty and the perfect reason of contingent truths is known to God only, who embraces the infinite in one intuition. And when this secret is known, the difficulty as to the absolute necessity of all things is removed, and it appears what the difference is between the infallible and the necessary.

G. VII. 200. Any truth which is incapable of analysis, and cannot be proved from its reasons, but takes its ultimate reason and its certainty from the divine mind alone, is not necessary. And such are all those that I call *truths of fact.* And this is the source of contingency, which no one, to my knowledge, has hitherto explained.

V. § 27. *The Law of Continuity : three forms of continuity maintained by Leibniz.*

G. V. 49 (N. E. 50; L. 376). Nothing happens all at once, and it is one of my great maxims, and among the most completely verified, that *nature never makes leaps :* which I called the *Law of Continuity....*I have remarked also that, in virtue of insensible variations, two individual things cannot be perfectly similar, and must always differ more than numerically.

G. V. 455 (N. E. 552). Everything goes by degrees in nature, and nothing by leaps, and this rule as regards changes is part of my law of continuity. But the beauty of nature, which desires distinguished perceptions, demands the appearance of leaps.

G. III. 52 (D. 33). A principle of general order which I have noticed...is of great utility in reasoning....It takes its origin from the infinite, it is absolutely necessary in Geometry, but it succeeds also in Physics, because the sovereign wisdom, which is the source of all things, acts as a perfect geometer, following a harmony to which nothing can be added....It [the principle] may be enunciated thus : " When the difference of two cases can be diminished below every given magnitude in the data or in what is posited, it must also be possible to diminish it below every given magnitude in what is sought or in what results," or, to speak more familiarly, " When the cases (or what is given) continually approach and are finally merged in each other, the consequences or events (or what is sought) must do so too." Which depends again on a still more general principle, namely : " When the data form a series, so do the consequences " (*datis ordinatis etiam quaesita sunt ordinata*).

G. II. 168. No transition happens by a leap....This holds, I think, not only of transitions from place to place, but also of those from form to form, or from state to state. For not only does experience confute all sudden changes, but also I do not think any *à priori* reason can be given against a leap from place to place, which would not militate also against a leap from state to state.

G. II. 182. Assuming that everything is always created by God, nothing prohibits a body, if we depart from the laws of order, from being transcreated by a leap from place to place, so that it jumps in one moment, and then all at once remains at rest for a while. A leap, a hiatus, a vacuum, and rest, are condemned by the same law.

G. II. 193. This hypothesis of leaps cannot be refuted, except by the principle of order, by the help of the supreme reason, which does everything in the most perfect way.

G. V. 473 (N. E. 575). I conceive things unknown or confusedly known only after the manner of those which we know distinctly; which renders philosophy very easy, and I even believe that we must do so... This is why I believe that there is no genius, however sublime, but has an infinity of others above him.

V. § 29. *Possibility and Compossibility.*

G. V. 286 (N. E. 334). I have reasons for believing that not all possible species are compossible in the universe, great as it is, and that this holds not only in respect to the things which exist together at one time, but even in relation to the whole series of things. That is, I believe that there necessarily are species which never have existed and never will exist, not being compatible with that series of creatures which God has chosen....The law of continuity states that Nature leaves no gap in the order which she follows; but not every form or species belongs to every order.

G. III. 573. The Universe is only the collection of a certain kind of compossibles; and the actual Universe is the collection of all existent possibles, *i.e.* of those which form the richest compound. And as there are different combinations of possibles, some better than others, there are many possible Universes, each collection of compossibles making one of them.

V. § 31. *The three kinds of necessity.*

G. III. 400 (D. 170). The whole universe might have been made differently; time, space, and matter being absolutely indifferent to motions and figures; and God has chosen among an infinity of possibles what he judged to be the most suitable. But as soon as he has chosen, it must be admitted that everything is comprised in his choice, and that nothing can be changed, since he foresaw and arranged everything once for all....It is this necessity, which can be attributed now to things in the future, which is called hypothetical or consequential....But though all the facts of the universe are now certain in relation to God,...it does not follow that their connection is always truly necessary, *i.e.* that the truth, which pronounces that one fact follows from another, is necessary.

G. VII. 389 (D. 255). We must distinguish between an absolute and an hypothetical necessity. We must also distinguish between a necessity which takes place because the opposite implies a contradiction (which necessity is called logical, metaphysical, or mathematical), and a necessity which is moral, whereby a wise being chooses the best, and every mind follows the strongest inclination.

VI. § 33. *The existence of the external world has only "moral certainty."*

G. I. 372 (*ca.* 1676). This variety of thoughts cannot come from what thinks, since a thing cannot itself be the cause of its own changes....Therefore there is outside of us some cause of the variety of our thoughts. And since we agree that there are certain subordinate causes of this variety, which nevertheless themselves need causes, we have established particular beings or substances in which we recognize some action, *i.e.* of which we conceive that from their change follows some change in ourselves. And we are marching with great strides towards the construction of what we call matter and body. But it is at this point that you [Foucher] are right in delaying us a little, and renewing the complaints of the ancient Academy. For all our experiences, at bottom, assure us of only two things, namely, that there is a connection between our appearances which gives us the means of successfully predicting future appearances, and that this connection must have a constant cause. But from all this it does not follow, strictly speaking, that matter or bodies exist, but only that there is something which presents well-ordered appearances to us. For if an invisible power took pleasure in making dreams, well connected with our previous life and agreeing with each other, appear to us, should we be able to distinguish them from realities until we had been awakened? Or what prevents the whole course of our life from being a great orderly dream, of which we might be disillusioned in a moment? And I do not see that this Power would for that reason be imperfect, as M. Des Cartes assures, besides that its imperfection does not enter into the question.

G. V. 275 (N. E. 318). God has ideas (of substances) before creating the objects of these ideas, and nothing prevents him from also communicating such ideas to intelligent creatures : there is not even any exact demonstration proving that the objects of our senses, and of the simple ideas which our senses present to us, are outside of us.

G. V. 355 (N. E. 422). I believe the true *criterion* as regards objects of sense is the connection of phenomena, *i.e.* the connection of what happens in different times and places, and in the experience of different men, who are themselves, in this respect, very important phenomena to one another.....But it must be confessed that all this certainty is not of the highest degree.....For it is not impossible, metaphysically speaking, that there should be a dream as connected and lasting as the life of a man; but it is a thing as contrary to reason as would be the fiction of a book produced by chance in throwing the printer's types pell-mell.

G. VII. 320 (N. E. 719). It cannot be absolutely demonstrated, by any argument, that there are bodies, and nothing prevents some well-ordered dreams from being offered to our minds, which would be judged by us to be true. ..Nor is the argument of great weight, which is commonly adduced, that thus God would be a deceiver; undoubtedly no one fails to see how far this is from a demonstration giving metaphysical certainty, since, in asserting something without accurate investigation, we should be deceived not by God, but by our own judgment.

G. V. 205 (N. E. 229). It is very true that the existence of spirit is more certain than that of sensible objects.

G. II. 516. From the reason of things we judge (even without respect to the divine wisdom) that we do not exist alone, since there appears no reason of a privilege in favour of one. Nor will you be able otherwise to convince by reason any one who contends that he alone exists, and that others are merely dreamed by him. But there is a reason for the privilege of existents over non-existents, or why not all possibles exist. Moreover even if no creatures existed except the percipient, the order of perceptions would show the divine wisdom. Thus there is no circle here, although the wisdom of God is also derived à *priori*, and not only from the order of phenomena. For from the mere fact that there are contingents it follows that there is a necessary Being.

VII. § 35. *Various meanings of* matter *and* body.

G. III. 657 (D. 234). *Primary* and pure *matter*, taken without the souls or lives which are united to it, is purely passive; also, properly speaking, it is not a substance, but something incomplete. And *secondary matter* (*e.g.* an organic body) is not a substance, but for another reason, namely, that it is a collection (*amas*) of several substances, like a pond full of fish, or a flock of sheep, and consequently it is what is called *unum per accidens*—in a word, a phenomenon. A true substance (such as an animal) is composed of an immaterial soul and an organic body, and it is the compound of these two which is called *unum per se.*

G. VII. 501 (N. E. 722). *Matter* is what consists in Antitypia, or what resists penetration; and thus bare matter is merely passive. But *body* has, besides matter, active force also. Now *body* is either corporeal substance, or a mass composed of corporeal substances. I call *corporeal substance* what consists in a simple substance or monad (*i.e.* a soul or something analogous to a soul) and an organic body united with it. But *mass* is the aggregate of corporeal substances, as cheese sometimes consists of a concourse of worms.

G. II. 252. I distinguish (1) the primitive entelechy or soul, (2) primary matter or primitive passive power, (3) the monad, completed by these two, (4) mass or secondary matter or the organic machine, to which innumerable subordinate monads concur, (5) the animal, or corporeal substance, which is made into one machine by the dominant monad.

VII. § 36. *Relation of Leibnizian and Cartesian Dynamics.*

G. IV. 497 (D. 88). You know that M. Des Cartes believed that the same quantity of motion is preserved in bodies. It has been shown that he was mistaken in this; but I have shown that it is always true that the same motive force is preserved, for which he had taken the quantity of motion. However the changes which happen in bodies in consequence of modifications of the soul embarrassed him, because they seemed to violate this law. He believed, therefore, that he had found an expedient, which is certainly ingenious, by saying that we must distinguish between motion and direction; and that the soul cannot augment or diminish the moving force, but alters the direction, or determination of the course of the animal spirits, and that it is through this that voluntary motions take place....But it must be known that there is another law of nature, which I have discovered and proved, and which M. Des Cartes did not know: this is that not only the quantity of moving force is conserved, but also the same quantity of direction [momentum] towards whichever part it may be taken in the world.... This law, being as beautiful and general as the other, was also worthy of not being violated: and this is what my system effects, by conserving force and direction, and in a word all the natural laws of bodies, notwithstanding the changes which happen in them in consequence of those of the soul.

G. VI. 540 (D. 164). If people had known, at the time of M. Des Cartes, that new law of nature, which I have proved, which asserts that not only the total force of bodies that have connection with each other is conserved, but also their total direction, he would apparently have come to my System of the pre-established Harmony.

G. IV. 286 (D. 5) (1680). The Physics of M. Des Cartes has a great defect; this is that his rules of motion, or laws of nature, which are intended to be the foundation, are for the most part false. There is proof of this: and his great principle, that the same quantity of motion is conserved in the world, is a mistake. What I say here is recognized by the ablest people in France and England.

VII. § 37. *The essence of matter is not extension.*

G. I. 58 (*ca.* 1672). In natural philosophy I am perhaps the first to have proved thoroughly...that there is a vacuum. [It follows that the essence of matter is not extension.]

G. II. 71 (1686). [Assuming that bodies are substances] it can be inferred that corporeal substance does not consist of extension or divisibility; for it will be admitted that two bodies remote one from another, *e.g.* two triangles, are not really one substance; let us suppose now that they approach so as to make a square; will mere contact make them into one substance? I think not. Now every extended mass can be considered as composed of two or a thousand others; we have merely extension by contact. Thus we shall never find a body of which we can say that it is truly one substance. It will be always an aggregate of many. Or rather it will not be a real being, because the parts which compose it are subject to the same difficulty....But also the general notion of individual substance...proves the same thing. Extension is an attribute which cannot constitute a complete being, no action or change can be derived from it, it expresses merely the present state, but not at all the future or the past, as the notion of a substance should. When two triangles are joined, we cannot from this conclude how the junction came about.

G. III. 97. We cannot conceive that resistance should be a modification of extension.

G. III. 453. Impenetrability is not a consequence of extension; it presupposes something more. Place is extended, but not impenetrable.

G. II. 233. You admit that existence and continuity, which are constituents of the notion of extension, differ formally, and I demand no more; but in truth that of which the notion is formed of different formal concepts, is not primitive. It is one of the primary errors of the Cartesians that they conceived extension as something primitive and absolute, and as what constitutes substance.

G. II. 169. I do not think that extension alone can constitute a substance, since the notion of extension is incomplete; and I hold that extension cannot be conceived *per se*, but is a resolvable and relative notion; for it is resolved into plurality, continuity, and coexistence or the existence of parts at one and the same time. Plurality is also contained in number, continuity also in time and motion, while coexistence is only added in extension.

VII. § 38. *Meaning of* materia prima *in Leibniz's Dynamics.*

G. II. 171. The resistance of matter contains two things, impenetrability or antitypia, and resistance or inertia; and in these, since they are everywhere equal in a body, or proportional to its extension, I place the nature of the passive principle or matter; as, in active force, displaying itself variously in motions, I recognize the primitive entelechy, or so to speak something analogous to a soul, whose nature consists in a perpetual law of its series of changes, which it describes uninterruptedly.

G. II. 170. I observed that Des Cartes in his letters, following the example of Kepler, had recognized inertia everywhere in matter.

This you [de Volder] deduce from the force which anything has of remaining in its (present) state, which force does not differ from its own nature. Thus you judge that the simple concept of extension suffices even for this phenomenon. ...But it is one thing to retain the actual state until there is something which changes it, which is done even by what is in itself indifferent to either, while it is something other and much more that a thing should not be indifferent, but have a force, and as it were an inclination, to retain its state and should resist the cause of change. ...And a world can be imagined, as at least possible, in which matter at rest would obey a cause of motion without any resistance ; but such a world would be a mere chaos.

G. V. 206 (N. E. 231). I believe that perfect fluidity belongs only to *materia prima, i.e.* in abstraction, and as an original quality, like rest; but not to *materia secunda,* such as it actually occurs, invested with its derivative qualities.

G. V. 325 (N. E. 383). It is not so useless as is supposed to reason about *materia prima* in general Physics, and to determine its nature, so as to know whether it is always uniform, whether it has any other property besides impenetrability (as in fact I have shown, after Kepler, that it has also what may be called inertia) etc., though it never occurs quite bare.

G. IV. 393 (N. E. 699). There is in body something passive besides extension, that namely by which a body resists penetration.

G. IV. 395 (N. E. 701). τὸ δυναμικὸν or power in body is twofold, passive and active. Passive force properly constitutes matter or mass, active force constitutes ἐντελέχειαν or form. Passive force is that resistance by which a body resists not only penetration, but also motion, and in virtue of which another body cannot come into its place unless it gives way, while it does not give way except by somewhat retarding the motion of the impelling body, and thus tries to persevere in its former state. ...Thus there are in it two resistances or masses : the first is called antitypia or impenetrability, the second, resistance, or what Kepler calls the natural inertia of bodies.

G. VII. 328. I call antitypia that attribute in virtue of which matter is in space. ...The modification or variety of antitypia consists in the variety of place.

VII. § 39. *Materia secunda.*

G. M. VI. 235 (N. E. 671). There is in corporeal things something besides extension, nay prior to extension, namely the very force of nature everywhere implanted by its Author, which consists, not in the simple faculty with which the schools seem to have been content, but is provided, besides, with a conation or effort which will have its full effect unless impeded by a contrary conation.

G. IV. 470 (D. 70). Corporeal substance never ceases to act, any more than does spiritual substance.

G. M. VI. 237 (N. E. 673). Because of form, every body always acts; and because of matter, every body always endures and resists.

G. IV. 513 (D. 122). Not only is a body at the present moment of its motion in a place commensurate to it, but it has also a conation or effort to change its place, so that the succeeding state follows of itself from the present state by the force of nature; otherwise in the present, and also in any moment, a body A which is in motion would differ in no way from a body B which is at rest.

G. IV. 396 (N. E. 702). Many things compel us to place active force in bodies, especially that experience which shows that there are motions in matter, which, though they are attributable originally to the general cause of things, God, yet are immediately and specially attributable to the force placed by God in things. For it is nothing to say that God in creation gave bodies a law of action, unless he gave them, at the same time, something by which the law was to be observed; otherwise he himself would always have to procure the observation of the law by extraordinary means.

G. III. 60. There is always conserved in the world the same quantity of motor action, *i e.* rightly understood, there is as much motor action in the universe in one hour as in any other hour whatever. But in moments themselves it is the same quantity of force which is conserved. And in fact action is nothing but the exercise of force, and amounts to the product of the force and the time.

G. IV. 510 (D. 119). That bodies are of themselves inert is true if it be rightly understood, to this extent namely, that what is, for some reason, once assumed to be at rest cannot set itself in motion, and does not allow itself without resistance to be set in motion by another body; any more than it can of itself change the degree of velocity or the direction which it once has, or allow it easily and without resistance to be changed by another body. And also it must be confessed that extension, or what is geometrical in body, if taken simply, has nothing in it which can give rise to action and motion; on the contrary, matter rather resists motion by a certain *natural inertia*, as Kepler has well called it, so that it is not indifferent to motion and rest, as is generally supposed, but needs, in order to move, an active force proportional to its size. Wherefore I make the very notion of *materia prima*, or of mass, which is always the same in a body and proportional to its size, consist of this very passive forċe of resistance (involving both impenetrability and something more); and hence I show that entirely different laws of motion follow than if there were in body and in matter itself only impenetrability together with extension ; and that, as there is in matter a natural inertia opposed to motion, so in body, and what is more in every substance, there is a natural constancy opposed to change. But this doctrine does not defend, but rather opposes, those who deny action to things; for just as certain as it is that matter of itself does not begin motion, so certain is it (as is shown by excellent experiments on the motion communicated by a moving body) that a body retains of itself the impetus which it has once acquired, and that it is stable in its levity, or makes an effort to persevere in that very series of changes upon which it has entered. As these activities and entelechies cannot be modifications of primary matter or mass, a thing essentially passive,...it may be hence inferred that there must be found in corporeal substance a first entelechy or πρῶτον δεκτικόν for activity ; *i.e.* a primitive motor force which, joined to extension (or what is purely geometrical) and to mass (or what is purely material) always indeed acts, but nevertheless, in consequence of the meeting of bodies, is variously modified through efforts and impetus. And it is this same substantial principle which is called *soul* in living beings, and *substantial form* in others.

VII. § 41. *Force and absolute motion.*

G. IV. 400 (N. E. 706). If forces are taken away, motion itself has nothing real left in it, for from the mere variation of position we cannot tell where the true motion or cause of variation is.

G. II. 137 (D. 39). As regards Physics, we must understand the nature of force, a thing quite different from motion, which is something more relative.

G. IV. 369 (D. 60). If motion is nothing but change of contact ‾or immediate vicinity, it will follow that we can never determine which thing is moving....Thus if there is nothing in motion but this relative change, it follows that there is **no**

reason in nature for ascribing motion to one thing rather than others. The consequence of which will be, that there is no real motion. Thus in order to say that anything moves, we require not only that it should change its situation relatively to other things, but also that it should contain the cause of change, the force or action.

G. VII. 403 (D. 269). Motion does not depend upon being observed, but it does depend upon being possible to be observed. ...When there is no change that can be observed, there is no change at all....I find nothing in the eighth definition of the *Mathematical Principles of Nature*, nor in the scholium belonging to it, that proves, or can prove, the reality of space in itself. However, I grant there is a difference between an absolute true motion of a body, and a mere relative change of its situation with respect to another body. For when the immediate cause of the motion is in the body, that body is truly in motion.

G. M. II. 184. As for the difference between absolute and relative motion, I believe that if motion, or rather the moving force of bodies, is something real, as it seems we must recognize, it is necessary that it should have a *subject*....You [Huygens] will not deny, I believe, that really each [body in impact] has a certain degree of motion, or if you will, of force, notwithstanding the equivalence of hypotheses. It is true, I derive hence the consequence that there is in bodies something other than Geometry can determine in them. And this is not the least among several reasons which I use to prove that, besides extension and its variations (which are something purely geometrical), we must recognize something superior, which is force. Mr Newton recognizes the equivalence of hypotheses in the case of rectilinear motions; but as regards circular motions, he believes that the effort which revolving bodies make, to recede from the centre or axis of revolution, makes known their absolute motion. But I have reasons which make me believe that nothing breaks the general law of equivalence.

G. II. 91 (1687). What is real in the state called motion proceeds just as much from corporeal substance as thought and will proceed from the mind.

G. II. 115 (1687). A corporeal substance gives itself its own motion, or rather what is real in the motion at each instant, *i.e.* the derivative force, of which it is a consequence; for every present state of a substance is a consequence of its preceding state....If God ever reduces a body to perfect rest, which could only be done by miracle, a new miracle will be required to restore any motion to it.

G. IV. 486 (D. 80; L. 318). As to absolute motion, nothing can determine it mathematically, since all ends in relations, with the result that there is always a perfect equivalence of hypotheses, as in Astronomy....Yet it is reasonable to attribute to bodies real motions, according to the supposition which explains the phenomena in the most intelligible way, for this denomination is in harmony with the notion of activity.

G. V. 370 (N. E. 440). The infinitesimal analysis has given us the means of allying Geometry with Physics.

G. M. VI. 247 (N. E. 684). It must be known, to begin with, that force is indeed something truly real, even in created substances; but space, time and motion are of the nature of rational entities, and are true and real, not of themselves, but in so far as they involve divine attributes—immensity, eternity, operation—or the force of created substances. Hence it follows at once that there is no vacuum in space or time; that motion, moreover, apart from force,... is in truth nothing else than a change of situation, and thus *motion, as far as phenomena are concerned, consists in a mere relation*....It follows also, from the relative nature of motion, that *the action of bodies on each other, or impact, is the same, provided they approach each other with the same velocity*....Meanwhile we speak as the matter requires, for a more suitable and simpler explanation of the phenomena, precisely as...in the theory of the planets we must use the Copernican hypothesis....For although force is something real and absolute, nevertheless motion pertains to the class of relative phenomena, and truth is looked for not so much in phenomena as in causes.

VII. § 42. *Metaphysical grounds for assuming force.*

G. III. 45. There is always a perfect equation between the complete cause and the whole effect....Though this axiom is wholly metaphysical, it is none the less one of the most useful that can be employed in Physics.

G. III. 48. I have shown that force must not be estimated by the compound of velocity and size, but by the future effect. However it seems that force or power is something already real, while the future effect is not so. Whence it follows that we must admit in bodies something different from size and velocity, unless we are willing to refuse to bodies all power of acting.

G. M. VI. 252 (N. E. 689). Since only force, and the effort which arises from it, exists at any moment (for motion never truly exists...), and every effort tends in a straight line, it follows that all motion is rectilinear, or composed of rectilinears.

G. VII. 305 (D. 103; L. 344). Metaphysical laws of cause, power, activity, are present in a wonderful way throughout the whole of nature, and are even superior to the purely geometrical laws of matter.

G. IV. 523. As for motion, what is real in it is force or power, *i.e.* what there is in the present state that brings with it a change for the future. The rest is only phenomena and relations.

VII. § 43. *Dynamical argument for plurality of causal series.*

G. V. 158 (N. E. 176). Though it is not true that a body [in impact] loses as much motion as it gives, it is always true that it loses some motion, and that it loses as much force as it gives.

G. M. VI. 251 (N. E. 688). The passion of every body is spontaneous, or arises from an internal force, though upon occasion of something external.

G. M. VI. 252 (N. E. 689) (1695). The action of bodies is never without reaction, and both are equal to each other and directly contrary.

G. M. VI. 230. This diminution of the total force [in a not perfectly elastic impact]...does not derogate from the inviolable truth of the conservation of the same force in the world. For what is absorbed by the small parts is not absolutely lost to the universe, though it is lost for the total force of the impinging bodies.

VII. § 45. *His grounds against extended atoms.*

G. I. 403. My axiom, that nature never acts by leaps, ...is of the greatest use in Physics; it destroys atoms, intervals of rest [*quietulas*], globes of the second element, and other similar chimeras.

G. M. II. 136. I confess that I have difficulty in understanding the reason of such infrangibility [as that of atoms], and I believe that for this effect we should have to have recourse to a kind of perpetual miracle.

G. M. II. 145. There is no absurdity in giving different degrees of rigidity to different bodies; otherwise we could prove by the same reason that bodies must have a zero or an infinite velocity. ...There are other inconveniences about atoms. For example, they could not be susceptible of the laws of motion, and the force of two equal atoms, which impinged directly with equal velocities, would have to be lost; for it seems that only elasticity makes bodies rebound.

G. M. II. 156. Matter, according to my hypothesis, would be divisible everywhere and more or less easily with a variation which would be insensible in passing from one place to another neighbouring place; whereas, according to the atoms, we make a leap from one extreme to the other, and from a perfect incohesion, which is in the place of contact, we pass to an infinite hardness in all other places. And these leaps are without example in nature.

G. M. II. 157. There is no last little body, and I conceive that a particle of matter, however small, is like a whole world, full of an infinity of still smaller creatures.

VII. § 46. *Against the vacuum.*

G. II. 475. The infinity of the physical continuum, in the hypothesis that there are only monads, does not depend so much on the reason of the best, as on the principle of sufficient reason, because there is no reason for limiting or ending, or for stopping anywhere.

G. V. 52 (N. E. 53; L. 385). We [Locke and Leibniz] seem also to differ as regards matter in this, that the author thinks there must be a vacuum in it for the sake of motion, because he believes that the small parts of matter are rigid. And I admit that if matter were composed of such parts, motion in the *plenum* would be impossible....But this supposition is not by any means granted.... Space must rather be conceived as full of an ultimately fluid matter, susceptible of all divisions, and even subjected actually to divisions and subdivisions *ad infinitum*....Consequently matter has everywhere some degree of rigidity as well as of fluidity.

G. IV. 395 (N. E. 701). Although some bodies appear denser than others, yet this happens because their pores are more filled with matter pertaining to the body, while on the contrary the rarer bodies have the nature of a sponge, so that another subtler matter washes through their pores, which is not reckoned with the body, and neither follows nor awaits its motion.

G. IV. 368 (D. 59). Not a few of those who defend a vacuum hold space to be a substance, nor can they be refuted by Cartesian arguments; there is need of other principles for ending this controversy.

G. VII. 356 (D. 240). The more matter there is, the more God has occasion to exercise his wisdom and power. Which is one reason, among others, why I maintain that there is no vacuum at all.

G. VII. 372 (D. 248). The same reason which shows that extramundane space is imaginary, proves that all empty space is an imaginary thing; for they differ only as greater and less. If space is a property or attribute, it must be the property of some substance. But what substance will that bounded empty space be an affection or property of, which its patrons [Clarke and Newton] suppose to be between two bodies?...Extension must be the affection of something extended. But if that space be empty, it will be an attribute without a subject, an extension without anything extended.

G. VII. 377 (D. 253). All those who maintain a vacuum are more influenced by imagination than by reason. When I was a young man, I also gave in to the notion of a vacuum and atoms; but reason brought me into the right way....I lay it down as a principle, that every perfection, which God could impart to things without derogating from their other perfections, has actually been imparted to them. Now let us fancy a space wholly empty. God could have placed some matter in it, without derogating in any respect from all other things: therefore he has actually placed some matter in that space: therefore there is no space wholly empty: therefore all is full.

G. VII. 396 (D. 261). Absolutely speaking, it appears that God can make the material universe finite in extension; but the contrary appears more agreeable to his wisdom.

VII. § 47. *Against action at a distance.*

G. III. 580. We disapprove the method of those [Newton and his followers] who suppose, like the scholastics formerly, unreasonable qualities, *i.e.* primitive qualities which have no natural reason, explicable by the nature of the subject to which this quality is to belong.... As we maintain that it [attraction] can only happen in an explicable manner, *i.e.* by an impulsion of subtler bodies, we cannot admit that attraction is a primitive quality essential to matter....According to these authors, not only are substances entirely unknown to us,...but it is even impossible for any one to know them ; and God himself, if their nature be such as they say, would know nothing of them.

G. II. 399. If God caused anything to act immediately at a distance, he would by that very fact give it multipresence.

G. II. 407. I reject the natural action of a body at a distance, but not the supernatural.

VII. § 48. *Force as conferring individuality.*

G. II. 116. Bodies, strictly speaking, are not pushed by others when there is an impact, but by their own motion, or by their elasticity (*ressort*), which again is a motion of their parts. Every corporeal mass, great or small, has already in it all the force which it can ever acquire, but the meeting with other bodies only gives its determination, or rather this determination only happens during the time of the meeting.

VII. § 49. *Primitive and derivative force.*

G. II. 262. Derivative force is the actual present state while tending to or pre-involving the following state, as everything present is big with the future. But that which persists, in so far as it involves all that can happen to it, has primitive force, so that primitive force is, as it were, the law of the series, while derivative force is the determination which designates a particular term of the series.

G. M. VI. 238 (N. E. 674). Force is twofold : the one elementary, which I also call *dead*, because motion does not yet exist in it, but only a solicitation to motion...; the other, however, is ordinary force, combined with actual motion, which I call *living*.

G. III. 457. There are two sorts of force in a body, the one primitive, which is essential to it (ἐντελέχεια ἡ πρώτη), and derivative forces, which depend upon other bodies also. And it should be considered that the derivative or accidental force, which one cannot refuse to bodies in motion, must be a modification of the primitive force, as shape is a modification of extension. Accidental forces could not occur in a substance without essential force, for accidents are only modifications or limitations, and cannot contain more perfection or reality than the substance.

G. IV. 396 (N. E. 702). Derivative force is what some call impetus, a conation or tendency, so to speak, to some determinate motion, by which primitive force or the principle of action is modified. I have shown that this is not preserved constant in the same body, but yet, however it be distributed among many, its sum remains constant, and that it differs from motion, whose quantity is not conserved.

G. IV. 533. In the soul, representations of causes are causes of representations of effects.

G. III. 636. As for the inertia of matter, as matter itself is nothing but a phenomenon, though well founded, resulting from monads, the same holds of inertia, which is a property of this phenomenon.

G. II. 92 (1687). Motions being real phenomena rather than beings, one motion as phenomenon is in my mind the immediate consequence or effect of another phenomenon, and similarly in the minds of others, but the state of one substance is not the immediate consequence of the state of another particular substance.

G. III. 623. The laws of motion, being founded in the perceptions of simple substances, come from final causes or causes due to fitness, which are immaterial and in each monad.

G. II. 419. The entelechy acts in matter according to the need of matter, so that the new state of matter is a consequence of the prior state, according to the laws of nature; but the laws of nature obtain their effect through entelechies. But also the present state of the entelechy itself follows from its prior state.

G. V. 196 (N. E. 219). As for motion, it is only a real phenomenon, because matter and mass, to which motion belongs, is not properly speaking a substance. There is, however, an image of action in motion, as there is an image of substance in mass; and in this respect we can say that a body *acts* when there is spontaneity in its change, and *suffers* when it is pushed or impeded by another.

VII. § 50. *Antinomy of dynamical causation.*

G. II. 233. I know not whether it can be said that, when two equal weights simultaneously pull a body, they have no common effect, but each separately has half the [total] effect. For we cannot assign one half of the body which they pull to each weight, but they act as if undivided.

VIII. § 51. *There must be simple substances, since there are compounds.*

G. VI. 598 (D. 209 ; L. 406). A substance is a being, capable of action. It is simple or compound. Simple substance is that which has no parts. Compound substance is a collection of simple substances or monads. ...Compounds or bodies are pluralities; and simple substances, lives, souls, spirits, are unities. And everywhere there must be simple substances, for without simple substances there would not be compound substances; and consequently all nature is full of life.

VIII. § 52. *Extension, as distinguished from space, is Leibniz's starting-point.*

G. VII. 399 (D. 265). Infinite space is not the immensity of God ; finite space is not the extension of bodies : as time is not their duration. Things keep their extension, but they do not always keep their space. Everything has its own extension, its own duration ; but it has not its own time, and does not keep its own space.

G. IV. 394 (N. E. 700). As in time we conceive nothing else than the disposition or series of variations which can happen in it, so by space we understand nothing but the possible disposition of bodies. And so when space is said to be extended, we take this in the same sense as when time is said to endure, or number to be numbered ; for, in truth, time adds nothing to duration, nor space to extension, but as successive variations are in time, so in body those things are diverse which can be simultaneously diffused.

G. V. 115 (N. E. 127). It must not be supposed that there are two extensions, the one abstract, of space, the other concrete, of body, the concrete being such as it is only through the abstract.

G. VI. 585. Extension, when it is the attribute of space, is the continuation or diffusion of situation or locality, as the extension of body is the diffusion of antitypia or materiality.

G. II. 261. You say, we must ask whether there are such unities in body [as mine are], and that, in order to prove these, I advocate entelechies. But on the contrary, I appeal to unities in order to prove the entelechies, although it is also true that, if the entelechies were otherwise proved, there would have to be true and real unities as well.

VIII. § 53. *Extension means repetition.*

F. de C. 28 (D. 176). Extension, or, if you prefer it, primary matter, is nothing but a certain indefinite repetition of things in so far as they are similar to each other or indiscernible. But just as number presupposes numbered things, so extension presupposes things which are repeated, and which have, in addition to common characteristics, others peculiar to themselves. These accidents, peculiar to each one, render actual the limits of size and shape, before only possible.

G. V. 94 (N. E. 102). I believe that the idea of extension is posterior to that of whole and part.

G. II. 510. That extension would remain if monads were removed I hold to be no more true than that numbers would remain if things were removed.

G. IV. 394 (N. E. 700). Since extension is a continuous simultaneous repetition, ...whenever the same nature is simultaneously diffused through many things, as, in gold, ductility or specific gravity or yellowness, in milk whiteness, in body generally resistance or impenetrability, there is said to be extension, although it must be confessed that this continuous diffusion in colour, weight, ductility, and other similar qualities that have a merely specious homogeneity, is only apparent, and does not occur in very small parts ; and thus the extension of resistance alone, which is diffused throughout matter, preserves this name with the rigorous investigator. But it is evident, from these considerations, that extension is not an absolute predicate, but relative to what is extended or diffused, and thus cannot be more separated from the nature of what is diffused than number from what is numbered. ...We now ask : What other nature is there whose diffusion constitutes body? We have already said that matter is constituted by the diffusion of resistance ; but in our opinion there is in body something else besides matter. ...This we say can consist in nothing but ἐν τῷ δυναμικῷ, or in the internal principle of change and persistence.

VIII. § 54. *Hence the essence of a substance cannot be extension, since a substance must be a true unity.*

G. V. 359 (N. E. 428). It is to be observed that matter, taken as a complete being (*i.e.* secondary matter, as opposed to primary, which is something purely passive, and consequently incomplete) is nothing but a collection (*amas*) or what results from it, and that every real collection presupposes simple substances or real unities, and when we consider further what belongs to the nature of these real unities, *i.e.* perception and its consequences, we are transferred, so to speak, into another world, that is, into the intelligible world of substances, whereas before we were only among the phenomena of the senses.

G. II. 269. The notion of extension is relative, or extension is the extension of something, as we say that multitude or duration is the multitude or duration of something. But the nature which is presupposed as diffused, repeated, continued, is what constitutes the physical body, and can only be found in the principle of action and passion, since nothing else is suggested to us by phenomena.

G. II. 135 (D. 38). Body is an aggregate of substances, and is not a substance properly speaking. It is consequently necessary that everywhere in body there should be indivisible substances, ingenerable and incorruptible, having something corresponding to souls.

G. II. 58 (1686). If body is a substance, and not a mere phenomenon like the rainbow, nor a being united by accident or by aggregation like a heap of stones, it cannot consist of extension, and it is necessary to conceive in it something which we call a substantial form, and which corresponds in some way to a soul.

VIII. § 55. *The three kinds of point. Substances not material.*

G. IV. 478 (D. 72; L. 300). At first, when I had freed myself from the yoke of Aristotle, I took to the vacuum and atoms, for that is the view which best satisfies the imagination. But having got over this, I perceived, after much meditation, that it is impossible to find the principles of a real unity in matter alone, or in that which is only passive, since everything in it is nothing but a collection or aggregate of parts *ad infinitum.* Now a multitude can derive its reality only from genuine units, which come from elsewhere, and are quite other than mathematical points, which are only extremities of the extended, and modifications of which it is certain that the continuum cannot be composed. Accordingly, in order to find these real units, I was constrained to have recourse to a real and animated point, so to speak, or to an atom of substance which must contain some kind of form or active principle, so as to make it a complete being. It was then necessary to recall, and, as it were, to rehabilitate the substantial forms, which are so much decried now-a-days, but in a way which rendered them intelligible, and separated the use to which they should be put from the abuse which they have suffered. I found, then, that the nature of substantial forms consists in force, and that from this follows something analogous to feeling and appetite; and that thus they must be conceived after the manner of the notion we have of souls.

G. III. 69. Thought, being the action of one thing on itself, does not occur in shapes and motions, which cannot show the principle of a truly internal action.

G. II. 96. I believe that where there are only beings by aggregation, there will not even be real beings; for every being by aggregation presupposes beings endowed with a veritable unity, because it derives its reality only from that of those of which it is composed, so that it will have none at all if each being of which it is composed is again a being by aggregation. ...I agree that in all corporeal nature there are nothing but machines (which are often animated), but I do not agree that there are only aggregates of substances, and if there are aggregates of substances, there must be true substances from which all these aggregates result.

G. II. 97. What is not truly *one* being (*un* être) is also not truly a *being* (un *être*).

G. II. 370. A point is not a certain part of matter, nor would an infinite number of points collected together make an extension.

G. II. 267. A thing which can be divided into several (already actually existing) is an aggregate of several, and...is not one except mentally, and has no reality but what is borrowed from its constituents. Hence I inferred that there must be in things indivisible unities, because otherwise there will be in things no true unity, and no reality not borrowed. Which is absurd. For where there is no true unity, there is no true multiplicity. And where there is no reality not borrowed, there will never be any reality, since this must in the end belong to some subject....But you [de Volder]... hold that the right conclusion from this is that in the mass of bodies no indivisible unities can be assigned. I, however, think that the contrary is to be concluded, namely that we must recur, in bodily mass, or in constituting corporeal things, to indivisible unities as prime constituents. Unless indeed you hold the right conclusion to be, that bodily masses are not themselves indivisible unities, which I say, but this is not the question. For bodies are always divisible, and even actually subdivided, but not so their constituents....

G. II. 268. From the very fact that the mathematical body cannot be resolved into first constituents, we can certainly infer that it is not real, but something mental, designating nothing but the possibility of parts, and not anything actual....And as a numbering number is not substance without the things numbered, so the mathematical body, or extension, is not substance without what is active and passive, or motion. But in real things, *i.e.* bodies, the parts are not indefinite (as in space, which is a mental thing), but are actually assigned in a certain way, since nature institutes actual divisions and subdivisions according to the varieties of motions, and although these divisions proceed to infinity, yet none the less everything results from certain primary constituents or real unities, but infinite in number. But strictly speaking, matter is not composed of constitutive unities, but results from them, for matter or extended mass is nothing but a phenomenon founded in things, like the rainbow or the parhelion, and all reality belongs only to unities. Therefore phenomena can always be divided into lesser phenomena, which might appear to other subtler animals, and never attain to least phenomena. In fact substantial unities are not parts, but foundations, of phenomena.

G. II. 275. I do not take away body, but I recur to what it is, for I show that corporeal mass, which is supposed to have something besides simple substances, is not substance, but a phenomenon resulting from simple substances, which alone have unity and absolute reality.

IX. § 57. *Difficulties about points.*

G. II. 98. The difficulties concerning the composition of the continuum will never be resolved, so long as extension is considered as making the substance of bodies.

G. II. 77 (1686). There is no exact and precise figure in bodies, on account of the actual subdivision of their parts. So that bodies would, no doubt, be something merely imaginary and apparent, if there were nothing in them but matter and its modifications.

IX. § 58. *Assertion of the actual infinite and denial of infinite number.*

G. I. 403. All magnitudes being infinitely divisible, there is none so small but that we can conceive in it an infinity of divisions, which will never be exhausted. But I do not see what harm comes of this, nor what need there is to exhaust them.

G. V. 144 (N. E. 161). Properly speaking, it is true that there are an infinity of things, *i.e.* that there are always more of them than can be assigned. But there is no infinite number, or line or any other infinite quantity, if these are understood as true wholes, as it is easy to prove....The true infinite exists, strictly speaking, only in the Absolute, which is anterior to all composition, and is not formed by addition of parts.

G. V. 145 (N. E. 163). You [Locke] are mistaken in wishing to imagine an absolute space which is an infinite whole composed of parts; there is no such thing, it is a notion which implies a contradiction, and these infinite wholes, with their opposed infinitesimals, are only in place in the calculations of geometers, just like imaginary roots in Algebra.

G. VI. 629. In spite of my Infinitesimal Calculus, I admit no true infinite number, though I confess that the multitude of things surpasses every finite number, or rather every number.

G. I. 338. Mons. Des Cartes in his reply to the second objections, article two, agrees to the analogy between the most perfect Being and the greatest number, denying that this number implies a contradiction. It is, however, easy to prove it. For the greatest number is the same as the number of all units. But the number of all units is the same as the number of all numbers (for any unit added to the previous ones always makes a new number). But the number of all numbers implies a contradiction, which I show thus: To any number there is a corresponding number equal to its double. Therefore the number of all numbers is not greater than the number of even numbers, *i.e.* the whole is not greater than its part.

G. V. 209 (N. E. 234). The idea of the infinite is not formed by extension of finite ideas.

G. II. 305. To pass from the ideas of Geometry to the realities of Physics, I hold that matter is actually broken into parts less than any given part, or that there is no part which is not actually subdivided into others exercising diverse motions.

G. II. 315. There is an actual infinite in the mode of a distributive whole, not of a collective whole. Thus something can be enunciated concerning all numbers, but not collectively. So it can be said that to every even number corresponds its odd number, and *vice versâ*; but it cannot therefore be accurately said that the multiplicities of odd and even numbers are equal.

G. M. IV. 91. It is not necessary to make mathematical analysis depend upon metaphysical controversies, nor to make sure that there are in nature strictly infinitesimal lines.... This is why, in order to avoid these subtleties, I thought that, to render the reasoning intelligible to everybody, it sufficed in this to explain the infinite by the incomparable, *i.e.* to conceive quantities incomparably greater or smaller than ours.

G. M. IV. 92. If an adversary wished to contradict our enunciation, it follows by our calculus that the error will be less than any error that he can assign.

G. M. IV. 93. It is found that the rules of the finite succeed in the infinite.

IX. § 59. *Continuity in one sense denied by Leibniz.*

G. IV. 394 (N. E. 700). All repetition...is either discrete, as in numbered things where the parts of an aggregate are discriminated; or continuous, where the parts are indeterminate and can be assumed in infinite ways.

G. II. 379. Space, just like time, is a certain order...which embraces not only actuals, but possibles also. Hence it is something indefinite, like every continuum whose parts are not actual, but can be taken arbitrarily, like the parts of unity, or fractions.... Space is something continuous but ideal, mass is discrete, namely an actual multitude, or being by aggregation, but composed of an infinite number of units. In actuals, single terms are prior to aggregates, in ideals the whole is prior to the part. The neglect of this consideration has brought forth the labyrinth of the continuum.

G. II. 475. The mathematical continuum, like numbers, consists of mere possibility; thus infinity is necessary to it from its very notion.

G. II. 278. Matter is not continuous but discrete, and actually infinitely divided, though no assignable part of space is without matter. But space, like time, is something not substantial, but ideal, and consists in possibilities, or in an order of coexistents that is in some way possible. And thus there are no divisions in it but such as are made by the mind, and the part is posterior to the whole. In real things, on the contrary, units are prior to the multitude, and multitudes exist only through units. (The same holds of changes, which are not really continuous.)

G. II. 282. In actuals there is nothing but discrete quantity, namely the multitude of monads or simple substances, which is greater than any number whatever in any aggregate whatever that is sensible or corresponds to phenomena. But continuous quantity is something ideal, which belongs to possibles, and to actuals considered as possibles. For the continuum involves indeterminate parts, while in actuals there is nothing indefinite—indeed in them all divisions which are possible are actual. ... But the science of continua, *i.e.* of possibles, contains eternal truths, which are never violated by actual phenomena, since the difference is always less than any assignable given difference.

G. III. 583. Unity is divisible, but is not resolvable; for the fractions which are parts of unity have less simple notions, because integers (less simple than unity) always enter into the notions of fractions. Several people who have philosophized, in mathematics, about the point and unity, have become confused, for want of distinguishing between resolution into notions and division into parts. Parts are not always simpler than the whole, though they are always less than the whole.

G. IV. 491. Properly speaking, the number $\frac{1}{2}$ in the abstract is a mere ratio, by no means formed by the composition of other fractions, though in numbered things there is found to be equality between two quarters and one half. And we may say as much of the abstract line, composition being only in concretes, or masses of which these abstract lines mark the relations. And it is thus also that mathematical points occur, which also are only modalities, *i.e.* extremities. And as everything is indefinite in the abstract line, we take notice in it of everything possible, as in the fractions of a number, without troubling ourselves concerning the divisions actually made, which designate these points in a different way. But in substantial actual things, the whole is a result or assemblage of simple substances, or of a multiplicity of real units. And it is the confusion of the ideal and the actual which has embroiled everything and produced the labyrinth concerning the composition of the continuum. Those who compose a line of points have sought first elements in ideal things or relations (*rapports*), otherwise than was proper; and those who have found that relations such as number, and space (which comprehends the order or relation of possible coexistent things), cannot be formed of an assemblage of points, have been mistaken in denying, for the most part, the first elements of substantial realities, as if they had no primitive units, or as if there were no simple substances.

G. V. 142 (N. E. 160). This definition, that number is a multiplicity of units, applies only to integers. The precise distinction of ideas, in extension, does not depend upon magnitude: for in order to recognize magnitude distinctly, recourse must be had to integers, or to other numbers known by means of integers, so that it is necessary to go back from continuous to discrete quantity, in order to have a distinct knowledge of magnitude.

IX. § 60. *In number, space and time, the whole is prior to the part.*

G. I. 416 (D. 64). As for indivisibles, when by these are meant mere extremities of a time or a line, we cannot conceive new extremities in them, or actual or potential parts. Thus points are neither large nor small, and no leap is needed to pass them. The continuum, however, though it has such indivisibles everywhere, is not composed of them.

G. III. 591. As regards the comparison between an instant and unity, I add that unity is part of any number greater than unity, but an instant is not properly a part of time.

G. II. 279. Extremities of a line and units of matter do not coincide. Three continuous points in the same straight line cannot be conceived. But two are conceivable: [namely] the extremity of one straight line and the extremity of another, out of which one whole is formed. As, in time, are the two instants, the last of life and the first of death. One unit is not touched by another, but in motion there is a perpetual transcreation, in this way: when a thing is in that condition that, by continuing its changes for an assignable time, there would have to be penetration in the next moment, each point will be in a different place, as the avoidance of penetration and the order of changes demand.

G. M. VII. 18. In either order (of space or of time) [points] are considered nearer or more remote, according as, for the order of comprehension between them, more or fewer are required.

G. II. 515. There is continuous extension whenever points are assumed to be so situated that there are no two between which there is not an intermediate point.

G. II. 300. I agree with you [Des Bosses] that being and one are convertible terms; and that unity is the beginning of numbers, if you are considering ratios (*rationes*) or priority of nature, not if you are considering magnitude, for we have fractions, which are certainly less than unity, to infinity. The continuum is infinitely divisible. And this appears in the straight line, from the mere fact that its part is similar to the whole. Thus when the whole can be divided, so can the part, and similarly any part of the part. Points are not parts of the continuum, but extremities, and there is no more a smallest part of a line than a smallest fraction of unity.

G. II. 304. Being and one are convertible terms, but as there is Being by aggregation, so also there is a unit by aggregation, although this entity and unity is semi-mental. Numbers, unities, fractions, have the nature of relations. And so far they can in some way be called beings. A fraction of unity is no less one being than unity itself. Nor must it be thought that formal unity is an aggregate of fractions, for its notion is simple, applying to divisibles and indivisibles, and there is no fraction of indivisibles.

G. VII. 404 (D. 270). As for the objection [Clarke's] that space and time are quantities, or rather things endowed with quantity, and that situation and order are not so : I answer, that order also has its quantity ; there is that in it which goes before, and that which follows ; there is distance or interval. Relative things have their quantity, as well as absolute ones. For instance, ratios or proportions in mathematics have their quantity, and are measured by logarithms ; and yet they are relations. And therefore, though time and space consist in relations, yet they have their quantity.

IX. § 62. *Summary of the argument from the continuum to monads.*

G. VII. 552. In order to judge by reason whether the soul is material or immaterial, we must conceive what the soul and matter are. Everybody agrees that matter has parts, and is consequently a multiplicity of many substances, as would be a flock of sheep. But since every multiplicity presupposes true unities, it is evident that these unities cannot be matter, otherwise they would in turn be multiplicities, and by no means true and pure unities, such as are finally required to make a multiplicity. Thus the unities are properly substances apart, which are not divisible, nor consequently perishable. For whatever is divisible has parts, which can be distinguished even before their separation. However, since we are concerned with unities of substance, there must be force and perception in these unities themselves, for otherwise there would be no force or perception in all that is formed of them.

IX. § 63. *Since aggregates are phenomenal, there is not really a number of monads.*

G. II. 261. Whatever things are aggregates of many, are not one except for the mind, nor have any other reality than what is borrowed, or what belongs to the things of which they are compounded.

G. II. 517. Aggregates themselves are nothing but phenomena, for everything except the component monads is added by perception alone, from the very fact of their being simultaneously perceived.

G. II. 304. Instead of an infinite number, we ought to say, there are more than any number can express....It is of the essence of a number, a line, or any whole, to be terminated. Hence even if the world were infinite in magnitude, it would not be one whole, nor could God be conceived, with certain of the ancients, as the soul of the world, not only because he is the cause of the world, but also because such a world would not be one body, nor could be regarded as an animal, nor would have, indeed, any but a verbal unity.

X. § 66. *Leibniz's arguments against the reality of space.*

G. V. 100 (N. E. 110). Things which are uniform and contain no variety are never anything but abstractions, like time, space, and the other entities of pure mathematics.

G. VII. 363 (D. 243). These gentlemen [Newton and Clarke] maintain...that space is a real absolute being. But this involves them in great difficulties; for such a being must needs be eternal and infinite. Hence some have believed it to be God himself, or one of his attributes, his immensity. But since space consists of parts, it is not a thing which can belong to God. As for my own opinion, I have said, more than once, that I hold space to be something merely relative, as time is....For space denotes, in terms of possibility, an order of things which exist at the same time, considered as existing together, without inquiring into their particular manner of existing. And when many things are seen together, one perceives that order of things among themselves....If space was an absolute being, there would something happen, for which it would be impossible there should be a sufficient reason. Which is against my Axiom. And I prove it thus. Space is something absolutely uniform; and without the things placed in it, one point of space does not absolutely differ in any respect whatsoever from another point of space. Now from hence it follows (supposing space to be something in itself, besides the order of bodies among themselves), that it is impossible there should be a reason why God, preserving the same situation of bodies among themselves, should have placed them in space after one particular manner, and not otherwise; why everything was not placed the quite contrary way, for instance by changing east into west. But if space is nothing else but that order or relation; and is nothing at all without bodies, but the possibility of placing them; then those two states, the one such as it now is, the other supposed to be the quite contrary way, would not at all differ from one another. Their difference, therefore, is only to be found in our chimerical supposition of the reality of space in itself. But in truth the one would exactly be the same thing as the other, they being absolutely indiscernible; and consequently there is no room to enquire after a reason of the preference of the one to the other.

The case is the same with respect to time....The same argument proves that instants, considered without the things, are nothing at all; and that they consist only in the successive order of things.

G. VII. 372 (D. 247). To suppose two things indiscernible, is to suppose the same thing under two names. And therefore to suppose that the universe could have had at first another position of time and place, than that which it actually had; and yet that all the parts of the universe should have had the same situation among themselves, as that which they actually had; such a supposition, I say, is an impossible fiction.

X. § 67. *Leibniz's theory of position.*

G. II. 277. The essential order of singulars, or relation to time and place, is to be understood of their relations to the things contained in time and space, both near and far, which must be expressed by any singular, so that in it the universe could be read, if the reader were infinitely perspicacious.

G. V. 115 (N. E. 128). Time and place are only kinds of order.

G. II. 347. Position is, without doubt, nothing but a mode of a thing, like priority or posteriority. A mathematical point itself is nothing but a mode, namely an extremity. And thus when two bodies are conceived as touching, so that two mathematical points are joined, they do not make a new position or whole, which would be greater than either part, since the conjunction of two extremities is not greater than one extremity, any more than two perfect darknesses are darker than one.

G. V. 140 (N. E. 157). This vacuum which can be conceived in time indicates, as it does in space, that time and space extend to possibles as well as existents.

G. V. 142 (N. E. 159). If there were a vacuum in space (*e.g.* if a sphere were empty inside) its magnitude could be determined; but if there were a vacuum in time, *i.e.* a duration without changes, it would be impossible to determine its length. Hence it follows that we can refute a man who says that two bodies, between which there is a vacuum, touch...but we cannot refute a man who says that two worlds, of which one is after the other, touch as regards duration, so that one necessarily begins when the other stops.... If space were only a line, and if body were immovable, it would not be possible either to determine the length of the vacuum between two bodies.

G. VII. 400 (D. 265). I will here show how men come to form to themselves the notion of space. They consider that many things exist at once, and they observe in them a certain order of coexistence, according to which the relation of one thing to another is more or less simple. This order is their situation or distance. When it happens that one of those coexistent things changes its relation to a multitude of others, which do not change their relations among themselves; and that another thing, newly come, acquires the same relation to the others, as the former had; we then say it is come into the *place* of the former; and this change we call a motion in that body, wherein is the immediate cause of the change. And though many, or even all the coexistent things should change according to certain known rules of direction and swiftness; yet one may always determine the relation of situation, which every coexistent acquires with respect to every other coexistent; and even that relation which any other coexistent would have to this, or which this would have to any other, if it had not changed, or if it had changed any otherwise. And supposing or feigning that among those coexistents there is a sufficient number of them which have undergone no change; then we may say that those that have such a relation to those fixed coexistents, as others had to them before, have now the same place which those others had. And that which comprehends all those places, is called space. Which shows that, in order to have an idea of place, and consequently of space, it is sufficient to consider these relations, and the rules of their changes, without needing to fancy any absolute reality out of the things whose situation we consider; and, to give a kind of definition : *place* is that, which we say is the same to A and to B, when the relation of the coexistence of B with C, E, F, G, *etc.*, agrees perfectly with the relation of the coexistence, which A had with the same C, E, F, G, *etc.*, supposing there has been no cause of change in C, E, F, G, *etc.* It might be said also, without entering into any farther particularity, that *place* is that, which is the same in different moments to different existent things, when their relations of coexistence with certain other existents, which are supposed to continue fixed from one of those moments to the other, agree entirely together. And fixed existents are those, in which there has been no cause of any change of the order of their coexistence with others; or (which is the same thing) in which there has been no motion. Lastly *space* is that which results from places taken together. And here it may not be amiss to consider the difference between place, and the relation of situation, which is in the body that fills up the place. For the *place* of A and B is the *same*; whereas the relation of A to fixed bodies is not precisely and individually the same as the relation which B (that comes into its place) will have to the same fixed bodies; but these relations agree only. For two different subjects, as A and B, cannot have precisely the *same* individual affection; it being impossible that the same individual accident should be in two subjects, or pass from one subject to another. But the mind, not contented with an agreement, looks for an identity, for something that should be truly the same; and conceives it as being extrinsic to these subjects : and this is what we here call place and space. But this can only be an ideal thing; containing a certain order, wherein the mind conceives the application of relations.

G. II. 271. Unless I am mistaken, the order of singulars is essential to particular parts of space and time, and from these [the singulars] universals are abstracted by the mind.

X. § 68. *The relation of monads to space a fundamental difficulty of monadism.*

G. II. 305. There is no part of matter which does not contain monads.

G. II. 112 (1687). Our body must be affected in some way by

the changes in all others. Now to all motions of our body correspond certain more or less confused perceptions or thoughts of our
soul; hence the soul also will have some thought of all the motions
of the universe.

G. II. 438. Between the appearance of bodies to us and their
appearance to God, there is the same kind of difference as between
a scenograph and an ichnograph. For scenographs are different
according to the situation of the spectator, while the ichnograph, or
geometrical representation, is unique.

G. VI. 608 (D. 218; L. 220). If simple substances did not
differ in their qualities, there would be no means of perceiving any
change in things....Assuming the *plenum*, each place would only
receive, in any motion, the equivalent of what it had had, and one
state of things would be indiscernible from another.

G. V. 24 (N. E. 25). The least impression reaches every body,
and consequently reaches the one whose motions correspond to the
actions of the soul.

X. § 69. *Leibniz's early views on this subject.*

G. I. 52 (1671). My proofs [of immortality, and of the nature
of God and the mind] are based on the difficult doctrine of the
point, the instant, indivisibles, and conation; for just as the actions
of body consist of motion, so the actions of mind consist of
conation, or, so to speak, the minimum or point of motion; while
mind itself consists properly in only a point of space, whereas a
body occupies a place. Which I clearly prove—to speak of it only
popularly—by the fact that the mind must be in the place of
concourse of all the motions which are impressed on us by the
objects of sense; for if I am to conclude that a body presented to
me is gold, I perceive together its lustre, clink, and weight, and
thence conclude that it is gold; so that the mind must be in a
position where all these lines of sight, hearing, and touch meet, and
consequently in a point. If we give the mind a greater place than
a point, it is already a body, and has parts external to each other;
it is therefore not intimately present to itself, and accordingly
cannot reflect on all its parts and actions....But assuming that the
mind does consist in a point, it is indivisible and indestructible....
I almost think that every body (*Leib*), whether of men or animals,
vegetables or minerals, has a kernel of its substance, which is
distinguished from the *caput mortuum*....

G. I. 54. If now this kernel of substance, consisting in a physical point (the proximate instrument, and as it were the vehicle, of the soul, which is constituted in a mathematical point), always remains, it matters little whether all gross matter...is left over.

X. § 70. *His middle views.*

G. IV. 482 (D. 76; L. 311) (1695). Only *atoms of substance*, *i.e.* real units absolutely devoid of parts, are the sources of actions, and the absolute first principles of the composition of things, and, as it were, the ultimate elements in the analysis of substantial things. They might be called *metaphysical points*; they have something of the nature of life and they have a kind of perception, and *mathematical points* are their *points of view* for expressing the universe. But when corporeal substances are contracted, all their organs together make but one *physical point* for us. Thus physical points are only apparently indivisible. Mathematical points are exact, but they are only modalities. None but metaphysical or substantial points (consisting of forms or souls) are exact and real.

G. IV. 484 (D. 78; L. 314) (1695). The organised mass, in which is the point of view of the soul, is more nearly expressed by the soul.

G. IV. 512 (D. 122) (1698). Nothing hinders souls, or at least things analogous to souls, from being everywhere, although the dominant, and hence intelligent, souls, like those of men, cannot be everywhere.

X. § 71. *His later views.*

G. IV. 574 (*ca.* 1700). It seems that it is more exact to say that spirits are where they operate immediately than to say...that they are nowhere.

G. II. 450 (1712). The explanation of all phenomena by nothing but the mutually conspiring perceptions of monads, setting aside corporeal substance, I hold to be useful for the fundamental inspection of things. And in this manner of exposition, space becomes the order of coexistent phenomena, as time of those that are successive; and there is no spatial or absolute distance or propinquity of monads: to say that they are massed together in a point, or disseminated in space, is to make use of certain fictions of our soul, since we take pleasure in imagining things which can only be conceived. In this way of looking at things, there is no extension or composition of the continuum, and all difficulties about points vanish.

G. V. 205 (N. E. 230) (1704). The schools have three kinds of *ubiety*, or ways of existing somewhere. The first is called *circumscriptive*, which we attribute to bodies that are in space, which are in it *punctatim*, so that they are measured according as points can be assigned to the situated thing corresponding to the points of space. The second is *definitive*, where we can define, *i.e.* determine, that the situated thing is in a certain space, without being able to assign precise points or proper places exclusively to what is there. It is thus people judge that the soul is in the body, not believing it possible to assign an exact point, where is the soul, or something of the soul, without its being also in some other point....The third sort of ubiety is *repletive*, which is attributed to God, who fills the whole universe even more eminently than spirits are in bodies, for he operates immediately on all creatures by continually producing them, whereas finite spirits cannot exercise any immediate influence or operation. I know not whether this doctrine of the schools deserves to be turned into ridicule, as it seems people endeavour to do. However we can always attribute a kind of motion to souls, at least in relation to the bodies with which they are united, or in relation to their manner of perception.

G. VI. 598 (D. 209; L. 408) (1714). There are simple substances everywhere, separated from each other, in fact (*effectivement*), by their own actions, which continually change their relations.

G. III. 623 (1714). We must not conceive extension as a real continuous space, strewn with points. These are fictions proper to content the imagination, but in which reason does not find what it requires. Nor must we conceive that Monads, like points in a real space, move, push, or touch each other; it is enough that phenomena make it seem so, and this appearance partakes of truth in so far as these phenomena are founded, *i.e.* agree with each other.

G. II. 339 (1707). A simple substance, though it has no extension in itself, yet has position, which is the foundation of extension, since extension is the simultaneous continuous repetition of position.

G. II. 370 (1709).   I do not think it fitting to consider souls as in points.   Some one might perhaps say that they are only in a place by operation...or rather,...that they are in a place by correspondence, and are thus in the whole organic body which they animate.   Meanwhile I do not deny a certain real metaphysical union between the soul and the organic body...according to which it could be said that the soul really is in the body.

G. II. 378 (1709).   Although the places of monads are designated by modifications or terminations of parts of space, yet the monads themselves are not modifications of a continuous thing. Mass and its diffusion result from monads, but not space.   For space ...is a certain order, embracing not only actuals but also possibles.

G. II. 436 (1712).   We ought not to say of monads, any more than of points and souls, that they are parts of bodies, that they touch each other, or that they compose bodies.

G. II. 438 (1712).   God sees not only single monads and the modifications of each monad, but also their relations, and in this consists the reality of relations and truths.

G. II. 444 (1712).   Monads *per se* have not even any relative situation—*i.e.* no real one—which extends beyond the order of phenomena.

G. II. 253 (1703).   Monads, though they are not extended, yet have something of the nature of position in extension, *i.e.* they have a certain ordered relation of coexistence to other things, through the machine which they dominate (*cui praesunt*).   And I do not think that any finite substances exist separated from every body, nor consequently are without position or order in regard to the other things which coexist in the universe.   Extended things involve in themselves many things having position, but things which are simple, though they have no extension, yet must have position in extension, although it is impossible to designate this *punctatim* as in incomplete phenomena.

G. II. 277 (1704–5).   My unities or simple substances are not diffused,...nor do they constitute a homogeneous whole, for the homogeneity of matter is obtained only by a mental abstraction, when we consider only things that are passive and therefore incomplete.

X. § 72.   *Time and change.*

G. VII. 373 (D. 249).   It is a similar, *i.e.* impossible, fiction, to imagine that God might have created the world some millions of years sooner. Those who agree to fictions of this sort will be unable to reply to those who would argue for the eternity of the world. For since God does nothing without a reason, and since no reason is assignable why he should not have created the world sooner, it will follow, either that he created nothing at all, or that he produced the world before every assignable time, *i.e.* that the world is eternal. But when it is shown that the beginning, whatever it is (*quel qu'il soit*), is always the same thing, the question why it was not otherwise ceases.

G. VII. 402 (D. 268). It cannot be said that a certain *duration* is eternal; but that things which continue always are eternal, by always gaining new extension. Whatever exists of time and of duration, being successive, perishes continually; and how can a thing exist eternally which (to speak exactly) does never exist at all? For how can a thing exist, whereof no part does ever exist? Nothing of time does ever exist, but instants; and an instant is not even itself a part of time.

G. VII. 408 (D. 274). From extension to duration, *non valet consequentia*. Though the extension of matter were unlimited, yet it would not follow that its duration would be also unlimited; nay even, *a parte ante*, it would not follow that it had no beginning. If it is of the nature of things in the whole to grow uniformly in perfection, the universe of creatures must have had a beginning.... Besides, the world's having a beginning does not derogate from the infinity of its duration *a parte post*; but bounds of the universe would derogate from the infinity of its extension.

G. III. 581. As for succession, where you [Bourguet] seem to judge, Sir, that one must conceive a first fundamental instant, as unity is the foundation of numbers, and as the point is also the foundation of extension : to this I might answer that the instant is also the foundation of time, but as there is no point in nature which is fundamental with regard to all other points, and so to speak the seat of God, so I do not see that it is necessary to conceive a principal instant. I admit, however, that there is this difference between instants and points, that one point of the universe has not the advantage of priority of nature over another, whereas the preceding instant has, over the succeeding instant, the advantage of priority not of time only, but also of nature. But it is not necessary on that account that there should be a first instant. There is a difference, in this, between the analysis of necessary things and that of contingent things....Thus the analogy from numbers to instants does not hold here. It is true that the notion of numbers is resolvable at last into the notion of unity, which is no longer resolvable, and may be considered as the primitive number. But it does not follow that the notions of the various instants are resolvable at last into a primitive instant. However, I do not venture to deny that there was a first instant. Two hypotheses may be formed, either that nature is always equally perfect, or that it always grows in perfection. ...[In the first case] it is more likely that there is no beginning. [In the second case]...the matter could still be explained in two ways, namely by the ordinates of a hyperbola or by those of a triangle. According to the hypothesis of the hyperbola, there would be no beginning...but according to the hypothesis of the triangle, there would have been a beginning....I see no way of showing demonstratively by pure reason which should be chosen.

G. VII. 415 (D. 281). The author [Clarke] objects here, that time cannot be an order of successive things, because the quantity of time may become greater or less, and yet the order of successions continue the same. I answer, this is not so. For if the time be greater, there will be more successive and like states interposed; and if it be less, there will be fewer; seeing there is no vacuum, nor condensation, nor penetration (if I may so speak) in times, any more than in places.

G. II. 183. Time is neither more nor less a being of reason than space. To coexist and to pre- or post-exist, are something real; they would not be so, I admit, according to the ordinary view of matter and substance.

G. V. 139 (N. E. 156). Time is the measure of motion, *i.e.* uniform motion is the measure of non-uniform motion.

X. § 74. *Leibniz held confusedly to an objective counterpart of space and time.*

G. VII. 329. Every primitive entelechy must have perception. For every first entelechy has internal variation, according to which its external actions also vary. But perception is nothing but that very representation of external by internal variation. Since, therefore, primitive entelechies are dispersed everywhere throughout matter—which can easily be shown from the fact that principles of motion are dispersed throughout matter—the consequence is, that souls also are dispersed everywhere throughout matter.

G. VI. 405. As soon as we admit that God exists, we must admit that he exists necessarily. Now this privilege does not belong to the three things of which we have been speaking [motion, matter and space].

G. VII. 375 (D. 251). God perceives things in himself. Space is the place of things, and not the place of God's ideas.

XI. § 75. *Perception.*

G. VI. 599 (D. 209; L. 409). Perceptions in the Monad are produced one from another according to the laws of appetites or of the final causes of good and evil, which consist in observable perceptions, regular or irregular.

G. I. 383 (1686). It is not necessary that what we conceive of things outside us should be perfectly similar to them, but that it should express them, as an ellipse expresses a circle seen obliquely, so that to each point of the circle a point of the ellipse corresponds, and *vice versâ*, according to a certain law of relation. For...each individual substance expresses the universe in its own way, much as the same town is diversely expressed according to different points of view.

G. V. 101 (N. E. III). A state without thought in the soul, and an absolute rest in body, seem to me equally contrary to nature, and without example in the world. A substance which is once in action will be so always, for all impressions remain, and are only mixed with other new ones.

G. VI. 576 (D. 187). When Mr Locke declares that he does not understand how the variety of ideas is compatible with the simplicity of God, it seems to me that he ought not hence to derive an objection to Father Malebranche; for there is no system which can make such a thing intelligible.

G. VI. 577 (D. 188). Mr Locke asks whether an indivisible and unextended substance can have at the same time modifications which are different and even refer to inconsistent objects. I answer that it can. What is inconsistent in the same object is not inconsistent in the representation of different objects, which are conceived at the same time. For this it is not necessary that there should be different parts in the soul, as it is not necessary that there should be different parts in the point, though different angles meet in it.

G. VI. 608 (D. 219; L. 222). I assume as admitted that every created being, and consequently the created Monad, is subject to change, and further that this change is continual in each. It follows from what has just been said, that the natural changes of the Monads come from an internal principle, since an external cause can have no influence upon their inner being. But besides the principle of the change, there must be a particular series of changes [*un détail de ce qui change*], which constitutes, so to speak, the specific nature and variety of the simple substances. This particular series of changes must involve a multiplicity in the unit, or in that which is simple. For, as every natural change takes place gradually, something changes and something remains unchanged; and consequently a simple substance must be affected and related in many ways, although it has no parts.

G. VI. 609 (D. 220; L. 226). We have in ourselves experience of a multiplicity in a simple substance, when we find that the least thought of which we are conscious involves variety in its object. Thus all those who admit that the soul is a simple substance should admit this multiplicity in the Monad.

G. VI. 327. It is true that the same thing can be represented differently; but there must always be an exact relation between the representation and the thing, and consequently between different representations of the same thing.

G. VII. 410 (D. 275). The author [Clarke] speaks as if he did not understand how, according to my opinion, the soul is a representative principle. Which is, as if he had never heard of my pre-established harmony. I do not assent to the vulgar notions, that the images of things are conveyed by the organs of sense to the soul. For, it is not conceivable by what passage, or by what means of conveyance, these images can be carried from the organ to the soul. This vulgar notion in philosophy is not intelligible, as the new Cartesians have sufficiently shown. It cannot be explained, how immaterial substance is affected by matter: and to maintain an intelligible notion thereupon, is having recourse to the scholastic chimerical notion of I know not what inexplicable *species intentionales*, passing from the organs to the soul. Those Cartesians saw the difficulty, but they could not explain it....But I think I have given the true solution of that enigma.

G. II. 71 (1686). It is the nature of the soul to express what is happening in bodies, being so created originally that the series of its thoughts agrees with the series of motions.

G. II. 74 (1686). The nature of every substance involves a general expression of the whole universe, and the nature of the soul involves more particularly a more distinct expression of what is now happening in relation to its body.

G. III. 575. Perception is, for me, the representation of a multiplicity in what is simple; and appetite is the tendency from one perception to another : now these two things are in all Monads, for otherwise a monad would have no relation to other things. I do not know, Sir, how you [Bourguet] can derive any Spinozism from this; that is jumping to conclusions rather too fast. On the contrary, it is just by means of these monads that Spinozism is destroyed, for there are as many true substances, and, so to speak, living mirrors of the universe always subsisting, or concentrated universes, as there are Monads, whereas according to Spinoza there is only a single substance. He would be right, if there were no monads; then everything except God would be passing, and would sink into mere accidents and modifications, since there would not be in things the basis of substances, which consists in the existence of monads.

F. de C. 62 (D. 182). [Spinoza] is wrong in thinking that affirmation or negation is volition, since volition involves also the reason of the good.

G. II. 317. A universal is one in many, or the similarity of many; but when we perceive, many are expressed in one, namely the percipient. You see how far apart these are.

G. II. 256. I recognize monads that are active *per se*, and in them nothing can be conceived except perception, which in turn involves action.

XI. § 77. *Perception not due to action of the perceived on the percipient.*

G. IV. 495 (D. 86). I take care not to admit that the soul does not know bodies, though this knowledge arises without influence of the one on the other.

G. IV. 484 (D. 77 ; L. 313). God at first so created the soul, or any other real unity, that everything must arise in it from its own inner nature, with a perfect spontaneity as regards itself, and yet with a perfect conformity to things outside of it....And accordingly, since each of these substances accurately represents the whole universe in its own way and from a certain point of view, and the perceptions or expressions of external things come into the soul at their appropriate time, in virtue of its own laws, as in a world by itself, and as if there existed nothing but God and the soul, ...there will be a perfect agreement between all these substances, which will have the same result as if they had communication with one another by a transmission of species or qualities, such as the mass of ordinary philosophers suppose.

G. VI. 607 (D. 218; L. 219). There is no way of explaining how a Monad can be altered in quality or internally changed by any other created thing; since it is impossible to change the place of anything in it or to conceive in it any internal motion which could be produced, directed, increased or diminished therein, although all this is possible in the case of compounds, in which there are changes among the parts. The monads have no windows, through which anything could come in or go out. Accidents cannot separate themselves from substances nor go outside of them, as the "sensible species" of the scholastics used to do. Thus neither substance nor accident can come into a monad from outside.

G. II. 12 (1686). Every singular substance expresses the whole universe in its own way, and in its notion are comprised all its events with all their circumstances, and the whole series of external things.

G. II. 136 (D. 38). Each of these substances contains in its nature *legem continuationis seriei suarum operationum*, and all that has happened and will happen to it. All its actions come from its own nature, except for its dependence upon God.

G. II. 503. I do not believe that a system is possible, in which Monads act on each other, because there seems to be no possible way of explaining such action. I add that an influence is also superfluous, for why should a monad give to another monad what it already has? For this is the very nature of substance, that its present should be big with the future, and that all things can be understood by means of one, unless indeed God should miraculously interfere.

G. IV. 440 (1686). Nothing can happen to us but thoughts and perceptions, and all our future thoughts and perceptions are only consequences, though contingent ones, of our previous thoughts and perceptions, so much so that if I were capable of considering distinctly all that happens or appears to me at the present time, I could see in it all that will happen or appear to me for ever; which would not fail, and would happen to me just the same, if all that is outside of me were destroyed, provided only that God and I remained.

G. II. 119. Only indivisible substances and their different states are absolutely real.

XI. § 79. *The pre-established harmony.*

G. II. 58 (1686). Only the hypothesis of the concomitance or agreement of substances *inter se* explains everything in a manner which is conceivable and worthy of God; it is even demonstrative and inevitable, in my opinion, according to the proposition which we have just established [that in every proposition the notion of the predicate is contained in that of the subject].

G. I. 382 (1686). I believe that every individual substance expresses the whole universe in its own way, and that its following state is a consequence (though often a free one) of its preceding state, as if there were nothing but God and it in the world; but as all substances are a continual production of the sovereign Being, and express the same universe or the same phenomena, they agree exactly with each other.

G. VII. 311. Every substance has something of the infinite, in so far as it involves its cause, *i.e.* God, that is, it has some trace of omniscience and omnipotence; for in the perfect notion of each individual substance there are contained all its predicates, alike necessary and contingent, past, present, and future; nay each substance expresses the whole universe according to its situation and aspect, in so far as other things are referred to it; and hence it is necessary that some of our perceptions, even if they be clear, should be confused, since they involve things which are infinite, as do our perceptions of colour, heat, etc.

G. II. 68 (1686). The hypothesis of concomitance is a consequence of the notion which I have of substance. For according to me the individual notion of a substance involves all that will ever happen to it.

G. II. 136 (D. 38). Each substance expresses the whole universe, but some more distinctly than others, especially each in regard to certain things, and according to its point of view. The union of soul and body, and even the operation of one substance on another, consists only in this perfect mutual agreement, purposely established by the order of the first creation, in virtue of which each substance, following its own laws, falls in with what the others demand, and the operations of the one thus follow or accompany the operation or change of the other.

G. II. 226. Certainly, in my opinion, there is nothing in the universe of creatures which does not need, for its perfect concept, the concept of every other thing in the universe of things, since everything influences everything else, so that if it were taken away or supposed different, all the things in the world would have been different from those that now are.

G. III. 143. It is true there is miracle in my system of pre-established Harmony, and that God enters into it extraordinarily, but it is only in the beginning of things, after which everything goes its own way in the phenomena of nature, according to the laws of souls and bodies.

G. III. 144. It seems to me that I may say that my hypothesis (concerning the pre-established Harmony) is not gratuitous, since I believe I have made it appear that there are only three possible hypotheses [the *influxus physicus*, occasionalism, and the pre-established harmony], and that only mine is at once intelligible and natural; but it can even be proved *à priori*.

XII. § 83. *The three classes of monads.*

G. VI. 600 (D. 211; L. 411). It is well to make a distinction between *perception*, which is the internal state of the Monad representing external things, and *apperception*, which is the *consciousness* or the reflective knowledge of this internal state, and which is not given to all souls, nor to the same soul at all times. It is for lack of this distinction that the Cartesians have made the mistake of ignoring perceptions of which we are not conscious....Genuine reasoning depends upon necessary or eternal truths, such as those of logic, of number, of geometry, which produce an indubitable connection of ideas and infallible inferences. The animals in which these inferences do not appear are called the *brutes*; but those which know these necessary truths are properly those which are called *rational animals*, and their souls are called *spirits* [*esprits*]. These souls have the power to perform acts of reflection, and to consider what is called the ego, substance, soul, spirit, in a word, immaterial things and truths.

G. VI. 604 (D. 215; L. 420). As regards the rational soul or spirit, there is in it something more than in the monads or even in mere souls. It is not only a mirror of the universe of created beings, but also an image of the Deity....It is for this reason that all spirits, whether of men or genii, entering in virtue of reason and of eternal truths into a kind of fellowship with God, are members of the City of God, *i.e.* of the most perfect state, formed and governed by the greatest and best of Monarchs.

G. VI. 610 (D. 220; L. 230). If we are to give the name of Soul to everything which has perceptions and appetites in the general sense which I have just explained, then all simple substances or created Monads might be called souls ; but as feeling is something more than a bare perception, I think it right that the general name of Monads or Entelechies should suffice for simple substances which have perception only, and that the name of *Souls* should be given only to those in which perception is more distinct and accompanied by memory.

G. IV. 479 (D. 73; L. 303). We must not confound or indifferently mix, with other forms or souls, *Spirits* or the reasonable soul, which are of a higher order, and have incomparably more perfection than these forms buried in matter—which in my opinion are to be found everywhere—being like little gods in comparison with these, being made in the image of God, and having in them some ray of the Divine light. For this reason, God governs spirits as a prince governs his subjects, and indeed as a father cares for his children ; while, on the other hand, he deals with other substances as an engineer works with his machines. Thus spirits have special laws, which put them above the revolutions of matter through the very order which God has placed there ; and it may be said that everything else is made only for them, these revolutions themselves being arranged for the felicity of the good and the punishment of the wicked.

G. V. 218 (N. E. 245). The consciousness or feeling of the *Ego* proves a moral or personal identity. And it is by this that I distinguish the *incessability* of a brute's soul from the *immortality* of the soul of man : both preserve *physical and real identity*, but as for man, it is conformable to the rules of the Divine Providence that the soul should retain also a moral identity apparent to ourselves, so as to constitute the same person, capable consequently of feeling chastisements and rewards.

G. V. 219 (N. E. 247). As for the *Self*, it will be well to distinguish it from the *appearance of Self* and from consciousness. The *Self* constitutes real and physical identity, and the *appearance of Self*, accompanied by truth, joins personal identity to it.

G. III. 622. [All monads] have *perception*...and *appetite*..., which is called *passion* in animals, and *will* where perception is an understanding.

G. V. 284 (N. E. 331). It is essential to substances to act, to created substances to suffer, to spirits to think, to bodies to have extension and motion. That is, there are sorts or species to which an individual cannot (naturally at least) cease to belong, when it has once belonged to them.

G. V. 290 (N. E. 338). [In man] reason is a fixed attribute, belonging to each individual, and never lost, though we cannot always perceive it.

G. VII. 529 (D. 190). You next ask my definition of *soul.* I reply, that *soul* may be employed in a broad and in a strict sense. Broadly speaking, *soul* will be the same as life or vital principle, *i.e.* the principle of internal action existing in the simple thing or monad, to which external action corresponds. And this correspondence of internal and external, or representation of the external in the internal, of the composite in the simple, of multiplicity in unity, really constitutes perception. But in this sense soul is attributed not only to animals, but also to all other percipient beings. In the strict sense, *soul* is employed as a nobler species of life, or sentient life, where there is not only the faculty of perceiving, but in addition that of feeling, inasmuch, indeed, as attention and memory are added to perception. Just as, in turn, mind is a nobler species of soul, *i.e.* mind is rational soul, where reason, or ratiocination from universality of truths, is added to feeling. As, therefore, mind is rational soul, so soul is sentient life, and life is perceptive principle.

XII. § 84. *Activity and passivity.*

G. IV. 486 (D. 79; L. 317). The customary ways of speaking can still be quite well preserved [in my system]. For we may say that the substance whose disposition explains a change in an intelligible way (so that we may hold that it is this substance to which the others have on this point been adapted from the beginning, according to the order of the decrees of God) is the substance which, in respect of this change, we should conceive as *acting* upon the others.

G. VI. 615 (D. 225; L. 245). A creature is said to *act* outwardly in so far as it has perfection, and to *suffer* in relation to another in so far as it is imperfect. Thus *action* is attributed to a Monad in so far as it has distinct perceptions, and passion in so far as its perceptions are confused. And one created thing is more perfect than another in this, that there is found in the more perfect that which serves to explain *à priori* what takes place in the other, and it is on this account that the former is said to act upon the latter. But in simple substances the influence of one Monad upon another is only ideal, and it can have its effect only through the mediation of God, in so far as in the ideas of God one Monad rightly claims that God, in regulating the others from the beginning of things, should have regard to it....And it is thus that, among creatures, activities and passivities are mutual. For God, comparing two simple substances, finds in each reasons which oblige him to adapt the other to it, and consequently what is active in certain respects is passive from another point of view ; *active* in so far as what we distinctly know in it serves to give a reason for what takes place in another, and *passive* in so far as the reason for what takes place in it is to be found in that which is distinctly known in another.

 G. IV. 441 (1686). When a change occurs by which several substances are affected (as in fact every change affects them all), I believe we may say that the one which thereby immediately passes to a greater degree of perfection or to a more perfect expression, exerts its power, and acts, and that which passes to a less degree makes known its feebleness, and *suffers*. Also I hold that every action of a substance which has perception implies some *joy*, and every passion some *pain*.

 G. II. 13 (1686). The action of one finite substance on another consists only in the increase in the degree of its expression joined to the diminution of that of the other, inasmuch as God has formed them beforehand so that they should agree together.

 G. V. 201 (N. E. 224). I do not know whether one can say that the same being is called action in the agent and passion in the patient, and is thus in two subjects at once, like a relation, or whether it is not better to say that they are two beings, one in the agent, the other in the patient.

  XII. § 86. Materia prima *as an element in each monad.*

 G. VII. 322 (N. E. 720). Substances have metaphysical matter or passive power in so far as they express anything confusedly, active power in so far as they express anything distinctly.

G. III. 636. As Monads (except the primitive one) are subject to passions, they are not pure forces; they are the foundation, not only of actions, but also of resistances or passivities, and their passions are in confused perceptions. It is this which involves matter or the infinite in number.

G. II. 516. A substance acts as much as it can, unless it is impeded; even a simple substance, however, is impeded, but not naturally unless internally by itself. And when a monad is said to be impeded by another, this is to be understood of the representation of the other in itself.

G. II. 306. *Materia prima*...[is] the primitive passive power, or principle of resistance, which does not consist of extension, but of what extension needs, and complements the entelechy or primitive active power, so as to produce the complete substance or Monad....We hold that such matter, *i.e.* the principle of passion, persists, and adheres to its own Entelechy.

G. II. 325. Although God could, by his absolute power, deprive a created substance of *materia secunda*, yet he cannot deprive it of *materia prima*; for he would thus make it *Actus purus*, such as he alone is.

G. II. 368. [The *materia prima* of one Monad] does not increase mass, or the phenomenon resulting from Monads, any more than a point increases a line.

XII. § 87. Materia prima *the source of finitude, plurality and matter.*

G. VI. 546 (D. 169). God alone is above all matter, since he is its Author; but creatures free or freed from matter would be at the same time detached from the universal connection, and like deserters from the general order.

G. II. 324. To remove these [Intelligences] from bodies and place, is to remove them from the universal connection and order of the world, which is made by relations to time and place.

G. II. 412. Whoever admits the pre-established Harmony, cannot but admit also the doctrine of the actual division of matter into infinite parts.

G. II. 460. You [Des Bosses] ask further, why there should be actually infinitely numerous monads? I answer, for this their possibility will suffice, since it is better that the works of God should be as splendid as possible; but the same is required by the order of things, otherwise phenomena will not correspond to all assignable percipients. And indeed in our perceptions, however distinct, we conceive that confused ones are contained to any degree of smallness ; and thus monads will correspond to these, as to greater and more distinct ones.

G. II. 248. You [de Volder] desire a necessary connection between matter (or resistance) and active force, so as not to join them arbitrarily. But the cause of the connection is, that every substance is active, and every finite substance is passive, while resistance is connected with passion. Therefore such a conjunction is demanded by the nature of things.

XII. § 90. *First theory of Soul and Body.*

G. VI. 539 (D. 163). When I am asked if these [principles of life] are substantial forms, I reply by a distinction : for if this term is taken, as M. Des Cartes takes it, when he maintains...that the reasonable soul is the substantial form of man, I should answer *yes*. But I should say *no*, if any one understood the term as those do who imagine that there is a substantial form of a piece of stone, or of some other non-organic body ; for principles of life belong only to organic bodies. It is true...that there is no portion of matter in which there are not numberless organic and animated bodies....But for all this, it must not be said that each portion of matter is animated, just as we do not say that a pond full of fish is an animated body, although a fish is so.

G. VI. 543 (D. 167). Not only the soul, but also the same animal, subsists....What does not begin to live, does not cease to live either ; and death, like generation, is only the transformation of the same animal, which is sometimes increased, sometimes diminished....The machines of nature being machines even in their smallest parts, are indestructible, because of the envelopment of a small machine in a larger one *ad infinitum*. Thus we are obliged to maintain at the same time both the pre-existence of the soul as of the animal, and the substance of the animal as of the soul.

G. VII. 530 (D. 191). To each primitive entelechy or each vital principle there is perpetually united a certain natural machine, which comes to us under the name of organic body : which machine, although it preserves its form in general, consists in a flux, and is, like the ship of Theseus, perpetually repaired. And we cannot be certain that the smallest particle received by us at birth remains in our body....Some animal always remains, although no particular animal ought to be called everlasting.

G. V. 214 (N. E. 240). Organization or configuration, without a subsistent principle of life, which I call a Monad, would not suffice for the continuance of *idem numero*, or the same individual; for configuration may remain specifically without remaining individually....Organized bodies, as well as others, remain the same only in appearance....But as for Substances, which have in them a true and real substantial unity..., and as for substantial beings, which...are animated by a certain indivisible spirit, it is right to say that they remain perfectly the *same individual*, through this soul or spirit, which makes the *Ego* in those which think.

G. III. 356. I have said, not absolutely, that organism is essential to matter, but to matter arranged by a sovereign wisdom.

G. II. 100. I admit that the body apart, without the soul, has only a unity of aggregation, but the reality which remains to it comes from the parts which compose it, and which retain their substantial unity because of the numberless living bodies which are enveloped in them. However, though it is possible for a soul to have a body composed of parts animated by separate souls, the soul or form of the whole is not on that account composed of the souls or forms of the parts.

G. VI. 619 (D. 229; L. 258). It must not be imagined... that each soul has a quantity or portion of matter belonging exclusively to itself or attached to it for ever, and that it consequently owns other inferior living beings....For all bodies are in a perpetual flux, like rivers....There is often metamorphosis in animals, but never metempsychosis or transmigration of souls; nor are there souls entirely separate or disembodied spirits. God alone is completely without body.

G. II. 58 (1686). Each [soul and body] following its laws, and one acting freely, the other without choice, agrees (*se rencontre*) in the same phenomena. The soul, however, is none the less the form of its body, because it expresses the phenomena of all other bodies according to their relation to its own.

G. VI. 595. I should have been much mistaken if I had objected to the Cartesians that the agreement which, according to them, God maintains immediately between the soul and the body, does not make a veritable union, since assuredly my pre-established Harmony cannot do so either....However I do not deny that there is something of this nature; and this would be analogous to *presence*, of which hitherto, as applied to incorporeal things, the notion has not been sufficiently explained.

G. VI. 598 (D. 209; L. 408). Each specially important simple substance or Monad, which forms the centre of a compound substance (*e.g.* of an animal) and the principle of its unity, is surrounded by a *mass* composed of an infinity of other Monads, which constitute the particular body of this central Monad....This body is organic, when it forms a kind of automaton or natural machine, which is a machine not only as a whole, but also in the smallest parts of it that can come into observation.

G. II. 306. It is not to be thought that an infinitesimal portion of matter is to be assigned to each entelechy; there is no such piece.

G. II. 378. Although there is no absolute necessity for every organic body to be animated, yet we must judge that God would not have neglected the opportunity for a soul, since his wisdom produces as much perfection as it can.

G. III. 363. Simple substance...cannot have extension in it, for all extension is composite.

G. VII. 468. Our substantial matter has only potential parts, but the human body is an aggregate.

XII. § 91. *Second theory of Soul and Body.*

G. III. 657 (D. 234). A true substance (such as an animal) is composed of an immaterial soul and an organic body, and it is the compound of these two which is called *unum per se*.

G. IV. 391 (D. 63). Just as all things are full of souls, so also they are full of organized bodies.

G. V. 309 (N. E. 362). Perfect unity must be reserved for bodies which are animated, or endowed with primitive entelechies.

G. II. 75 (1686). Our body in itself, apart from the soul,... can only be called *one* substance improperly, like a machine or a heap of stones.

G. II. 77 (1686). If I am asked, in particular, what I say of the sun, the globe of the earth, the moon, trees and similar bodies, and even beasts, I could not affirm absolutely that they are animated, or at least that they are substances, or whether they are merely machines or aggregates of several substances. But at least I can say that if there are no corporeal substances such as I want, it follows that bodies will be only true phenomena, like the rainbow....

We shall never come to anything of which we can say: "there is truly a being," except when we find animated machines to which their soul or substantial form gives a substantial unity independent of the external union of contact. And if there are none such, it follows that except man there would be nothing substantial in the visible world.

G. II. 371. I do not deny *a certain real metaphysical union* between the soul and the organic body..., according to which it could be said, that the soul really is in the body.... But you see that I have been speaking, not of the union of the Entelechy or active principle with *materia prima* or passive power, but of the union of the soul, or the Monad itself (resulting from both principles) with mass or with other monads.

G. VII. 502. Every created monad is provided with some organic body....Every mass contains innumerable monads, for although every organic body in nature has its corresponding monad, yet it contains in its parts other monads similarly provided with their organic bodies, which are subservient to the primary organic body.

G. IV. 511 (D. 120). So far as by its union with matter [the substantial form] constitutes a substance truly one, or a thing that is one *per se*, it forms what I call a *monad*.

G. II. 118. As for the other difficulty which you [Arnauld] make, Sir, namely that the soul joined to matter does not make a being truly one, since matter is not truly one in itself, and the soul, as you judge, gives it only an extrinsic denomination, I answer that it is the animated substance, to which this matter belongs, which is truly one being, and matter taken as mere mass is only a pure phenomenon or well-founded appearance.

G. II. 120. A whole which has a true unity can remain the same individual, strictly speaking, though it gains or loses parts, as we experience in ourselves.

G. II. 368. A new entelechy can be created, even if no new part of mass is created; for although mass already has unities everywhere, yet it is always capable of new ones, dominating many others; as if you were to imagine that God should make an organic body out of a mass which, as a whole, is inorganic, *e.g.* a lump of stone, and should set its soul over it; for there are as many entelechies as there are organic bodies.

G. II. 370. Every part of an organic body contains other entelechies.

G. II. 304. A fraction or half of an animal is not one Being *per se*, because this can only be understood of the animal's body, which is not one being *per se*, but an aggregate, and has an arithmetical, but not a metaphysical unity.

G. II. 251. A primitive entelechy can never arise or be extinguished naturally, and can never be without an organic body.

XII. § 92. *The* vinculum substantiale.

G. II. 399. Since the bread is really not a substance, but a being by aggregation or a *substantiatum*, resulting from innumerable monads by a certain superadded union, its substantiality consists in this union; thus it is not necessary according to you [the Catholics] that God should abolish or change those monads, but only that he should take away that by means of which they produce a new being, namely this union; thus the substantiality which consists in it will cease, though the phenomenon will remain, arising now not from those monads, but from some divine equivalent substituted for the union of those monads.   Thus there will really be no substantial subject present.   But we, who reject transubstantiation, have no need, of such theories.   [This passage precedes the first suggestion of the *vinculum substantiale*.]

G. II. 435. We must say one of two things : either bodies are mere phenomena, and thus extension also is nothing but a phenomenon, monads alone are real, and the union is supplied by the operation of the percipient soul in the phenomenon; or, if faith leads us to corporeal substances, this substance will consist in the reality of the union, which adds something absolute (and therefore substantial), though temporary, to the monads which are to be united. ...If this substantial bond of monads were absent, all bodies with all their qualities would be only well-founded phenomena.

G. II. 461. Supernatural matters being opposed to philosophy, we need nothing else than monads and their internal modifications.

G. II. 481. I have changed my mind, so that I think nothing absurd will follow if we hold the *vinculum substantiale* also...to be ingenerable and incorruptible; since indeed I think no corporeal substance should be admitted except where there is an organic body with a dominant monad. ...Since, therefore, I deny...not only that the soul, but also that the animal can perish, I shall say that the *vinculum substantiale* also...cannot arise or cease naturally.

G. II. 516. This *vinculum substantiale* is naturally, but not essentially, a bond.   For it requires monads, but does not essentially involve them, since it can exist without monads, and monads without it.

G. II. 517. If monads alone were substances, it would be necessary either that bodies should be mere phenomena, or that the continuum should arise out of points, which is certainly absurd. Real continuity cannot arise except from the *vinculum substantiale.*

G. II. 520. Monads alone do not compose the continuum, since *per se* they are destitute of all connection, and each monad is like a world apart. But in *materia prima* (for *materia secunda* is an aggregate), or in the passive element of a composite substance, is involved the foundation of continuity, whence the true continuum springs from juxtaposed compound substances....And in this sense I may perhaps have said that extension is a modification of *materia prima,* or of what is formally non-extended.

XII. § 94. *Preformation.*

G. VII. 531 (D. 192). I hold that the souls, latent in seminal animalcules from the beginning of things, are not rational until, by conception, they are destined for human life; but when they are once made rational and rendered capable of consciousness and of society with God, I think that they never lay aside the character of citizens in the Republic of God....Death...can render perceptions confused, but cannot entirely blot them from memory, the use of which returning, rewards and punishments take place.

G. VI. 152. I hold that souls, and simple substances generally, can only begin by creation, and end by annihilation : and as the formation of animated organic bodies does not seem explicable in the order of nature, unless we suppose an already organic *preformation,* I have hence inferred that what we call the generation of an animal is only a transformation and augmentation : thus since the same body was already organized, it is to be believed that it was already animated, and that it had the same soul....I should believe that souls which will one day be human, like those of the other species, have been in the seeds, and in the ancestors up to Adam, and have consequently existed since the beginning of things, always in a sort of organized body....But it seems proper, for several reasons, that they should have existed then only as sensitive or animal souls... and that they remained in that state until the time of the generation of the man to whom they were to belong, but that then they received **reason, whether there be a natural** method of elevating a sensitive soul to the degree of a reasonable soul (which I have difficulty in conceiving), or that God gave reason to this soul by a special operation, or (if you will) by a kind of *transcreation*.

G. VI. 352. I should prefer to do without miracle in the generation of man, as of the other animals; and this could be explained by conceiving that, among the great number of Souls and Animals, or at least of organic living bodies, which are in the seed, those souls alone which are destined to attain some day to human nature contain the reason which will some day appear in them.

G. III. 565. The question always remains whether the basis of the transformation, or the preformed living being, is in the ovary... or the sperm....For I hold that there must always be a preformed living being, whether plant or animal, which is the basis of the transformation, and that it must contain the same dominant monad.

G. VI. 543 (D. 167). I am of the opinion of Mr Cudworth... that the laws of mechanism alone could not form an animal, where there is as yet nothing organized.

XIII. § 96. *Unconscious mental states.*

G. V. 107 (N. E. 118). What is noticeable must be composed of parts which are not so....It is impossible for us to think expressly upon all our thoughts; otherwise, the mind would reflect upon each reflection to infinity, without ever being able to pass to a new thought.

G. V. 109 (N. E. 120). These sense-ideas [heat, softness, cold] are simple in appearance, because, being confused, they do not give the mind the means of distinguishing their contents.

G. V. 48 (N. E. 49; L. 373). These insensible perceptions also mark and constitute the same individual, who is characterized by traces or expressions, which they preserve, of the preceding states of this individual....It is also by the insensible perceptions that we explain that admirable pre-established Harmony of the soul and the body, and even of all monads.

G. V. 49 (N. E. 51; L. 377). I have also noticed that, in virtue of insensible variations, two individual things cannot be perfectly alike, and that they must always differ more than numerically.

G. V. 79 (N. E. 84). *Philalethes* [Locke]: It is very difficult to conceive that a truth should be in the mind, if the mind has never thought of this truth. *Theophilus* [Leibniz]:...This reasoning proves too much ; for if truths are thoughts, we shall be deprived, not only of truths of which we have never thought, but also of those we have thought of, but are no longer actually thinking of ; and if truths are not thoughts, but habits and aptitudes, natural or acquired, nothing hinders there being some in us of which we never have thought and never will think.

G. V. 148 (N. E. 166). We have always an infinity of minute perceptions without perceiving them. We are never without *perceptions*, but it is necessary that we should be often without *apperceptions*, namely when there are no perceptions which are noticed [*distinguées*].

G. V. 97 (N. E. 105). In order that knowledge, ideas or truths should be in our mind, it is not necessary that we should have ever actually thought of them ; they are only natural habits. that is to say, active and passive dispositions and attitudes, and more than a *tabula rasa*.

XIV. § 99. *Innate ideas and truths.*

G. V. 70 (N. E. 75). I agree that we learn innate ideas and truths, whether by attending to their source, or by verifying them through experience. Thus I do not make the supposition you [Locke] suppose, as if, in the case of which you speak, we learnt nothing new. And I cannot admit this proposition : *Whatever we learn is not innate.*

G. V. 71 (N. E. 76). *Ph.*: Is it not possible that not only the terms or words which we use, but also the ideas, come to us from without? *Th.*: It would then be necessary that we should ourselves be outside of ourselves, for intellectual ideas, or ideas of reflection, are drawn from our mind : And I should much like to know how we could have the idea of being, if we were not ourselves Beings, and did not thus find being in us?

G. V. 76 (N. E. 80). If [the mind] had only the mere capacity for receiving knowledge...it would not be the source of necessary truths, as I have just shown that it is ; for it is incontestable that the senses do not suffice for showing their necessity.

G. V. 79 (N. E. 84). The proposition, *the sweet is not the bitter*, is not innate, according to the sense we have given to the term *innate truth*. For the feelings of sweet and bitter come from the external senses....But as for the proposition, *the square is not a circle*, we may say that it is innate, for, in considering it, we make a subsumption or application of the principle of contradiction to what the understanding itself furnishes.

G. V. 100 (N. E. 111). I shall be opposed by this axiom, admitted among philosophers, *that nothing is in the soul which does not come from the senses.* But we must except the soul itself and its affections. *Nihil est in intellectu, quod non fuerit in sensu,* excipe : *nisi ipse intellectus.* Now the soul contains being, substance, unity, identity, cause, perception, reasoning, and many other notions, which the senses cannot give.

G. V. 139 (N. E. 156). A succession of perceptions awakes in us the idea of duration, but does not create it.

G. V. 279 (N. E. 325). [Ideas] express only possibilities ; thus, if there had never been a parricide,...parricide would be a possible crime, and its idea would be real.

G. V. 324 (N. E. 380). The purpose of the predicaments is very useful, and we ought to think rather of rectifying than of rejecting them. Substances, quantities, qualities, actions or passions, and relations...may suffice, with those formed by their composition.

G. V. 338 (N. E. 400). It is quite true that truth is always founded in the agreement or disagreement of ideas, but it is not true generally that our knowledge of truth is a perception of this agreement or disagreement.

G. V. 347 (N. E. 410). As for the primitive truths of fact, they are immediate internal experiences of an immediacy of feeling. And it is here that the first truth of the Cartesians or of St. Augustine occurs : *I think, therefore I am,* i.e. *I am a thing which thinks.* But...it is not only immediately clear to me that *I think,* but it is just as clear to me that *I have different thoughts.*...Thus the Cartesian principle is sound, but is not the only one of its kind.

G. V. 391 (N. E. 469). We may always say that the proposition *I exist* is of the highest evidence, being a proposition which cannot be proved by any other, or an *immediate truth.* And to say : *I think, therefore I am,* is not properly to prove existence by thought, for to think and to be thinking are the same thing ; and to say *I am thinking* is already to say *I am.* You may, however, with some reason, exclude this proposition from among the Axioms, for it is a proposition of fact, founded on an immediate experience, and not a necessary proposition, whose necessity is seen in the immediate agreement (*convenance*) of the ideas. On the contrary, only God sees how these two terms, *I* and *Existence,* are connected, *i.e.* why I exist.

G. V. 415 (N. E. 499). The immediate apperception of our existence and of our thoughts furnishes us the first *à posteriori* truths or truths of fact, *i.e.* the *first experiences*, as identical propositions contain the first *à priori* truths or truths of reason....Both are incapable of being proved, and may be called *immediate*; the former, because there is immediacy between the understanding and its object, the latter, because there is immediacy between the subject and the predicate.

G. VII. 263 (N. E. 716). By the word *idea* we understand something which is in our mind; therefore marks impressed upon the brain are not ideas....But many things are in our minds—*e.g.* thoughts, perceptions, affections—which we recognize not to be ideas, though they cannot occur without ideas. For an idea does *not* consist for us *in any act of thought, but in a faculty.*...There is nevertheless, in this also, a certain difficulty; for we have a remote faculty of thinking about all things, even those whose ideas we are perhaps destitute of, because we have the faculty of receiving them; therefore an idea demands *some near faculty or facility of thinking of a thing.* But even this does not suffice....It is therefore necessary that there should be something in me *which not only leads to the thing, but also expresses it.* [See XI. § 75.]

G. IV. 357 (D. 48). The first of the truths of reason is the principle of contradiction....The first truths of fact are as many as the immediate perceptions.

G. V. 15 (D. 95; N. E. 15). As for the question whether there are ideas and truths born with us, I do not find it absolutely necessary for the beginnings, nor for the practice of the art of thinking, to decide it....The question of the origin of our ideas and maxims is not preliminary in philosophy; and we must have made great progress to solve it well.

G. VI. 505 (D. 155). Since the senses and inductions can never teach us perfectly universal truths, nor what is absolutely necessary, but only what is, and what is found in particular examples, and since we nevertheless know necessary and universal truths...it follows that we have derived these truths in part from what is within us.

G. II. 121. I agree that the idea we have of thought is clear, but not everything clear is distinct....It is an abuse to wish to employ confused ideas, however clear, to prove that something cannot be.

G. III. 479. The soul is innate to itself, so to speak, and

consequently existence, substance, unity, sameness, diversity, etc.,...
are so also.

G. V. 156 (N. E. 175). *Ph.*: Bodies do not furnish us by
means of the senses with so clear and distinct an idea of active
power as that which we have of it by the reflections which we make
on the operations of our mind....*Th.*: These considerations are very
good.

G. V. 340 (N. E. 402). Since all belief consists in memory of
past life, of proofs or of reasons, it is not in our power or in our free
will to believe or not to believe, since memory is not a thing which
depends on our will.

G. V. 66 (N. E. 70). I have always been, as I still am, in
favour of the innate idea of God...and consequently of other innate
ideas, which cannot come to us from the senses. Now I go still
further, in conformity to the new system, and I even think that all
the thoughts and actions of our soul come from its own nature, and
that it is impossible they should be given to it by the senses....But
at present I will set aside this investigation, and accommodating
myself to the received expressions,...I shall examine how we ought
to say, in my opinion, even in the usual system (speaking of the
action of bodies on the soul, as the Copernicans, like other men,
speak, with good foundation, of the motion of the sun) that there
are ideas and principles which do not come to us from the senses,
which we find in us without forming them, though the senses give
us occasion to notice them.

G. III. 659. There is no necessity (it seems) to take [ideas] as
something which is outside us. It is sufficient to consider ideas as
notions, *i.e.* as modifications of our soul.

XIV. § 102. *Distinction of sense and intellect.*

G. IV. 436 (1686). It can even be proved that the notion of
magnitude, of figure and of motion, is not so distinct as is supposed,
and that it involves something imaginary and relative to our perceptions, as do also (though far more) colour, heat, and other similar
qualities, concerning which we may doubt whether they really are
found in the nature of things external to us.

G. V. 77 (N. E. 82). The intellectual ideas which are the
source of necessary truths do not come from the senses. ...The ideas
which come from the senses are confused, and the truths which
depend upon them are so also, at least in part; whereas the intellec-

tual ideas and the truths which depend upon them are distinct, and neither have their origin in the senses, though it is true we should never think without the senses.

G. V. 108 (N. E. 119). I distinguish between ideas and thoughts; for we always have all pure or distinct ideas independently of the senses; but thoughts always correspond to some sensation.

G. V. 117 (N. E. 130). It seems that the senses cannot convince us of the *existence* of sensible things without the aid of reason. Thus I should hold that the consideration of existence comes from reflection.

G. V. 197 (N. E. 220). The senses provide us with the matter for reflections, and we should never even think of thought, if we did not think of something else, *i.e.* of the particulars which the senses provide.

G. V. 220 (N. E. 248). Present or immediate memory, or the recollection of what has just happened, *i.e.* the consciousness or reflection which accompanies internal action, cannot naturally deceive; otherwise we should not even be sure that we are thinking of such and such a thing....If immediate internal experiences are not certain, there will be no truth of fact of which we can be sure.

G. V. 363 (N. E. 432). The ideas of sensible qualities are confused, and the powers, which ought to produce them, consequently also furnish only ideas in which there is an element of confusion; thus we cannot know the connections of these ideas otherwise than by experience, except in so far as they are reduced to distinct ideas which accompany them, as has been done (for example) in regard to the colours of the rainbow and prisms.

G. V. 373 (N. E. 445). Our certainty would be small, or rather nothing, if it had no other foundation for simple ideas but that which comes from the senses....Ideas are originally in our mind, and even our thoughts spring from our own nature, without the other creatures being able to have an immediate influence on the soul. Moreover the foundation of our certainty in regard to universal and eternal truths is in the ideas themselves, independently of the senses, as also pure and intelligible ideas do not depend upon the senses....But the ideas of sensible qualities...(which in fact are only phantoms) come to us from the senses, *i.e.* from our confused perceptions. And the foundation of the truth of contingent and particular things is in success, which shows that the phenomena of sense are connected rightly, as the intelligible truths demand.

G. VI. 499 (D. 149). We may say that sensible qualities are in fact occult qualities, and that there must certainly be others more manifest, which could make them explicable. And far from our understanding only sensible things, they are just what we understand least.

G. VI. 500 (D. 150). However, we must do the senses this justice, that besides these occult qualities, they make us know other more manifest qualities, which furnish more distinct notions. These are those attributed to *common sense*, because there is no external sense to which they are specially attached and peculiar....Such is the idea of numbers....It is thus also that we perceive figures.... Though it is true that, to conceive numbers and figures themselves distinctly,...we must come to things which the senses cannot furnish, and which the understanding adds to the senses.

G. VI. 502 (D. 152). There are therefore three classes of notions : those which are *sensible only*, which are the objects appropriated to each particular sense, those which are *at once sensible and intelligible*, which belong to common sense, and those which are *intelligible only*, which are peculiar to the understanding.

G. I. 352. The mark of imperfect knowledge, for me, is when the subject has properties of which we cannot yet give the proof. Thus geometers, who have not yet been able to prove the properties of the straight line, which they have taken as acknowledged, have not yet had a sufficiently distinct idea of it.

G. II. 412. Would that incomprehensibility were an attribute of God only ! We should then have better hope of understanding nature. But it is too true that there is no part of nature which we can perfectly understand....No creature however noble can distinctly perceive or comprehend an infinity at one time ; nay more, whoever understood one piece of matter, would understand the whole universe.

XIV. § 103. *The quality of ideas.*

G. V. 243 (N. E. 273). I have this idea [a distinct one] of it [a chiliagon], but I cannot have the image of a chiliagon.

G. II. 265. The ways of action of the mind, you say, are more obscure. I should have thought they were the clearest, and were almost alone clear and distinct.

G. V. 472 (N. E. 574). God alone has the advantage of having only intuitive knowledge.

XIV. § 104. *Definition.*

G. V. 248 (N. E. 279). When there is only an incomplete idea, the same subject is susceptible of several mutually independent definitions, so that we cannot always derive the one from the other, ...and then only experience teaches us that they all belong to it together.

G. V. 274 (N. E. 317). The real [definition] shows the possibility of the thing defined, and the nominal definition does not do so.

G. V. 275 (N. E. 319). Simple terms cannot have a nominal definition : but...when they are simple only in relation to us (because we have not the means of analyzing them in order to reach the elementary perceptions of which they are composed), like hot, cold, yellow, green, they can receive a real definition, which will explain their cause.

G. V. 300 (N. E. 353). When the question is concerning fictions and the possibility of things, the transitions from species to species may be insensible....This indeterminateness would be true even if we knew perfectly the interior of the creatures concerned. But I do not see that it could prevent things from having real essences independently of the understanding, or us from knowing them.

G. IV. 424 (D. 30) (1684). We have a distinction between *nominal definitions*, which only contain the marks of the thing which is to be distinguished from others, and *real definitions*, from which it appears that the thing is possible ; and by this Hobbes is answered, who held truths to be arbitrary, because they depended on nominal definitions, not considering that the reality of the definition is not arbitrary, and that not any notions can be conjoined.

G. IV. 450 (1686). When [definition] pushes analysis until it reaches primitive notions, without presupposing anything whose possibility requires an *à priori* proof, the definition is perfect or *essential.*

XIV. § 105. *The* Characteristica Universalis.

G. V. 460 (N. E. 559). I hold that the invention of the form of syllogisms is one of the most beautiful which the human mind has made, and even one of the most considerable. It is a kind of *universal mathematics* whose importance is not sufficiently known.

G. V. 461 (N. E. 560). Further it should be known that there are *good asyllogistic conclusions...e.g.*: Jesus Christ is God, therefore the mother of Jesus Christ is the mother of God...If David is the father of Solomon, without doubt Solomon is the son of David. And these consequences do not fail to be demonstrable by truths upon which common syllogisms themselves depend.

G. I. 57 (*ca.* 1672). In Philosophy, I have found a means of accomplishing in all sciences what Des Cartes and others have done in Arithmetic and Geometry by Algebra and Analysis, by the *Ars Combinatoria.* ...By this all composite notions in the whole world are reduced to a few simple ones as their Alphabet; and by the combination of such an alphabet a way is made of finding, in time, by an ordered method, all things with their theorems and whatever is possible to investigate concerning them.

G. III. 216. I had considered this matter...when I was a young man of nineteen, in my little book *de Arte Combinatoria,* and my opinion is that truly real and philosophic characters must correspond to the analysis of thoughts. It is true that these characters would presuppose the true philosophy, and it is only now that I should dare to undertake their construction.

G. M. II. 104. What is best and most convenient about my new calculus [the infinitesimal calculus] is, that it offers truths by a kind of analysis, and without any effort of imagination, which often only succeeds by chance, and that it gives us over Archimedes all the advantages which Vieta and Des Cartes had given us over Apollonius.

G. VII. 185. [In an account of a boyish speculation Leibniz says] I came upon this remarkable consideration, namely, that a certain *Alphabet of human thoughts* could be invented, and that from the combination of the letters of this alphabet, and from the analysis of the words formed of them, everything could be both discovered and tested. ...At that time I did not sufficiently realize the greatness of the matter. But later, the more progress I made in the knowledge of things, the more confirmed I became in the resolve to pursue so great a matter.

G. VII. 20. Algebra itself is not the true characteristic of Geometry, but quite another must be found, which I am certain would be more useful than Algebra for the use of Geometry in the mechanical sciences. And I wonder that this has hitherto been remarked by no one. For almost all men hold Algebra to be the true mathematical art of discovery, and as long as they labour under this prejudice, they will never find the true characters of the other sciences.

G. VII. 198. The progress of the art of rational discovery depends in great part upon the art of characteristic (*ars characteristica*). The reason why people usually seek demonstrations only in numbers and lines and things represented by these is none other than that there are not, outside numbers, convenient characters corresponding to the notions.

XV. § 106. *Four proofs of the existence of God.*

G. VII. 302 (D. 100; L. 337). Besides the world or the aggregate of finite things, there is a certain unity which is dominant, not only as the soul is dominant in me, or rather as the Ego itself is dominant in my body, but also in a much higher sense. For the dominant unity of the universe not only rules the world but constructs or fashions it. It is higher than the world, and so to speak extramundane, and is indeed the ultimate reason of things. For the sufficient reason of existence cannot be found either in any particular thing or in the whole aggregate and series of things. Let us suppose that a book of the elements of Geometry existed from all eternity, and that in succession one copy of it was made from another, it is evident that, although we can account for the present book by the book from which it was copied, nevertheless, going back through as many books as we please, we could never reach a complete reason for it, because we can always ask why such books have at all times existed, *i.e.* why books at all, and why written in this way. What is true of books is also true of the different states of the world; for, in spite of certain laws of change, the succeeding state is, in some sort, a copy of that which precedes it. Therefore, to whatever earlier state you go back, you never find in it the complete reason of things, *i.e.* the reason why there exists any world, and why this world rather than some other.

You may indeed suppose the world eternal; but as you suppose only a succession of states, in none of which do you find the sufficient reason, and as even any number of them does not in the least help you to account for them, it is evident that the reason must be sought elsewhere. For in eternal things, even though there be no cause, there must be a reason, which, for permanent things, is necessity itself or essence; but for the series of changing things, if it be supposed that they succeed one another from all eternity, this reason would be, as we shall presently see, the prevailing of inclinations, which consist not in necessitating reasons...but in inclining reasons. From this it is manifest that, even by supposing the eternity of the world, we cannot escape the ultimate extramundane reason of things, *i.e.* God....Since the ultimate root of all must be in something which has metaphysical necessity, and since the reason of any existing thing is to be found only in an existing thing, it follows that there must exist one Being who has metaphysical necessity, one Being of whose essence it is to exist; and thus there must exist something different from that plurality of beings, the world, which, as we admitted and showed, has no metaphysical necessity.

G. VI. 614 (D. 224; L. 241). In God is the source, not only of existences, but also of essences in so far as they are real, *i.e.* the source of what is real in possibility. For the understanding of God is the region of eternal truths, or of the ideas on which they depend, and without him there would be nothing real in possibilities, and not only would there be nothing existing, but nothing would even be possible. For if there is a reality in essences or possibilities, or in eternal truths, this reality must needs be founded in something existing and actual, and consequently in the existence of the necessary Being, in whom essence involves existence, or in whom it suffices to be possible in order to be actual. Thus God alone (or the necessary Being) has this prerogative, that he must necessarily exist if he be possible. And as nothing can interfere with the possibility of that which involves no limits, no negation, and consequently no contradiction, this is sufficient of itself to make known the existence of God *à priori*. We have proved it also through the reality of eternal truths....We must not, however, imagine, as some do, that eternal truths, being dependent upon God, are arbitrary and depend upon his will....That is only true of contingent truths, whose principle is *fitness* or the choice of the *best*, whereas necessary truths depend solely on his understanding, and are its internal object. Thus God alone is the primary unity or original simple substance, of which all created or derivative Monads are products, and have their birth, so to speak, through continual fulgurations of the Divinity from moment to moment, limited by the receptivity of the created being, of whose essence it is to have limits. In God there is *Power*, which is the source of all, then *Knowledge*, whose content is the variety of ideas, and finally *Will*, which makes changes or products according to the principle of the best. These characteristics correspond to what in created monads forms the subject or basis [see Mr Latta's note, L. 245], to the faculty of Perception, and to the faculty of Appetition. But in God these attributes are absolutely infinite or perfect; and in the created Monads...there are only imitations of these attributes, according to the degree of perfection of the Monad.

XV. § 107. The ontological argument.

G. V. 419 (N. E. 504). [The ontological argument] is not a paralogism, but an imperfect demonstration, which presupposes something that it was still necessary to prove, to give the argument mathematical evidence; namely, it is tacitly supposed that this idea of the all-great or all-perfect Being is possible, and implies no contradiction. And it is already something that, by this remark, it is proved that *supposing God to be possible, he exists,* which is the privilege of the Divinity alone....The other argument of M. Des Cartes—which undertakes to prove the Existence of God, because the idea of him is in our soul, and must have come from the original —is still less conclusive.

G. V. 420 (N. E. 505). Almost all the means which have been employed for proving the existence of God are good, and might serve their purpose if they were perfected.

G. IV. 406 (D. 137). If the necessary Being is possible, he exists. For the necessary Being and the Being by his essence are one and the same thing....If the Being through self is impossible, all beings through others are so too, since they only are, in the end, through the Being through self; and thus nothing could exist....If there is no necessary Being, there is no possible being.

G. III. 572. I agree that the idea of possibles involves neces- sarily that (*i.e.* the idea) of the existence of a being who can produce the possible. But the idea of possibles does not involve the actual existence of this being, as it seems, Sir, that you take it, when you add : "If there were not such a being, nothing would be possible." For it suffices that a being who would produce the thing should be possible, in order that the thing should be possible. Generally speaking, in order that a being may be possible, it suffices that its efficient cause be possible; I except the supreme efficient cause, which must actually exist. But this is for another reason, because nothing would be possible if the necessary Being did not exist.

XV. § 108. *Proof that the idea of God is possible.*

G. VII. 261 (N. E. 714) (1676). *That the most perfect Being exists.* I call a *perfection* every simple quality which is positive and absolute, and expresses without any limits whatever it does express. Now since such a quality is simple, it is also irresolvable or indefinable, for otherwise it will either not be one simple quality, but an aggregate of several, or, if it is one, it will be circumscribed by limits, and will therefore be conceived by a negation of further progress, contrary to the hypothesis, for it is assumed to be purely positive. Hence it is not difficult to show that *all perfections are compatible inter se*, or can be in the same subject. For let there be such a proposition as

A and B are incompatible

(understanding by A and B two such simple forms or perfections— the same holds if several are assumed at once), it is obvious that this cannot be proved without a resolution of one or both of the terms A and B; for otherwise their nature would not enter into the reasoning, and the incompatibility of any other things could be shown just as well as theirs. But (by hypothesis) they are irresolvable. Therefore this proposition cannot be proved concerning them.

But it could be proved concerning them if it were true, for it is not true *per se*; but all necessarily true propositions are either demonstrable, or known *per se*. Therefore this proposition is not necessarily true. In other words, since it is not necessary that A and B should not be in the same subject, they can therefore be in the same subject; and since the reasoning is the same as regards any other assumed qualities of the same kind, therefore all perfections are compatible.

There is, therefore, or there can be conceived, a subject of all perfections, or most perfect Being.

Whence it follows also that he exists, for existence is among the number of the perfections....

I showed this reasoning to D. Spinoza, when I was at the Hague, and he thought it sound; for as at first he contradicted it, I wrote it down and read him this paper.

SCHOLIUM.

The reasoning of Des Cartes concerning the existence of the most perfect Being presupposed that the most perfect Being can be

conceived, or is possible....But it is asked whether it is in our power
to imagine such a Being....

XV. § 109. *The cosmological argument.*

G. V. 417 (N. E. 500). [Locke argues that, because we now
exist, therefore something has always existed. Leibniz replies:]
I find ambiguity in it [your argument] if it means *that there never
was a time when nothing existed.* I agree to this, and indeed it
follows from the preceding propositions by a purely mathematical
consequence. For if there had ever been nothing, there would have
always been nothing, since nothing cannot produce a Being; consequently we ourselves should not be, which is contrary to the first
truth of experience. But the consequence makes it first appear
that in saying something has existed from all eternity, you mean an
eternal thing. It does not follow, however, in virtue of what you
have advanced so far, that if there has always been something, then
there has always been a certain thing, *i.e.* an eternal Being. For
some adversaries will say that I have been produced by other things,
and these things by yet others.

G. IV. 359 (D. 51). That there is some necessary thing is
evident from the fact that contingent things exist.

G. IV. 360 (D. 51). From the fact that we now are, it follows
that we shall be hereafter, unless a reason of change exists. So
that, unless it were established otherwise that we could not even
exist except by the favour of God, nothing would be proved in
favour of the existence of God from our duration.

XV. § 111. *The argument from the eternal truths.*

G. VII. 310. A necessary being, if it be possible, exists. This
...makes the transition from essences to existences, from hypothetical
to absolute truths, from ideas to the world....If there were no eternal
substance, there would be no eternal truths; thus God is also deduced
hence, who is the root of possibility, for his mind is itself the region
of ideas or truths. But it is very erroneous to suppose that eternal
truths and the goodness of things depend on the divine will, since
all will presupposes the judgment of the intellect as to goodness,
unless some one by a change of names would transfer all judgment
from the intellect to the will, though even then no one could say
that the will is the cause of truths, since the judgment is not their

cause either. The reason of truths lies in the ideas of things, which are involved in the divine essence itself. And who would dare to say that the truth of God's existence depends upon the divine will?

G. VI. 226. We ought not to say, with some Scotists, that the eternal truths would subsist, even if there were no understanding, not even God's. For, in my opinion, it is the divine understanding that makes the reality of eternal truths: although his Will has no part in it. Every reality must be founded in something existent. It is true that an atheist may be a geometer. But if there were no God, there would be no object of Geometry. And without God, not only would there be nothing existent, but there would be nothing possible.

G. VII. 190 (1677). **A.** You hold that this [a certain proposition of Geometry] is true, even though it be not thought by you? **B.** Certainly, before either the geometers had proved it, or men had observed it. **A.** Therefore you think that truth and falsehood are in things, not in thoughts? **B.** Certainly. **A.** Is anything false? **B.** Not the thing, I think, but the thought or proposition about the thing. **A.** Thus falsity belongs to thoughts, and not to things? **B.** I am compelled to say so. **A.** Then is not truth also? **B.** It would seem so, though I doubt whether the consequence is valid. **A.** When the question is proposed, and before you are sure of your opinion, do you not doubt whether a thing is true or false? **B.** Certainly. **A.** You recognize therefore that the same subject is capable of truth and falsehood, since one or other follows according to the nature of the question? **B.** I recognize and affirm, that if falsity belongs to thoughts, not things, so does truth also. **A.** But this contradicts what you said above, that even what nobody thinks is true. **B.** You have puzzled me. **A.** Yet we must attempt a reconciliation. Do you think that all thoughts which can occur are actually formed, or, to speak more clearly, do you think that all propositions are thought? **B.** I do not think so. **A.** You see then that truth concerns propositions or thoughts, but possible ones, so that this at least is certain, that if any one thinks in one way or in the opposite way, his thought will be true or false. [The rest of the dialogue is concerned in refuting Hobbes's nominalism.]

XV. § 113. *Relation of knowledge to truth.*

G. VI. 230. This pretended fate [that of the necessity of eternal truths], which governs even the divinity, is nothing else but the very nature of God, his own understanding, which furnishes rules to his wisdom and goodness.

G. VI. 423. Is it by the will of God, for example, or is it not rather by the nature of numbers, that some numbers are more capable than others of being exactly divided in several ways?

G. II. 125. We may say that created spirits differ from God only as the less from the more, the finite from the infinite.

G. IV. 426 (D. 32) (1684). As to the controversy, whether we see all things in God,... or have ideas of our own, it must be understood that, even if we did see all things in God, it would still be necessary that we should also have ideas of our own, *i.e.* not, as it were, certain little images, but affections or modifications of our mind, answering to what we should see in God.

XV. § 114.   *Argument from the pre-established harmony.*

G. V. 421 (N. E. 507). These Beings [Monads] have received their nature, both active and passive,... from a general and supreme cause, for otherwise,... being independent of each other, they could never produce that Order, Harmony, and Beauty, which is observed in nature.   But this argument, which appears to have only a moral certainty, is brought to a perfectly metaphysical necessity, by the new species of harmony which I have introduced, which is the pre-established harmony.

F. de C. 70 (D. 184). God produces substances, but not their actions, in which he only concurs.

G. VII. 365 (D. 245). God is not present to things by *situation*, but by *essence*; his presence is manifested by his immediate *operation*.

G. VI. 107. Power is concerned with *Being*, wisdom or understanding with the *true*, and will with the *good*.

G. VI. 167. [God's] *goodness* led him *antecedently* to create and produce all possible good; but his *wisdom* made choice of it, and was the cause of his choosing the best *consequently*; and finally his *power* gave him the means of *actually* executing the great design which he had formed.

G. IV. 440 (1686). God alone (from whom all individuals continually emanate, and who sees the universe, not only as they see it, but also quite differently from all of them) is the cause of this correspondence of their phenomena, and causes what is private to one to be public to all; otherwise there would be no connection.

G. IV. 533. In order that an action should be not miraculous, it is not sufficient that it should conform to a general law. For if this law were not founded in the nature of things, perpetual miracles would be required to execute it....Thus it is not enough that God should order the body to obey the soul, and the soul to have perception of what happens in the body; he must give them a means of doing so, and I have explained this means.

G. VII. 390 (D. 255). God, being moved by his supreme reason to choose, among many possible series of things or worlds, that in which free creatures should take such or such resolutions, though not without his concourse, has thereby rendered every event certain and determined once for all; without derogating thereby from the liberty of those creatures : that simple decree of choice not at all changing, but only actualizing, their free natures, which he saw in his ideas.

G. VII. 358 (D. 242). If God is obliged to mend the course of nature from time to time, it must be done either supernaturally or naturally. If it be done supernaturally, we must have recourse to miracles to explain natural things, which is reducing an hypothesis *ad absurdum* ; for everything may easily be accounted for by miracles. But if it be done naturally, then God will not be *intelligentia supramundana* : he will be comprehended under the nature of things ; that is, he will be the soul of the world.

XV. § 117. *God's goodness.*

G. VII. 399 (D. 264). I have still other reasons against this strange imagination, that space is a property of God. If it be so, space belongs to the essence of God. But space has parts: therefore there would be parts in the essence of God. *Spectatum admissi.*

G. VII. 415 (D. 281). The immensity and eternity of God would subsist, though there were no creatures; but those attributes would have no dependence either upon times or places....These attributes signify only that God would be present and coexistent with all the things that should exist.

XVI. § 118. *Freedom and determinism.*

G. VI. 29. There are two famous labyrinths, where our reason very often goes astray ; one is concerned with the great question of the free and the necessary, especially in the production and origin of evil.

G. VI. 411. If the will determines itself without there being anything, either in the person choosing, or in the object chosen, which can lead to the choice, there will be neither cause nor reason in this election : and as moral evil consists in bad choice, this is to admit that moral evil has no source at all. Thus by the rules of good metaphysics, there should be no moral evil in nature; and also, by the same reason, there would be no moral good either, and all morality would be destroyed.

G. VI. 380 (D. 197). The necessity which is contrary to morality, which ought to be avoided, and would make punishment unjust, is an insurmountable necessity, which would make all opposition useless, even if we wished with all our hearts to avoid the necessary action, and though we made all possible efforts to this end. Now it is evident that this is not applicable to voluntary actions ; since we should not do them unless we wished it. Also their prevision and predetermination is not absolute, but presupposes the will : if it is certain we shall do them, it is no less certain that we shall wish to do them.

G. II. 419. I should not say that in Adam, or in any one else, there was a moral necessity of sinning, but only this : that the inclination to sin prevailed in him, and that thus there was a certain predetermination, but no necessity. I recognize that there is a moral necessity in God to do the best, and in confirmed spirits to act well. And in general I prefer to interpret the words thus, lest anything should follow which would sound bad.

G. V. 163 (N. E. 182). It seems to me that, properly speaking, though volitions are contingent, necessity should not be opposed to volition, but to contingency...and that necessity must not be confounded with determination, for there is no less connection or determination in thoughts than in motions....And not only contingent truths are not necessary, but also their connections are not always of an absolute necessity... ; physical things even have something moral and voluntary in relation to God, since the laws of motion have no other necessity than that of the best.

G. V. 165 (N. E. 184). [The advocates of free will] demand (at least several do so) the absurd and the impossible, in desiring a liberty of equilibrium, which is absolutely imaginary and impracticable, and would not even serve their purpose if it were possible for them to have it, *i.e.* that they should have liberty to will against all the impressions which may come from the understanding, which would destroy true liberty, and reason also.

G. V. 167 (N. E. 187). We do not will to will, but we will to do; and if we willed to will, we should will to will to will, and this would go to infinity.

G. IV. 362 (D. 54). To ask whether there is freedom in our will, is the same as asking whether there is will in our will. Free and voluntary mean the same thing.

G. VII. 419 (D. 285). All the natural powers of spirits are subject to moral laws.

G. VI. 130. The reason which M. Des Cartes has alleged, for proving the independence of our free actions by a pretended lively internal feeling, has no force. We cannot properly feel our independence, and we do not always perceive the often imperceptible causes upon which our resolution depends.

G. VI. 421. Not only free creatures are active, but also all other substances, and natures composed of substances. Beasts are not free, and yet they do not fail to have active souls.

G. I. 331 (1679). Whatever acts, is free in so far as it acts.

G. VI. 122. There is contingency in a thousand actions of nature; but when there is no judgment in the agent, there is no liberty.

XVI. § 119. *Psychology of volition and pleasure.*

G. V. 149 (N. E. 167). *Ph.* The *Good* is what is proper to produce and increase pleasure in us, or to diminish and abridge some pain. *Evil* is proper to produce or increase pain in us, or to diminish some pleasure. *Th.* I am also of this opinion.

G. V. 171 (N. E. 190). I would not have it believed...that we must abandon those ancient axioms, that the will follows the greatest good, or flies the greatest evil, which it feels. The source of the little application to the truly good comes, in great part, from the fact that, in the affairs and occasions where the senses scarcely act, most of our thoughts are surd (*sourdes*), so to speak,...*i.e.* void of perception and feeling, and consisting in the bare employment of symbols....Now such knowledge cannot move us; we need something lively (*vif*) in order to feel emotion.

G. V. 173 (N. E. 193). We must, once for all, make this law for ourselves: henceforth to await and to follow the conclusions of reason, once understood, though only perceived in the sequel usually by *surd thoughts,* and destitute of sensible attractions.

G. V. 175 (N. E. 194). Uneasiness is essential to the felicity of creatures, which never consists in complete possession, which would make them insensible and stupid, but in a continual and uninterrupted progress to greater goods.

G. VII. 73 (D. 130). Pleasure or delight is a sense of perfection, *i.e.* a sense of something which helps or assists some power.

G. V. 179 (N. E. 200). In the moment of combat, there is no longer time to use artifices; all that then strikes us weighs in the balance, and helps to form a compound direction, almost as in Mechanics.

G. VI. 385 (D. 202). [In answer to the proposition that he who cannot fail to choose the best is not free:] It is rather true liberty, and the most perfect, to be able to use one's free will in the best way, and always to use this power without being turned aside either by external force or by internal passions.

G. V. 179 (N. E. 201). I do not know whether the greatest pleasure is possible; I should rather think that it can grow infinitely.

G. V. 180 (N. E. 201). Although pleasure cannot receive a nominal definition, any more than light or colour, yet it can, like them, receive a causal definition, and I believe that, at bottom, pleasure is a feeling of perfection and pain a feeling of imperfection, provided they are sufficiently remarkable for us to be able to perceive them.

G. VI. 266. Properly speaking, perception is not enough to cause misery, if it is not accompanied by reflection. The same is true of felicity....We cannot reasonably doubt that there is pain in animals; but it seems that their pleasures and pains are not as lively as in man, they are not susceptible either of the sorrow (*chagrin*) which accompanies pain, or of the joy which accompanies pleasure.

XVI. § 120. *Sin.*

G. IV. 300 (D. 9) (ca. 1680). Immortality without memory is quite useless to morals; for it destroys all reward and all punishment.

G. VI. 118. Moral evil is so great an evil as it is only because it is a source of physical evils.

G. VI. 141. There is a kind of justice, and a certain sort of rewards and punishments, which appears inapplicable to those who act from an absolute necessity, if there were any such. This is the kind of justice which has not for its object amendment, or example, or even the reparation of evil. This justice is founded only in fitness, which demands a certain satisfaction as the expiation of a bad action.

G. IV. 454 (1686). It depends upon the soul to guard against the surprises of appearances by a firm will to make reflections, and neither to act nor to judge, in certain circumstances, without great and mature deliberation.

G. VII. 92. Virtue is an unchangeable precept of the mind, and a perpetual renewing of the same, by which we are as it were driven to perform what we believe to be good....Since our will is not drawn to obtain or avoid anything, except as the understanding presents it to the will as something good or bad, it will suffice that we should always judge rightly, in order to our always acting rightly.

G. VII. 99. The chief rule of our life is, that we should always, as far as possible, exactly do or leave undone what not the passions, but the understanding, shows to be the most useful or the most harmful; and that when we have done this, we should then, however it turns out, account ourselves happy.

XVI. § 121. *Meaning of good and evil; three kinds of each.*

G. VII. 74 (D. 130). The perfection of the universe, or harmony of things, does not allow all minds to be equally perfect. The question why God has given to one mind more perfection than to another is among senseless questions.

G. VI. 376 (D. 194). It must be admitted that there is evil in this world which God has made, and that it was possible to make a world without evil, or even to create no world at all...; but ...the better part is not always that which tends to avoid evil, since it may be that the evil is accompanied by a greater good.

G. IV. 427 (1686). We must know what a perfection is, and here is a sufficiently certain mark of one: forms or natures which are not capable of the last degree, are not perfections, as for example the nature of number or figure. For the greatest of all numbers (or the number of all numbers), as well as the greatest of all figures, imply a contradiction; but the greatest knowledge and omnipotence do not involve impossibility.

G. VII. 303 (D. 101; L. 340). Perfection is nothing but quantity of essence.

G. III. 33. The ultimate origin of evil must not be sought in the divine will, but in the original imperfection of creatures, which is contained ideally in the eternal truths constituting the internal object of the divine intellect, so that evil could not be excluded from the best possible system of things.

G. VII. 194 (*ca.* 1677?). Absolutely first truths are, among truths of reason, those which are identical, and among truths of fact this, from which all experiments can be proved *à priori*, namely : *Everything possible demands that it should exist*, and hence will exist unless something else prevents it, which also demands that it should exist and is incompatible with the former; and hence it follows that that combination of things always exists by which the greatest possible number of things exists; as, if we assume A, B, C, D to be equal as regards essence, *i.e.* equally perfect, or equally demanding existence, and if we assume that D is incompatible with A and with B, while A is compatible with any except D, and similarly as regards B and C; it follows that the combination ABC, excluding D, will exist; for if we wish D to exist, it can only coexist with C, and hence the combination CD will exist, which is more imperfect than the combination ABC. And hence it is obvious that things exist in the most perfect way. This proposition, that everything possible demands that it should exist, can be proved *à posteriori*, assuming that something exists; for either all things exist, and then every possible so demands existence that it actually exists; or some things do not exist, and then a reason must be given why some things exist rather than others. But this cannot be given otherwise than from a general reason of essence or possibility, assuming that the possible demands existence in its own nature, and indeed in proportion to its possibility or according to the degree of its essence. Unless in the very nature of Essence there were some inclination to exist, nothing would exist; for to say that some essences have this inclination and others not, is to say something without a reason*, since existence seems to be referred generally to every essence in the same way. But it is as yet unknown to men, whence arises the incompossibility of diverse things, or how it can happen that diverse essences are opposed to

---

* Leibniz remarks in the margin: If existence were anything other than what is demanded by essence (*essentiae exigentia*), it would follow that it itself would have a certain essence, or would add something new to things, concerning which it might again be asked, whether this essence exists, and why this rather than another.

each other, seeing that all purely positive terms seem to be compatible *inter se*.

G. VII. 195 (*ca.* 1677 ?). The *Good* is what contributes to perfection. But *perfection* is what involves the most of essence.

XVI. § 122. *Metaphysical evil the source of the other two kinds.*

G. VI. 162. God concurs in moral and physical evil, and in both in a moral and in a physical manner; man also concurs morally and physically in a free and active way, which renders him blameworthy and punishable.

G. VI. 237. It might be said that the whole series of things to infinity may be the best that is possible, although what exists throughout the universe in each part of time is not the best. It would be possible, therefore, for the universe to go always from better to better, if the nature of things were such that it is not permitted to attain the best all at once. But these are problems concerning which it is difficult for us to judge.

G. VI. 378 (D. 196). God is infinite, and the Devil is limited; the good can and does go to infinity, whereas evil has its bounds.

G. II. 317. Vice is not a potentiality of acting, but a hindrance to the potentiality of acting.

XVI. § 123. *Connection with the doctrine of analytic judgments.*

G. V. 242 (N. E. 272). If any one wished to write as a mathematician in Metaphysics and Morals, nothing would hinder him from doing so with rigour.

G. V. 18 (D. 98; N. E. 17). I strongly approve of Mr. Locke's doctrine concerning the demonstrability of moral truths.

G. II. 578 (D. 128). The felicity of God does not compose a part of our happiness, but the whole.

G. II. 581 (D. 129). To love truly and disinterestedly is nothing else than to be led to find pleasure in the perfections or the felicity of the object....This love has properly for its object substances capable of felicity.

XVI. § 124. *The kingdoms of nature and of grace.*

G. IV. 480 (D. 73; L. 304). Spirits have special laws which put them above the revolutions of matter through the very order which God has placed there; and it may be said that everything else is made only for them, these revolutions themselves being arranged for the felicity of the good and the punishment of the wicked.

G. VI. 168. I agree that the happiness of intelligent creatures is the principal part of God's designs, for they most resemble him; but I do not see how it can be proved that this is his sole aim. It is true that the kingdom of nature must be helpful to the kingdom of grace; but as everything is connected in God's great design, we must believe that the kingdom of grace is also in some way fitted to the kingdom of nature, in such a manner that this keeps the greatest order and beauty, so as to render the whole composed of both the most perfect possible.

G. IV. 462 (1686). Felicity is to persons what perfection is to beings. And if the first principle of the existence of the physical world is the decree giving it as much perfection as possible, the first design of the moral world or City of God, which is the noblest part of the universe, must be to distribute through it the greatest possible felicity.

G. IV. 391 (D. 63). Nature has, as it were, an empire within an empire, and so to speak a double kingdom, of reason and of necessity, or of forms and of particles of matter.

G. VI. 621 (D. 231; L. 266). Among other differences which exist between ordinary souls and minds [*esprits*]...there is also this: that souls in general are living mirrors or images of the universe of created things, but that minds are also images of the Deity or Author of nature himself, capable of knowing the system of the universe, and to some extent of imitating it....It is this that enables minds to enter into a kind of fellowship with God, and brings it about that in relation to them he is not only what an inventor is to his machine (which is the relation of God to other created things) but also what a prince is to his subjects, and even what a father is to his children. Whence it is easy to conclude that the totality of all minds must compose the City of God, *i.e.* the most perfect State that is possible, under the most perfect of Monarchs. This City of God, this truly universal monarchy, is a moral world in the natural world, and is the most exalted and the most divine among the works of God; and it is in it that the glory of God really consists, for he would have no glory were not his greatness and his goodness known and admired by minds. It is also in relation to this divine City that God properly has goodness, while his wisdom and his power are manifested everywhere. As we have shown above that there is a perfect harmony between the two realms in nature, the one of efficient, the other of final causes, we should here notice also another harmony, between the physical realm of nature and the moral realm of grace, *i.e.* between God considered as Architect of the machine of the universe and God considered as Monarch of the divine City of Spirits. A result of this harmony is that things lead to grace by the very ways of nature, and that this globe, for instance, must be destroyed and renewed by natural means at the very time when the government of spirits requires it, for the punishment of some and the reward of others. It may also be said that God as Architect satisfies in all respects God as Lawgiver, and thus that sins must bear their penalty with them, through the order of nature, and even in virtue of the mechanical structure of things; and similarly that noble actions will attain their rewards by ways which, in relation to bodies, are mechanical, although this cannot and ought not always to happen immediately.

Note to § 105. Many quotations relative to this subject (some from unpublished MS.) are given by Peano, "Formules de Logique Mathématique," *Revue de Mathématiques*, T. VII. No. 1.

INDEX TO APPENDIX.

INDEX.

Head Office: 40 Museum Street, London, WC1

Sales, Distribution and Accounts Departments:
Park Lane, Hemel Hempstead, Hertfordshire

Athens: 7 Stadiou Street, Athens 125
Barbados: Rockley New Road, St. Lawrence 4
Bombay: 103/5 Fort Street, Bombay 1
Calcutta: 2850 Bepin Behari Ganguli Street, Calcutta 12
Dacca: Alico Building, 18 Motijheel, Dacca 2
Hornsby, N.S.W.: Cnr. Bridge Road and Jersey Street, 2077
Ibadan: P.O. Box 62
Johannesburg: P.O. Box 23134, Joubert Park
Karachi: Karachi Chambers, McLeod Road, Karachi 2
Lahore: 22 Falettis' Hotel, Egerton Road
Madras: 2/18 Mount Road, Madras 2
Manila: P.O. Box 157, Quezon City, D-502
Mexico: Serapio Rendon 125, Mexico 4, D.F.
Nairobi: P.O. Box 30583
New Delhi: 4/21-22B Asaf Ali Road, New Delhi 1
Ontario: 2330 Midland Avenue, Agincourt
Singapore: 248C-6 Orchard Road, Singapore 9
Tokyo: C.P.O. Box 1728, Tokyo 100-91
Wellington: P.O. Box 1467, Wellington, New Zealand